THE PHILOSOPHY OF
MICHAEL MANN

Edited by
STEVEN SANDERS, AEON J. SKOBLE,
AND R. BARTON PALMER

K UNIVERSITY PRESS OF KENTUCKY

Scholarly publisher for the Commonwealth,
serving Bellarmine University, Berea College, Centre College of Kentucky, Eastern Kentucky University, The Filson Historical Society, Georgetown College, Kentucky Historical Society, Kentucky State University, Morehead State University, Murray State University, Northern Kentucky University, Transylvania University, University of Kentucky, University of Louisville, and Western Kentucky University.
All rights reserved.

Editorial and Sales Offices: The University Press of Kentucky
663 South Limestone Street, Lexington, Kentucky 40508-4008
www.kentuckypress.com

Library of Congress Cataloging-in-Publication Data

The philosophy of Michael Mann / edited by Steven Sanders, Aeon J. Skoble, and R. Barton Palmer.
     pages cm.
  Includes bibliographical references and index.
  ISBN 978-0-8131-4471-9 (hardcover : alk. paper) — ISBN 978-0-8131-4473-3 (pdf) (print)— ISBN 978-0-8131-4472-6 (epub)
  1. Mann, Michael, 1943—Criticism and interpretation. I. Sanders, Steven, 1945- editor of compilation. II. Skoble, Aeon J. editor of compilation. III. Palmer, R. Barton, 1946- editor of compilation.
  PN1998.3.M338835P46 2014
  791.4302'33092—dc23   2014003470

CONTENTS

AN INTRODUCTION TO THE PHILOSOPHY OF MICHAEL MANN

Steven Sanders

Michael Mann's personal involvement as a writer, director, and producer has given him the reputation of being an unusually talented triple threat in Hollywood. He has been called "one of the most breathtaking cinematic stylists of his era" and "Hollywood's foremost urbanist."[1] His ability to re-create the language and visualize the circumstances of the crime cultures he so often infiltrates is as uncanny as it is illuminating. His diagnosis of the circumstances of his existential protagonists in the alienated urban space of postmodern capitalism incorporates a film noir sensibility even as it investigates the cultural dilemmas of the twenty-first century. His numerous television-scriptwriting credits, directorial achievements, and executive-producing expertise have earned him the respect of his peers and the gratitude of fans worldwide.

Mann's work bears the unique signature of his probing intelligence and aesthetic flair in many and diverse formats and forms: from documentaries to biopics, from period interpretations of classic literature to neo-noir urban-crime feature films; from socially conscious examinations of corporate misconduct to stunning automobile advertisements for Mercedes-Benz and Ferrari; from a network television series about undercover police work in 1980s Miami to one about mob turf wars in early 1960s Chicago, Las Vegas, and Central America to an HBO series about horse racing in Southern California. Add to these credits Mann's new projects in development (about which there is always speculation), and it is easy to see why those who would take the full measure of his career achievements have their work cut out for them. *The Philosophy of Michael Mann* is the first collection of original essays by scholars in philosophy, film criticism, literature, and elsewhere to identify, describe, and open up for discussion some of the most interesting philosophical themes in Mann's ten feature films, his early telefilm, *The Jericho Mile* (1979), and the network television series he executive-produced, *Miami Vice* (1984–1989) and *Crime Story* (1986–1988).[2] The essays, some of which provide readings of Mann's work inspired by existentialism, postmodernism, and film noir, keep faith with readers who have made the Philosophy of Popular Culture Series an important, admired, and accessible forum for the philosophical discussion of the work of such film exemplars as Stanley Kubrick, Martin Scorsese, and Steven Spielberg and of such genres as neo-noir, science fiction, and the Western. Throughout this book, such themes as existential choice, evil and power, style and its discontents, justice, law, and ethics are introduced, elucidated, applied to Mann's work, and evaluated. Rather than trying to pinpoint *the* philosophy of Michael Mann, as the volume's title might lead some readers to expect, the contributors are remarkably eclectic in their approaches, areas of interest, and presuppositions. Some invoke historical figures such as Aristotle, Locke, Kant, and Rousseau, whereas others utilize contemporary European philosophers such as Foucault, Deleuze, Guattari, and Levinas, and still others revisit recent film theorists and critics such as David Bordwell and Sean Cubitt to fashion an understanding of Mann's work. Some of the essays emphasize Mann's existentialist ideas, others focus on his aesthetics of horror, and still others discuss his critique of the corporatization of crime and his creation of a new noir that brings together images of relationships, work, and individual striving in the megalopolises of Los Angeles and Miami and the evolution of a wholly new model of criminal trafficking on a global scale.

Authorship and the Rise of the Crime Auteur

Mann's well-known involvement as a writer-director-producer of feature films, television series, and documentaries as well as his transformation of the urban-crime genre from a redoubt of film noir into a contemporary commercial sector, which some have thought comparable to the work of his contemporary Martin Scorsese, would seem to put him in a strong position to bear the honorific *auteur*. In *The Cinema of Michael Mann: Vice and Vindication*, Jonathan Rayner discusses the question of Mann's authorship and writes, "Mann's authorship must be viewed in several chronological, industrial, and formal contexts: the post-classical context, inflected by television but still marked by the influence of experimentation in American film of the 1960's and 1970's, in which his career begins; the brand name, commercial American auteurist cinema of the 1980's and 1990's in which Mann's signature and success become established; and the emerging digital cinema of the new millennium, in which Mann's films are proving instrumental in defining."[3] And in defining Mann as a "crime auteur," Steven Rybin remarks that "it is fair to call Mann a crime auteur, given his career-long predilection for crime as a genre and a narrative trope, even in his noncrime films. Indeed, crime may be the key trope for understanding [the] vexed relationship between Mann's men and the world they inhabit."[4] Nevertheless, Mann's designation as an auteur, the creator or author of the cinematic or televisual work of art, has been challenged both by those who have never adopted auteur analysis and by those who think there might be something to the notion of the auteur but do not think Mann qualifies as one.[5] This controversy heated up when, in the full flush of the popularity of *Miami Vice* and *Crime Story,* the 1980s television series that Mann executive-produced for NBC, the mantle of auteur was bestowed upon him.[6] Just as Chris Carter, Dick Wolf, and David Chase put their distinctive stamp on *The X-Files* (1993–2002), *Law and Order* (1990–2010), and *The Sopranos* (1999–2007), respectively, Mann oversaw the creation of a total atmosphere on *Miami Vice*—visual, sonic, and narrative.

The term *auteur* is typically used as a term of praise denoting not only accomplishment in the development of a personal style and the articulation of a worldview, but also control, and there is often a significant factual basis for explaining whose vision or point of view has guided a particular film or television series. Identifying the themes, narratives, visual realization, sound design, casting, and direction of a film or series by reference to the decisions of an individual—typically a director (Alfred Hitchcock, Orson Welles, Howard Hawks, John Ford), but sometimes a producer or even a studio head (David O. Selznick, Darryl F. Zanuck)—is part of such an explanation. Of course, explanations by reference to an auteur do not mean that there are no other factors involved in bringing a feature film or television series to fruition, from the contingencies of financing to the vicissitudes of location, weather, production costs, labor disputes, cast availability, star demands, and so on. And Mann himself has spoken of the fact that even those who *are* in control have to make difficult decisions in light of the many factors that bear on the making of a film. "I have to make a lot of really difficult, hard, heart-breaking decisions sometimes about material that I really love, and people do fabulous work in," Mann has said, alluding to the "fast boat" race sequence that originally opened the *Miami Vice* (2006) feature film but was subsequently cut.[7] "I always felt the story should be tight," Mann explains. "You should be dropped into [Sonny Crockett and Rico Tubbs's] lives, and I wanted it to have an intensity, and a drive, where bang, you're in it, and when that movie ends, it goes to black, and that's as much of this story as we're telling right now."[8]

Mann and Existentialist Philosophy

The link between the philosophy of existentialism and Mann's cinema can be found in the frequency with which existentialist concepts and themes are given dramatic expression in his work. Indeed, if there is a connection between his feature films and the predominantly French and German philosophical and literary movement, it is because both have a common source in the attempt to dramatize and explain human experience in terms of alienation, authenticity, freedom, and existential choice. The works of the existentialists were written out of the depths of their (often conflicted) personalities, and the way in which personality is woven into the fabric of Mann's protagonists—so often outliers, loners, rebels, and mavericks—gives his work philosophical significance: a concern with the dilemmas and paradoxes of freedom and personal identity; the central issue of troubled pasts; alienation and rootlessness in the protagonists' character formation; and the competitive and combative nature of human relationships.

Architecture also figures prominently in Mann's work, and his use of it has an important existential dimension, as Robert Arnett analyzes in detail in his resourceful essay "Michael Mann and Nonplace: A Nietzschean Element in Mann's Modern Crime Films." Arnett argues that Mann's later crime films establish what he calls a "digital noir" profoundly concerned with identity and sameness. He suggests that the core of Mann's evolving philosophy is that identity is intrinsically tied to one's ability to control the physical and digital surrounding space. In this connection, Arnett finds echoes of Nietzsche's philosophy of power and draws attention to relevant portions of the nineteenth-century philosopher's work to support this interpretation.

In "'Awakened to Chaos': Outsiders in *The Jericho Mile* and *Thief*," an essay incorporating philosophy, literature, and film criticism, volume coeditor R. Barton Palmer provides a conceptual portrait of the outsider as he is found in these early works directed by Mann. Palmer argues that unlike some protagonists who "in the end offer only despairing displays of cynical antiheroism or unpersuasive restorations of the status quo, Mann's protagonists consistently mold their own destinies, choose loss, destruction, or even death over either a surrender to the system or an abrogation of their personal truth."[9] In this way, Palmer argues convincingly that Mann provides a fascinating alternative to the characterization of the outsider so often found in cinema. Taking up this motif of the rootless, alienated protagonist, I argue in "Existential Mann" that although many of Mann's protagonists are given to actions that express an existential impasse, they are also strongly moved by the ideas of freedom, authenticity, and existential choice. For them, Jean-Paul Sartre's idea that we are condemned to be free gives rise not only to anguish, but also to the prospect of attaining the authentic existence they seek. I call attention to these themes in *Thief* (1981) and in key episodes of *Miami Vice*. I then discuss some contrasts between the *Miami Vice* television series and Mann's feature film of the same title.

Evil, Power, and the Aesthetics of Horror

Mann has not been reluctant to explore evil and horror in his films. In the essay "Do You See? Reflecting on Evil in *Manhunter*," volume coeditor Aeon J. Skoble examines the conception of evil in the killers Francis Dollarhyde and Hannibal Lecktor and by the FBI profiler Will Graham, whose methodology includes trying to think as the killers think. Skoble shows how Graham is able to do this and, effectively invoking both Socrates and Nietzsche, explains why it is dangerous to him, both physically and psychologically. He also adds to the auteurist case by citing connections between *Manhunter* (1986) and *Miami Vice* that are hardly likely to be coincidental. In "Mann and *Übermensch*: Evil and Power in *Manhunter*," David Sterritt acutely and persuasively explores evil, power, and voyeurism as well as, in his words, "the notion of 'law' in relation to the psychic economy of heroes and villains in Mann's seminal horror film, linking the operations of its corrupted and corrupting enjoyment to Friedrich Nietzsche's concepts of power, amorality, and evil as a propulsive, productive force."[10] And in "'Blood in the Moonlight': Toward an Aesthetics of Horror in *The Keep* and *Manhunter*," Ivo Ritzer provides close readings of two of Mann's early films in the light of the contribution they make to an aesthetics of horror. He contrasts *The Keep*'s (1983) supernatural power threatening humans with *Manhunter*'s manlike monster, the diabolical sovereign Hannibal Lecktor. Ritzer argues that Mann's aesthetics of horror is an *aestheticization* of horror because in both films the terrible is transformed into the beautiful through mise-en-scène and montage.

Style and Its Discontents

As noted earlier, a key achievement of Mann's cinema is the way he brings together existentialist ideas and noir themes, spiked with emotional resonance. Unfortunately, the elaborate and often thrilling orchestrations that are characteristic of Mann's crime cinema have given him the reputation among some as a filmmaker with a style-heavy hand. As a case in point, consider film historian and critic David Thomson's appraisal of Mann, which has swung wildly in successive editions of his influential source book *The New Biographical Dictionary of Film* and elsewhere. He has gone from saying in 2004 that "no one does film with better touch"[11] and writing in 2008 of "Mann's exhilarating prowess, his unmatched capacity for holding the screen," and his "faultless hiring of players as well as an unerring ear for movie talk"[12] to calling the *Miami Vice* feature film in 2010 "so style-oriented it left you screaming. And *Public Enemies* was enough to erase the legend that Michael Mann deserves to be regarded as a talent."[13]

Although most of Mann's critics have not been as erratic as Thomson or reflected such seemingly conflicting judgments (to say nothing of expressing them in such indefensibly harsh terms), commentary on Mann's work typically has weighed in on one side or the other of this critical divide, lending significance to the discussions of Mann and style in the chapters that examine in detail the relations between style and meaning in his cinema. Examples of the way Mann's visuals have a functional role in the elaboration of story and character can be found in most of the chapters in this book. Several make the point that even Mann's action sequences are concerned with character delineation and plot as a way to deflect the criticism that he emphasizes style at the expense of content, a canard that has shadowed Mann throughout much of his career.

Few commentators on Mann have analyzed the intensification of themes and particular meanings through style as acutely as Steven Rybin. His essay "Style, Meaning, and Myth in *Public Enemies*" is an intensive case study of Mann's 2009 film and an implicit rejoinder to Thomson's judgment. According to Rybin, Mann's films are consistent with the director's career-long desire for authenticity and realism even as they also call attention to themselves as striking aesthetic objects through a creative use of high-definition digital technology. With his analysis of key sequences in *Public Enemies* (2009), Rybin shows how Mann synthesizes style and content, framing acting as both a component of style and a vehicle for the gradual development of narrative meaning. In a characteristically inventive and minutely observed study of his essay's subject, Murray Pomerance argues in "Interiorization in *Public Enemies*" that the film is about modernity, despite being a period gangster film. He demonstrates this through a close examination of several of Mann's techniques, such as contrasts in setting, exposition of personality types, and conflicting perspectives on where the audience's loyalties are expected to lie. In this light, Pomerance discusses how the very notion of interiors is fluid and treated differently by the gangster film. Tom Paulus and Vito Adriaensens adapt the notion of mannerism as a means to achieve a better understanding of Mann's cinema. In their carefully documented essay "Mannerism: Neoclassical Style in the Films of Michael Mann," they observe both changes and continuities in his directorial development while identifying the relevant and rapidly accumulating literature on cinematic style before boldly proposing a conception of Mann's cinema as "mannerist in the sense of its being image conscious and thereby both constructive and instructive of viewing skills."

Ethics, Justice, and Law

In a number of his films, Mann addresses the postmodern theme of the relativity of truth and all modes of representing it and giving it expression. This idea is closely related to the theme of the representation of persons and events in the mass media, a key theme of *The Insider* (1999). David LaRocca discusses in "The Ethics of Contracts, Conscience, and Courage in *The Insider*" three interrelated topics of philosophical significance at the center of Mann's film. He skillfully draws from the work of philosophers such as Epictetus, Aristotle, Emerson, Kant, and J. L. Austin to assess the ways in which Mann's film illustrates and complicates an understanding of performative speech and the nature of promises and contracts, individual conscience in its social context, especially in a marriage, and the quality and conditions for moral courage. In "The Commodification of Justice: Michael Mann and Postmodern Law," Mark Wildermuth argues that "Mann's televisual and cinematic works show concern for the collapse of collective social action under the influence, in part, of a modern legal system that commodifies the idea of justice and thereby ensures that the law serves mainly the violently acquisitive members of society at the top of the economic hierarchy." Analyzing such films as *The Last of the Mohicans* (1992) and *Collateral* (2004) as well as episodes of *Miami Vice* and *Crime Story,* he argues that in Mann's view law is a coercive force for controlling human identity and corrupting human society in late-capitalist America. And in "Subjectivity and the Ethics of Duty in Michael Mann's Cinema," Aga Skrodzka explores ethics in Mann's feature films *Thief* and *Collateral.* In her exploration of Mann's preoccupation with human subjectivity and the process of its constitution, Skrodzka draws on philosopher Emmanuel Levinas's ethics of unconditional responsibility in the face of the demands of the Other. In this way, she endeavors to determine whether this ethics will resolve tensions that might otherwise remain in Mann's outlook.

Love, Emotion, and the Methodology of Philosophy

Alan Woolfolk's reflections on the clash of cultures in *The Last of the Mohicans* in his essay "Natural Man, Natural Rights, and Eros: Conflicting Visions of Nature, Society, and Love in *The Last of the Mohicans*" are carried out with an eye toward showing how "Mann has chosen to inject full-blown moral agents into what Rousseau originally conceived to be an amoral natural state. The state of nature has been moralized and pitted against the corrupting influences of European civilization within the American colonies." Situating much of his discussion historically, Woolfolk provides a richly textured and carefully documented account of the ways in which Mann has woven both Lockean and Rousseauian motifs into *The Last of the Mohicans.*

A recurring theme in Mann's work is the emotional, if not moral, similarity between cop and criminal. It is on full display, for example, in *Heat* (1995) by allowing police Lieutenant Vincent Hanna (Al Pacino) and thief Neil McCauley (Robert De Niro) to reveal enough of themselves to convince us that they have similar psychologies. In *Heat's* famous café conversation between McCauley and Hanna, each concedes that there is nothing else he knows how to do or wants to do more than rob banks and catch criminals, respectively. Until McCauley meets Eady (Amy Brenneman), he is isolated from the feelings of ambivalence that would affect any normal person who must be prepared in thirty seconds flat to walk away from any attachments he may have if he is to achieve McCauley's form of professionalism in his chosen endeavor. Hanna's susceptibility to the same isolation from feeling is reflected in the words that his wife, Justine (Diane Venora), has for him: "You don't live with me; you live among the remains of dead people. You sift through the detritus, you read the terrain, you search for signs of passing, for the scent of your prey, and then you hunt them down. That's the only thing you're committed to."[14] When Hanna returns home to find his wife entertaining a would-be lover, he begins a tirade against Justine's exhusband's "dead-tech, postmodernistic, bullshit house." In "Emotion, Truth, and Space in *Heat*," Jonah Corne argues that Hanna's outburst offers us a highly fruitful way to understand *Heat*'s overlapping preoccupations with emotion, truth, and space. He argues that Hanna resists strict identification with any one side of the binaries that frame such contrasts: dead/alive, warm/cold, bullshit/truth. Rather, he is a character marked by fierce antagonisms who keeps Mann's complex philosophico-architectural vision absorbingly open and unresolved.

In the end, McCauley and Hanna are driven by a need that defines who and what each man is. These commitments and needs characteristic of the two are exposed in the film's finale. McCauley seems to have decided to move to Australia with Eady, a woman he thinks he cannot live without. But he hesitates on their way to the airport long enough to make the fateful choice to hunt down the psychopathic Waingro (Kevin Gage), who shot and killed an armored car guard on an earlier McCauley heist, forcing McCauley and his crew to kill the remaining guards. It is a fateful choice because although he finds and kills Waingro in the airport hotel, he cannot get back to Eady without encountering Hanna, who pursues McCauley into the field on the outskirts of the airport tarmac in a deadly finale.

David Rodríguez-Ruiz discusses in "Mann's Biopics and the Methodology of Philosophy: *Ali* and *The Insider*" the philosophical background of Mann's concerns with definitions and examines the challenges that his biopics raise for the methodology of philosophy. He argues that in *Ali* "the protagonists' fights outside the ring are fought with words and actions, and their goal is to confront received notions, and in *The Insider* corporations influence public opinion and hide valuable information by playing with the meaning of terms, making up legal concepts, and undermining the reputation of their opponents."[15] Using Mann's biopics as illustrative instances, Rodríguez-Ruiz asks whether philosophy's task is to spell out common conceptions or to confront them or both.

Television Mann

The chapters in this volume encompass Michael Mann's career to date as a feature filmmaker, but no introduction to his work should fail to comment on his extensive contributions to television. He wrote scripts for *Police Story* (1973–1977), *Starsky & Hutch* (1975–1979), and the pilot for *Vega$* (1978–1981). That pilot depicted the transition from the old Las Vegas to the new as a move from downtown to the Strip. The neo-noir dimensions that Mann might have brought to the series evidently were not going to be realized, however, so Mann decamped to Chicago and North Wales, respectively, to direct two feature films: *Thief*, starring James Caan, and *The Keep*, starring Scott Glenn. Both films have music tracks by the German electronic group Tangerine Dream that reflect the dark and foreboding nature of their respective themes and surroundings. With the recognition in the industry that the exposure from the two films brought him, Mann was hired to executive-produce *Miami Vice*, an assignment that put him in the public eye and gave him the opportunity to helm a broadcast crime drama as noteworthy as a cultural phenomenon as it was as a television milestone. During the series run, Mann also executive-produced the groundbreaking television series *Crime Story*. Both series are filmed extensively though by no means exclusively at night and wallpapered in sound. *Miami Vice* in particular has Jan Hammer's exquisite thematic scores and includes songs symbolic of the episodes they are found in, such as Todd Rundgren's "Tiny Demons," Russ Ballard's "Voices," Bryan Ferry's "Kiss and Tell," the Payola$' "Eyes of a Stranger," the Smithereens' "Blood and Roses," as well as a lengthy list of New Wave, soul, Latin, and rock-and-roll hits, all in their original renditions—a rarity on broadcast television at the time.

Mann's legendary hands-on approach to executive-producing suggests that he had a say in virtually everything that concerned the look and sound of *Miami Vice* (at least during its first two years), including scripts, locations, wardrobe, and music.[16] In addition to foregrounding Miami's status as a "sunshine noir" city, Mann's influence as executive producer is especially clear in the attention the series gives to the themes of existential crises and threats to personal identity as well as to important social and political issues of the day. He is especially mindful of the show's story lines and narrative boldness, about which he told John Maguire in 2007: "I looked again at the pilot and some of the early episodes and I got kind of captured afresh by the deep currents and the emotional power of those stories, and I'm talking here about the first two seasons. The way the issues were brought in from the outside world into the lives of Crockett and Tubbs and the way the stories impacted on them. To me, these stories summed up *Miami Vice* as it originally was."[17]

Although much of *Miami Vice* engages us through its style, Mann's comments remind us that the series did not neglect narrative, character, or performance, including performances by guest stars that were often tours de force. The episode "Heart of Darkness" (September 28, 1984) is a case in point. It features an FBI agent (Ed O'Neill) who, while working undercover to entrap a Miami porn dealer, must make an existential choice between living the glamorous life of money and beautiful, available women that he has become accustomed to and maintaining his identity as a law enforcement professional and faithful husband, and who knows he cannot do both. Other examples include "Shadow in the Dark" (October 31, 1986), in which Sonny Crockett (Don Johnson) tries to hold on to his identity while simultaneously entering the mental life of a bizarre cat burglar (Vincent Caristi). The episode ends in a scene associated with all the narrative ambiguity of neo-noir: an abrupt cut away from Crockett behind a two-way mirror observing the interrogation of the Shadow to Crockett suddenly waking, which provokes viewers to wonder whether the episode they have been watching has been Crockett's dream all along. In "Out Where the Buses Don't Run" (October 18, 1985), a former vice detective's (Bruce McGill) past haunts him and enters his present. In existential conflict, he obsessively seeks the drug kingpin who disappeared after charges against him were dismissed—unable, either psychologically or existentially, to accept that he murdered the criminal long ago. In "Death and the Lady" (October 16, 1987), an avant-garde filmmaker (Paul Guilfoyle) accused of murdering an actress during the making of a snuff flick engages in cat-and-mouse play with Crockett, defying him by introducing him to alternative models, each of whom bears a startling resemblance to the actress he is accused of killing. Other episodes dramatize how Crockett "becomes" his undercover criminal alter ego, Sonny Burnett, after he suffers a concussion while on an undercover assignment. Working for a crime syndicate in the underworld that is Burnett's milieu, Crockett engages in criminal activity even as he begins to have flashbacks to his life as a vice detective. So begins an existential struggle to confront the killer inside him and recover his true identity.

In *Crime Story*, a prime-time period drama in serial format, two deeply alienated adversaries, Chicago police detective lieutenant Mike Torello (Dennis Farina) and ruthless criminal Ray Luca (Anthony Denison), demonize each other in a Manichean struggle for dominance. Torello, sworn to uphold the law, pursues Luca from Chicago to Las Vegas, where Luca operates an international criminal enterprise. As Torello's obsession to put Luca behind bars begins to take its toll, and with the authority of a federal Major Crime Unit task force he now heads, he resorts to acts of professional misconduct on a massive scale. Shot on location and described by Mann as "a 22-hour picture," this neo-noir masterpiece has been contrasted with its illustrious predecessor: Julia Cameron writes, "If *Miami Vice* renders a vision of our near future in pastel neons, *Crime Story* gives us a past that is black and blue and purple: the colors of a bruise."[18] Writing about the series in the *New York Times* in 2001, thirteen years after NBC had cancelled the show at the end of its second season and A&E began to air the entire series, Thelma Adams called *Crime Story* "one of the best television series you've probably never seen."[19]

In 1989, with both *Miami Vice* and *Crime Story* behind him, Mann wrote, directed, and executive-produced the TV movie *L.A. Takedown,* a precursor to *Heat.* In 1990, he produced the Emmy Award–winning miniseries *Drug Wars: The Camarena Story,* and in 2002–2003 in the early days of high-definition broadcasting he co-executive-produced *Robbery Homicide Division,* starring Tom Sizemore. The series ran for ten episodes. In 2011–2012, Mann co-executive-produced and directed the pilot of *Luck,* the ironically titled series for HBO created by David Milch and starring Dustin Hoffman. After several incidents led to the death of three racehorses during production, HBO cancelled the series. In 2012, Mann and filmmaker David Frankham executive-produced *Witness* for HBO, a documentary in four installments about the experiences of photojournalists whose work involves reporting on conflict situations around the world. In mid-2013, shooting commenced in Los Angeles and Hong Kong on *Cyber,* a thriller written, directed, and produced by Mann. He is at work on a digital restoration of *Thief* to be released on DVD in 2014.[20]

Notes

1. Jonathan Romney, "Mann and His Movies," *Guardian* (London), April 18, 1996.

2. To date, Mann has directed the following films: *Thief* (1981), *The Keep* (1983), *Manhunter* (1986), *The Last of the Mohicans* (1992), *Heat* (1995), *The Insider* (1999), *Ali* (2001), *Collateral* (2004), *Miami Vice* (2006), and *Public Enemies* (2009).

3. Jonathan Rayner, *The Cinema of Michael Mann: Vice and Vindication* (London: Wallflower Press, 2013), 172.

4. Steven Rybin, *Michael Mann: Crime Auteur* (Lanham, MD: Scarecrow Press, 2013), xiii.

5. Discussions of Mann as television auteur can be found in Jeremy G. Butler, *Television Style* (New York: Routledge, 2010), 87–108; James Lyons, *Miami Vice* (West Sussex, UK: Wiley, Blackwell, 2010), 29–57; and Steven Sanders, *Miami Vice* (Detroit: Wayne State University Press, 2010), 7–16, 19–33.

6. The *Miami Vice* pilot was written by Anthony Yerkovich and directed by Thomas Carter. Anthony Yerkovich is officially credited with creating the series.

7. The sequence featured a spectacular bit of underwater technology and can be seen in its entirely on the director's cut edition of the DVD.

8. Quoted in Iain Blair, "Michael Mann: *Miami Vice*," *Post* magazine, August 1, 2006, http://www.postmagazine.com /publications/Post-Magazine/ 2006/August-1-2006/ Michael/Mann/Miami/Vice/aspx, accessed October 8, 2013.

9. This quote is from Palmer's original abstract for his essay in this volume.

10. This quote is from Sterritt's original abstract for his essay in this volume.

11. David Thomson, *The New Biographical Dictionary of Film* (New York: Knopf, 2004), 576.

12. David Thomson, *"Have You Seen . . . ?" A Personal Introduction to 1,000 Films* (New York: Knopf, 2008), 362.

13. David Thomson, *The New Biographical Dictionary of Film, Updated and Expanded Edition* (New York: Knopf, 2010), 625.

14. Although audiences may well sympathize with Justine, it might be argued that this is not on point because the issue for Mann is how *Hanna* understands his life-defining principles and commitments.

15. This quote is from Rodríguez-Ruiz's abstract for his essay in this volume.

16. John Nicolella, the show's Miami-based producer during its first two seasons, told reporter Emily Benedek, "Michael was in charge of the whole visual sense of the show, all this slick stuff—which car, what the clothes look like, the colors, the kind of film cutting. He said, 'It'll be this and this and this,' and he has maintained that all along." Emily Benedek, "Inside *Miami Vice*," *Rolling Stone*, March 28, 1985, 61.

17. John Maguire, "Michael Mann Interview: *Miami Vice*," *Maguiresmovies*, http:// blogspot.com/2006/07/Michael-mann-interview-miami-vice.html.

18. Julia Cameron, "The Difference Between 'Vice,' 'Crime Story,'" *Chicago Tribune*, October 28, 1986, http://www.articles.sun-tentinel.com/1986-10-28/ features/8603060900_1_crime-story-miami-vice-darlene-fluegel, accessed June 7, 2013. The quote from Mann also comes from this article.

19. Thelma Adams, "Mob Life Draped in Angst (Sounds Familiar, Right?)," *New York Times*, August 5, 2001, http://www.nytimes.com/2001/08/05/arts/television-radio-mob-life-draped-in-angst-sounds-familiar-right.html, accessed June 7, 2013.

20. My thanks to Michael Henry Wilson for informing me of Mann's digital restoration of *Thief*.

MICHAEL MANN AND NONPLACE

A Nietzschean Element in Mann's Modern Crime Films

Robert Arnett

Early in *Collateral* (2004), Vincent (Tom Cruise), a hit man beginning a job, describes Los Angeles as "too sprawled out. Disconnected. . . . Seventeen million people . . . but nobody knows each other. Too impersonal. I read about this guy. Gets on the MTA, here, and dies. Six hours he's riding the subway before anybody notices. This corpse doing laps around LA, people on and off, sitting next to him, nobody notices." Buildings, bridges, roads, and other geographic structures act as key elements in Michael Mann's mise-en-scène and suggest, as Vincent alludes to, the "nonplace" of Marc Augé's supermodernity. Augé defines nonplace as space that "cannot be defined as relational, or historical, or concerned with identity."[1] Nonplaces separate people from their identity, creating mass groups, such as commuters, passengers, shoppers, consumers. Nonplaces induce physical and virtual sameness and soullessness, and Augé sees the points where large numbers of people collect, such as airports, large retail spaces, cable and wireless networks, as putting "the individual in contact only with another image of himself."[2] Sameness on a pervasive scale makes the essential quality of supermodernity excess: too many events, too many structures, and both filled with too many individuals stripped of their identity. Mann and Augé take a cue from Friedrich Nietzsche in their expression of place: "The language spoken by these buildings is far too rhetorical and unfree, reminding us that they are houses of God and ostentatious monuments of some supramundane intercourse."[3]

Michael Mann's storytelling engages a spatial sensibility, and in a previous essay I track how space influences narrative decisions.[4] In this essay, Nietzsche's writing provides a vehicle to illuminate the multiple levels of meaning found in Mann's modern crime films, from direction and mise-en-scène to the central characters' profound struggle to find meaning, or the lack thereof, in the spaces they inhabit and often to (re)define those spaces. The characters define the spaces they inhabit much as in Nietzsche's contention that "I do not see how we could remain content with such buildings even if they were stripped of their churchly purposes."[5] From an architectural theory point of view, Mark Rakatansky suggests that the constitution and management of people occur in "institutional space" (office buildings, homes, roads, parks) and that "institutional space may provide one of the more productive themes for a narrative architecture."[6] For Nietzsche, institutional space is religious/God space (churches, monasteries, etc.), and the architect, who "has always been under the spell of power," creates buildings that "are supposed to render pride visible, and a victory over gravity, the will to power."[7] Yet, for Nietzsche, architecture often fails in its aims and becomes institutionalized. He asserts, "We who are godless could not think *our thoughts* in such places."[8] Mann, as film director–architect, exerts a will to power with institutional spaces and adapts the management of the subjects within those spaces to fit his rhetorical means. The space often requires minimal "management/will to power" from Mann—that is, the bridge is supposed to be a bridge; lighting and composition enhance the bridge's rhetorical presence. In some cases, the will to power alters the meaning of the original space. For example, Atlanta's High Museum becomes the prison holding Dr. Hannibal Lecktor (Brian Cox) in *Manhunter* (1986). By rejecting its museum qualities, Mann frames the museum to fit a thematic design. For Mann, the museum becomes a prison, and its prevailing whiteness and sterility amplify the absence of identity he associates with prisons. Architecture, in other words, bears multiple levels of meaning in Mann's modern crime films, but Augé's supermodernity of nonplace provides only a beginning to understanding the potential in Mann's mise-en-scène. We turn, then, to Nietzsche for a more philosophical understanding of the excessive sameness of Augé's supermodernity in Mann's modern crime films, using the films as case studies, first, to explicate Mann's filmic style; second, to isolate the various levels of meaning and architectural representation; and third, to find in Mann's treatment of space elements resonating with Nietzsche's philosophy.

Mann's filmic style coordinates the camera elements (composition, lighting, color saturation) and built environs and uses them to frame the viewer's position on the characters and events. The camera frames structures in a way determined to connect space and character. Mann takes us through structures to see characters carefully positioned within a space. He sets Neil McCauley (Robert De Niro), the professional thief of *Heat* (1995), for example, in his beach house so that the interior frames the view of both Neil and the ocean beyond. Similar compositions appear in *Manhunter* and the film version of *Miami Vice* (2006). Consistent architectural representations go on to form a lexicon of structures. Mann's heroes usually live in beach homes, antagonists live in modern homes, parking garages become meeting places, office buildings are blue-collar work sites, confrontations occur beneath bridges, highways are places of meditation and contemplation, and diners or bars act as sites of negotiation and exchange. His film style interacts with architectural representations and demonstrates how space drives character and narrative.

On a broad level, Mann's modern crime films depict the arrival of the hero within a nonplace (e.g., Frank [James Caan] breaks into a safe in an office building in *Thief* [1981]; the cops deliver Will Graham [William Peterson] to the home of the murder victims in *Manhunter;* Neil arrives on a commuter train in *Heat;* Vincent arrives at the Los Angeles Airport in *Collateral;* and Crockett and Tubbs [Colin Farrell and Jamie Foxx] enter a drug organization network in an undercover operation in *Miami Vice*), and that space determines their action (a crime, an investigation, or an undercover operation). On a more detailed level, space defines character. For example, when members of the Aryan Brotherhood kidnap Trudy (Naomie Harris) in the 2006 *Miami Vice,* she manages to give away the location during the hostage phone call by referring to "trailer trash," which clues her colleagues to find trailer parks near airports. Similarly, the serial killer of *Manhunter,* whose home reflects his inner state, lives in a house that through framing devices makes visual the representational objects of his fantasy.

By giving emphasis to architectural space in the mise-en-scène, Mann's crime films can make statements, in the words of Mark Lamster, "about the built—or unbuilt—environment, or use that environment to comment metaphorically on any of a variety of subjects."[9] Mann's style within the crime film composes space as allusion, using the experience of inhabiting a space and moving through it as meaningful experience. He provides the frame through which the film's viewer enacts the experience of perception and allusion. In seeing the framing as rhetorical or, in Nietzsche's phrasing, as "think[ing] our thoughts," Mann exerts his will upon the viewer to connect the environs to the narrative so that space drives the events and reflects character.

Nowhere is it more evident that Mann's film style of space drives the narrative than in the television series *Miami Vice* (1984–1989). As executive producer, Mann supervised the production and established the look of the show, but he never directed an episode.[10] Mark Steensland explains: "To Mann, of course, this [*Miami Vice*] style was not gratuitous, but was instead 'an expression of place and content, the milieu the guys are moving through.'"[11] Mann was determined, as Steven Sanders puts it in his recent monograph, "to use the city not merely as a backdrop but as a character in its own right. A tourist destination, a once and future film location, and a safe haven for Cuban exiles, Miami is also a locus of the art deco, late modern, and vernacular architecture that provides not one but many cityscapes and makes a major contribution to the show's atmosphere."[12] Sanders further suggests that Mann, along with the show's creator, Anthony Yerkovich, "sensed that the quintessentially telegenic Greater Miami with its cycle of decline, decay, redevelopment, and renewal (invariably followed by further repetitions of the cycle), affirmed the indeterminacy and contingency of postmodern noir."[13] The Miami of the 1980s *Miami Vice* bears a similar dynamic to the Chicago of *Thief*: enough history and identity resonate with the structures, but that history conflicts with the encroaching excess of supermodernity. Miami's deco buildings of the 1920s and 1930s, slathered in pastels, provide a contrast to the modernity visualized by the characters (e.g., the cars, the fashions, the music). In contrast, in the 2006 feature-film version of *Miami Vice,* not only are the deco buildings nowhere in sight, but nonplaces also eclipse the modernity of the television series.

Although *Heat* visualizes a nonplace-dominated Los Angeles, it also exemplifies how Mann's film style reflects character. According to Janice Polley, *Heat*'s location manager, Mann "was very specific on this film that he wanted it to be a certain look, each character had an architectural style, and he also wanted it to be locations he had never photographed in Los Angeles before."[14] The film opens with images of a commuter train and train station to establish architectural design as generating attitudes about and an understanding of Neil, the bank robber.[15] In the absence of narrative context at the film's outset, the environs and their design frame the character-commuter, but with something different about him. The hospital in the second location provides another allusion. It alludes to a nonplace, the second nonplace in this minutes-old film, in which inhabiting the space determines the individuals. Neil "inhabits" the space, but his determined movement sets him apart from the other patients' excess. According to Mark Wildermuth, "Neil moves into the hospital—a place of electronics, computer screens, and antiseptic whiteness, until Neil glances in one room and we see a bleeding victim's body in close-up, [the] first sign of what this all means, anything can be invaded, nothing is secure, and nothing is sacred in this fragmented world of incongruities."[16]

The hospital elaborates the dangerous, fragmented world of supermodernity that began with the train station and provides an important example of how Mann's film style uses the camera to frame the perception of space to "manage" the characters inhabiting and reacting to the space. It performs at a surface level of meaning within images and narrative events. The space beneath the bridge determines the method of robbing the armored truck in *Heat* and propels the rest of the story. Similarly, Graham's "reading" of the victims' homes in *Manhunter* motivates the course of his investigation. The buildings Frank breaks into in *Thief* define his professional character. The breakdown of virtual and physical networks motivates the undercover operation in the 2006 *Miami Vice*. Hence, my claim that space drives the narrative in Mann's modern crime films.

With space driving the narrative and reflecting character, isolating the various levels of meaning and architectural representation becomes necessary to understanding the narratives and finding elements that resonate with Nietzsche. In Mann's first feature-length film, the made-for-television movie *The Jericho Mile* (1979), a single structure dominates the narrative, Folsom State Penitentiary. Because one structure dominates the film, the narrative plays more like a one-act story, reacting to a single event. Folsom tells a story of containment and institutional repression. At key moments, Folsom literally forces convicts into their solitude. Bells ring, and the cell bars close, shutting in each convict. Les Roberts, in applying Augé's theory to Pawel Pawlikowski's *Last Resort* (2000), classifies different zones of nonplaces: arrival and departure, transition, and stasis. Folsom fits the "zone of stasis," with its denial of movement and with connection beyond the boundaries becoming "the central element within the social practice of the diegetic characters."[17] Considered alone, Folsom offers little narrative, but its intertextual relationship to the prison experiences of Mann's other modern crime films, especially *Thief* and *Heat,* informs those narratives.

With *Thief,* Mann begins a depiction of the American city. *Thief* features either urban-based businesses or upper-middle-class homes. The decaying structures of *Thief* suggest the ending of place and the coming excess of supermodernity's nonplaces. *Thief* and the *Miami Vice* television series have a retro element to their architecture. The skyline shots of Chicago contain iconic structures, such as the Sears Tower, which emphasize the identity of the space. Mann purposefully frames his city view to make Chicago's identity and history (North Shore, blues clubs, State Street) distinct, emphasizing in *Thief* a narrative with polarities of place and nonplace.

More specifically, Mann shows the parts of the local architecture that emphasize the zone of arrival and departure within a structure: fire escapes in the alley, doorways, windows, bus station, police station, elevator shafts, and the industrial water front—all fringe, boundary, or transitional spaces. Mann's strategic framing finds the retro feel of Chicago architecture giving way to nonplace. For example, as Frank prepares a break-in, he goes to an old foundry, seemingly from the nineteenth century and about to collapse. The temporal quality of the architecture in *Thief* comes from its juxtaposition within single shots and to other architectural references. The urban architecture's age contrasts to the contemporary suburban environment, as seen in the house Frank buys and the home of the crime boss, Leo. The only distinction Frank's and Leo's homes seem to have is that they are just like every other house in the neighborhoods of gridlike streets. The suburban architecture tells a story of an excess of conformity and the expansion of nonplaces, issues that parallel Frank's story.

Nonplaces become more elaborate as Mann's crime films progress. "Travelers," Augé's term, enter the network of nonplaces and thereby transform themselves into commuters or passengers or shoppers. In other words, the structures suggest a sequence of acts. In Act I, or the beginning, travelers enter supermodernity (zones of arrival and departure). Act II concerns the obstacles and conflicts that test the hero on his or her path to an important revelation. Within the network of nonplaces, Augé explains, the traveler "obeys the same code as others, receives the same messages, [and] responds to the same entreaties."[18] In Mann's crime cinema, the codes, messages, and entreaties of the architecture are often seductive: Larry "Rain" Murphy (Peter Strauss) in *The Jericho Mile* eschews the standard ethnic affiliations coded into the prison; Frank in *Thief* succumbs temporarily to suburban living; Graham of *Manhunter* reenters the network of nonplaces as an FBI investigator and fights to maintain his professionalism as evidence/architecture taunts him; a complex set of structures tempts both Neil and police lieutenant Vincent Hanna (Al Pacino) throughout *Heat* (to be good at what they do, they cannot inhabit traditional socially acceptable "spaces": Neil denies any attachments, and Vincent has to mimic Neil's actions to be able to track him); and in *Miami Vice* the film, the architecture of domesticity and a world outside of police work tempts Sonny Crockett. In Act III, the ending, the environs frame a story of affirming identity or the ultimate loss of identity. In the language of nonplace, Act III resolves the tension between the zone of arrival and departure and the zone of stasis. For example, the safe house at the end of *Miami Vice* suggests the stasis of domesticity with Isabella that Crockett denies; Graham's beach house tells as much of his ending as any element of the film; and the jets and airport frame the loss of Neil's life and Vincent's stasis at the end of *Heat*. Mann's strategically stylized architecture conveys a narrative, starting with crossing a threshold into supermodernity, then meeting conflicts of identity (deteriorating old buildings, juxtapositions of new and old, placement) and obstacles in realizing identity (place becomes nonplace, nonplace becomes place), and, in the end, returning to zones of arrival and departure, where structures connote the excess of time, space, and a loss of identity.

Again, Mann engages Augé's theory, first by establishing a visual vocabulary of space. As noted earlier, Les Roberts provides a rubric to categorize general nonplaces: zones of arrival and departure (airports, commuter train stations, bus stations, industrial piers—and, within those spaces, doors and windows), zones of transition (roads, parking garages, diners and bars, motels and hotels, the underside of bridges), and zones of stasis (homes, office buildings, physical and virtual networks, cars). When this lexicon is turned back on Mann's films, a progression of place to nonplaces emerges. The 1981 *Thief* contains much "place," the identity of Chicago, but in the 1995 *Heat* little of the Los Angeles that Mann depicts contains any "place" (we know it's Los Angeles only because the characters say it's Los Angeles). *Collateral* takes place entirely within nonplaces, and *Miami Vice* (Miami looking no different than Los Angeles) finds "place" only outside of Miami. Mann's film style does not change, but his architectural representations reflect the growing sameness of Augé's supermodernity. Augé's concept helps connect how Mann's film style and the architectural representations interact, an important layer of meaning just below the surface of image and narrative events, but making sense of the excessive sameness of supermodernity demands a more expansive philosophy, and in many ways this layer of meaning echoes the ideas of Friedrich Nietzsche.

The combination of film style and architectural representation has two broad effects on Mann's modern crime films. First, architecture and narrative intersect at crucial moments of a film. The characters redefine the space (e.g., the armored car robbery and the bank robbery in the streets in *Heat*), or the space redefines the characters and their situation (e.g., Max Durocher's

[Jamie Foxx] cab in *Collateral* or the victims' homes in *Manhunter*). Second, the architectural representations may reflect a character's inner state (the sparseness of Neil's beach house in *Heat*). The exterior/interior dynamic of the effect of film style and architectural representation demonstrates how pervasive "space" becomes in Mann's crime films.

The heroes in these films defy reduction to commuters or patients or diners or shoppers and suggest a narrative space negotiated between architecture and story world. In Nietzsche's words, the heroes of Mann's modern crime films are "the godless." Nietzsche's God/religion parallels Augé's supermodernity of excess. The "godless" struggle to not let God/religion/ morality reduce them to a member of the "herd." According to Nietzsche, "Morality trains the individual to be a function of the herd and to ascribe value to himself only as a function."[19] Mann's heroes defy the herd, and their interactions with the spaces they inhabit make this clear. Nietzsche seems particularly relevant to the relationship between the godless and institutional spaces: "The language spoken by these buildings is far too rhetorical and unfree . . . we who are godless could not think *our thoughts* in such surroundings."[20] An especially important place in Mann's modern crime film that is "far too rhetorical and unfree" is the prison. It becomes an intertextual convergence point, an institutional nonplace that strips away identity. We see the prison in *The Jericho Mile,* and Murphy asserts that he is "nothing." Frank, in *Thief,* explains prison as a negotiation between nonplace and a person and expresses a Nietzschean notion of becoming free or not becoming one of the herd: "I was twenty when I went in, thirty-one when I come out. . . . You don't count months and years. You don't do time that way. . . . You gotta forget time. You gotta not give a fuck if you live or die. You gotta get to where nothing means nothing."

For Nietzsche, getting to "where nothing means nothing" is indicative of freedom: "Such a spirit who has *become free* stands amid the cosmos with a joyous and trusting fatalism, in the *faith* that only the particular is loathsome, and that all is redeemed and affirmed in the whole—*he does not negate any more.*"[21] In Nietzsche's language, the heroes in Mann's modern crime films are Dionysian. In *Heat,* Neil's crew formed in prison, and they learned the following lesson from an older thief: don't keep anything in your life you're "not willing to walk out on in thirty seconds flat if you feel the heat around the corner."[22] In Mann's crime films, the prison represents the institutional space that erases individual identity. The hero suffers metaphorical death, then resurrects as a new identity within the prison: a thief who violates the definitions of institutional space. Prison, then, is the space in which the hero negotiates his freedom from the herd and, in Nietzschean terms, becomes godless. Creating a new life and family or returning to family life drives the hero, and because of the emphasis on living and creating "place," Mann's heroes qualify as Dionysian.

The home acts as another site of confrontation between the herd and the godless in Mann's modern crime films and appears to be more Apollonian. In *Manhunter,* the victims' homes contain the story of the murders and the clues to finding the serial killer, if Graham can break their code. In reference to his wife's house, Vincent in *Heat* refers to it as "postdead tech," the house becoming the visualization of the dope and Prozac "prisoners" of the city as a zone of stasis. Steven Rybin periodically connects the interaction of architecture and narrative in his analysis, and of *Collateral* he notes that "richly realized city images figure as an overarching metaphor for postmodern contingency in innumerable scenes throughout the film."[23] The living spaces in *Miami Vice*—trailer parks, mansions, glass-walled beachfront homes—define the characters as much as their actions do. The Atlanta and Birmingham homes of *Manhunter* become rhetorical and unfree, tragic redefinitions imposed by an Apollonian sense of order and form as defined by Nietzsche. Francis Dollarhyde (Tom Noonan) acts as a violent Apollonian in his "becoming" as he redefines the home space into his own art and religion ("You owe me awe," he tells one of his victims). At this level of meaning, Mann's modern crime films become tragedies of identity within a supermundane intercourse/supermodernity.

In the 2006 *Miami Vice* and in *Heat,* the heroes enact an important variation on a Dionysian redefinition of nonplace. The heroes of *Miami Vice* penetrate the nonplace of physical and virtual networks and negotiate and renegotiate identity. As undercover agents, the space they inhabit insists they establish the credibility of their "identities." What could be more Dionysian for Nietzsche? As Nietzsche claims, "In the Dionysian state . . . the whole affective system is excited and enhanced: [it] drives forth simultaneously the power of representation, imitation, transfiguration, transformation, and every kind of mimicking and acting."[24] The cops and robbers of *Heat* renegotiate physical and virtual space to see each other's acts as forms of Apollonian (Vincent) and Dionysian (Neil) artistic expression. They change rooftops, freeways, parking garages, and the underside of bridges into sophisticated forms of expression. Vincent, for example, arrives at the armored-car robbery site and immediately inflicts order and form on the workspace, decoding the evidence and even complimenting the quality of the work ("M.O. is that they are good"). Throughout the film, Neil assumes different identities (he enters the hospital at the beginning in the coveralls of an ambulance driver, and at the end he assumes the identity of a hotel worker), until he reveals something close to the truth of himself to Eady (Amy Brenneman) near the end and to Vincent at the very end.

The meeting between the FBI and Miami police in *Miami Vice* takes place on the top of an empty parking garage, surrounded by the digital grid of buildings lit for the night. The nonplace parking garage frames scenes in which Mann's Dionysian characters redefine or elaborate self-definition/ transformations. Crockett and Tubbs go undercover; Neil learns about his nemeses from Nate (Jon Voight) in a parking garage; and Dollarhyde sends the flaming Freddy Lounds (Stephen Lang) to the FBI in a parking garage. At the end of *Miami Vice,* Crockett and Tubbs succeed in stopping the traitor within the drug organization who used the Aryan Brotherhood to take over the organization. In effect, Crockett and Tubbs expose and eliminate the viral infection within the network of nonplaces. The implication is clear in the ending: the networks of the drug organization and the networks of law enforcement will renegotiate the meaning of a few intersecting spaces and then, as in Nietzsche's eternal recurrence, continue as before. The American city of supermodernity exists as a sprawling mass of stasis and is, in Nietzsche's words, "rhetorical" and "unfree."

The endings of Mann's crime films become the moments when architecture and narrative achieve a Nietzschean "frenzy" of convergence. *Thief* involves Frank's invasion of the mob boss's home. The "frenzy" of violence ends with Frank still standing, free, but adrift in the excess of nonplace. In *Manhunter,* the frenzy involves Graham crashing through the window into Dollarhyde's home and a violent "frenzy" of "we the godless" not able to "think *our thoughts.*" Amid the frenzy of Waingro's (Kevin Gage) killing at the airport hotel in *Heat,* Neil and Vincent face each other (again, each in contact with an image of himself—the final sequence of consistent shot/ reverse shot of Neil and Vincent that runs through the film). Neil's death recalls Nietzsche's elaboration of the Dionysian pessimism: "I call this pessimism of the future—I see it comes! I see it coming!—Dionysian pessimism."[25] Max manages to kill Vincent on the commuter train in *Collateral,* offering the visual of a Dionysian victory over the Apollonian in the sense that Max exerts his will to power within the nonplace as Vincent mistakenly thinks he possesses a vision of power over the excess of nonplace. Max ultimately becomes capable of a metamorphosis that Vincent is unable or unwilling to achieve.

In *Miami Vice,* the showdown takes place at an industrial pier, a zone of arrival and departure, and reveals Crockett's true identity as a cop to Isabella. Mann suggests Augé's idea that existing in supermodernity amounts to role-playing. Crockett, in Augé's (very Nietzschean) words, "tastes for a while . . . the more active pleasure of role-playing."[26] By *Miami Vice,* nonplace dominates, in Mann's view, the American city. Film style and architectural representation negotiate a narrative from the tension between place and nonplace, and by Mann's latter films, which are set predominantly in nonplace, the characters negotiate identity within nonplace—to varying degrees of success. The affirmation is not of character or of identity, but of the hegemony of supermodernity. And as Nietzsche reminds us, "We who are godless could not think *our thoughts* in such surroundings."

Characters' internal conflict with supermodernity also relies on film style and architectural representation. For example, in *Manhunter* Mann fixes Dollarhyde's inner demons to the architecture and objects of his home. Thomas Harris's original novel describes a home much like the house from Hitchcock's *Psycho* (1960). In *Manhunter,* however, Dollarhyde's home becomes a richer symbol because of its purpose in visualizing Dollarhyde's interior and not, as in Harris's case, in reflecting his upbringing. "[*Manhunter's*] architecture," F. X. Feeney explains, "is not a passive backdrop defining milieu, but a dynamic and active part of the drama. Dollarhyde's house looks normal on the outside, but the inside is full of objects selected by Dollarhyde that express his delusions about what he seeks."[27]

When Graham breaks through the glass picture window (part of a broken glass/mirror motif) at Dollarhyde's home, he metaphorically succeeds in breaking into Dollarhyde's mind. The house is Dollarhyde's mindscape, including lots of glass to refract and distort the outside light into strange shadow plays on the walls, a lunar landscape mural, a strange planet-system light fixture, a television set droning only static, William Blake's *The Great Red Dragon and the Woman Clothed with the Sun* painting. The interior design of the home features a flow-through openness because Dollarhyde's mind contains no walls.

There seems to be only a kitchen and a main room, where windowpanes encase the front door. At the end of the fight, Dollarhyde lies on the floor with blood pouring out from him, forming red dragon wings—his final transformation literally soaks into the structure. In Harris's novel, Dollarhyde's house burns down and sets up a standard horror film genre ending in which Dollarhyde appears later at Graham's home, allowing Graham to reaffirm his identity and "home." Clearly, Mann adapts Harris's story away from its temporal narrative (i.e., When will Dollarhyde reappear?) to a spatially driven narrative of Graham breaking into Dollarhyde's home and mind and emphasizing Nietzsche's godless overcoming the religious.

The effect of film style and architectural representation appears in Mann's first film, *The Jericho Mile*. Rain Murphy's cell, in particular, makes visual Murphy's interiority of "nothing": it is virtually empty and completely unadorned, connecting to Frank's "nothing means nothing" in *Thief*. Murphy's only friend, in the next cell, offers the other side of the visual juxtaposition: a cell decorated with pictures of his family. Mann tints the shots of Murphy working out in the cell in a blue light, which connects this space to the oceanside homes in *Manhunter* and *Heat*. According to Rybin, "Mann often links blue and gray color schemes to the existential crisis of his characters."[28] The color signifies the narrative moment, but the surrounding architecture and the character's interaction with it express the character's interiority and the basis of the existential crisis ahead. And the characters' interiority reveals their status as "godless."

One of Mann's most profound examples of style, architecture, and character interiority comes in *Heat* and the first depiction of Neil's beach house. As noted earlier, the house frames the beach from the interior, emphasizing the glass wall facing the ocean, with the ocean horizon line neatly dividing the composition into equal halves. Jean-Baptiste Thoret sees a metaphor of separation in these fragmented glass surfaces in Mann's films, forming "a glass jar, but also set[ting] up a place of confrontation between a feeling of enclosure, or claustrophobia even, and that of an infinite openness."[29] The modernist style with its bright, clean, airy spaces appeals to Neil, the former convict. An artificially lit and cramped prison cell, as seen in *The Jericho Mile*, severely restricts opening to the exterior. The contracted cell offers nowhere for the spatial experience to go except for off another wall, and it denies the opportunity for mental or visual stimulation (see Frank's explanation of being state raised in *Thief*).

Neil's beach house displays the opposite, a place where the godless can think their thoughts. Windows facing the ocean constitute an entire wall made of glass, resulting in an airy interior awash in bluish lighting. The ocean so dominates this scene that it feels as if it were an extension of the house, making the house expansive—not, as Thoret suggests, an enclosure.[30] Neil's house becomes instrumental in visualizing the connection between Neil and the ocean. Water signs follow Neil throughout the film, and his inner motivation becomes tied to crossing the ocean with Eady to a new life. In Nietzsche's words, the crossing is ascension to being an "overman" and to deceiving "not even myself."[31] The excesses of supermodernity (nonplace) drive Neil's interior narrative and his existential crisis. The interaction of Mann's film style and architectural representation makes visual Neil's longing for identity in some meaning-filled space across the ocean (place), just as Nietzsche claims the godless seek to "see *ourselves* translated into stone and plants . . . to take walks *in ourselves* when we stroll around these buildings and gardens."[32] Yet Vincent kills Neil, not only denying Neil's ascension, but also sentencing Vincent himself to a life in the excess of supermodernity, similar to Murphy's prison sentence in *The Jericho Mile*, similar to Frank's wandering at the end of *Thief* and to Crockett's life at the end of the 2006 *Miami Vice*. The tragedy of *Manhunter* takes the form of Graham's dark descent into Dollarhyde's dreams. Graham's survival makes him stronger, and he returns to his family (the beach home), bearing yet more scars of his battles within supermodernity. Nietzsche helps us understand these films as tragedies.

Mann's film style connects architectural representations and story events. Because these modern crime films involve stories in which cops and criminals alter the physical and virtual space, interaction becomes inevitable. Place and nonplace appear in Mann's crime films so consistently that they form a lexicon. For example, the prison, both present (*The Jericho Mile, Manhunter*) and referenced (*Thief, Heat*), becomes a nonplace of existential self-awareness and redefinition—nonplace turns the hero into "nothing," and from there the hero begins a journey of new identity. Prison is the central metaphor of supermodernity. Prison and supermodernity turn individuals into "nothing," and the film characters become heroes because the prison forces them to reclaim their identity. The home becomes tragic space because families do not unite; they are often destroyed or torn apart there. Mann, the director as architect, exerts an artistic will through the use of space. Homes become crime scenes. The underside of bridges, often eerily lit, with cathedral-like arches, becomes a strange, underworld stadium where the professionals perform. These intersections of space and narrative motivate characters through the narrative and, in turn, motivate new meanings of the space.

Part of Mann's design resides with film style and architectural representation revealing character interiority. Mann's use of architectural design in the framing effect of Neil's beach house in *Heat* reveals Neil's connection to the ocean, the emptiness of his life, and the precision with which he lives; the open flow of windows and rooms in Dollarhyde's home in *Manhunter* becomes the landscape filled with the objects of his psychosis. For Mann, the relationship between architectural design and character interiority is a subtle means of making the inner life of the characters visual. He directs as if he were one of Nietzsche's architects: "The most powerful human beings have always inspired architects; the architect has always been under the spell of power. His buildings are supposed to render pride visible, and the victory over gravity, the will to power. Architecture is a kind of eloquence of power in forms—now persuading, even flattering, now only commanding."[33]

Michael Mann's films represent an alternative convergence of architecture space and film. His crime films move architecture from the background to the foreground. Most crime films rely on temporal elements to move the story and relegate architectural space to the background. At most, space accentuates a feeling or enhances the ambiance. Time, in most crime films, drives the conventional crime narrative and ultimately produces conventional results: reaffirming identity and place. The hero in *Memento* (2000, Christopher Nolan) moves backward through his memory to discover his identity; *L.A. Confidential* (1997, Curtis Hanson) uses the crime genre to evoke the heritage of a city's identity as the heroes establish their identities; *Reservoir Dogs* (1992, Quentin Tarantino) emphasizes its temporal discontinuities to express its characters.

Mann's crime films are different because the heroes do not win their confrontations with the modern urban spaces; nonplace triumphs over place. Philosophers such as Nietzsche help us understand the depth of this tragedy. At best, Mann's heroes survive the confrontation within the identityless American city *(Thief, Manhunter, Collateral,* and *Miami Vice)* and live to fight the hegemony of nonplace and supermodernity another day (eternal recurrence). *Heat* provides an operatic, multilayered culmination of the spatially driven film: Vincent, Apollonian enforcer of the law (for Nietzsche, religion, law, morality; for Augé, nonplace), kills Neil, the Dionysian seeking to exert his will to power, at the end of a runway at LAX (the airport—Augé's ultimate image of nonplace, a zone of arrival and exit), with jets (zones of transition) full of passengers flying in and out over the ocean. Moby's "God Moving over the Face of the Ocean" rises on the soundtrack, further enhancing the water–ocean imagery associated with Neil and his tragic ascension. Vincent, facing inland to the airport and city (nonplace), takes Neil's hand in an act of transference and acknowledgment (as in the opening, Vincent understands the meanings of the transformed space and that Neil almost became a Nietzschean overman). Neil dies facing the ocean, an important image in Mann's modern crime films because it suggests a mysterious, perfect place on its other, unseen shore. Mann's "eloquence of power in forms" in *Heat* makes for a grand tragedy of the Dionysian, attempting to construct their own "buildings," to think their thoughts, and, ultimately, to rise above the "ostentatious monuments of some supermundane intercourse." The excessive sameness of supermodernity/supermundane intercourse overwhelms them and underscores Mann's Nietzschean sense of tragedy or Dionysian pessimism:

> Saying Yes to life even in its strangest and hardest problems, the will to life rejoicing over its own inexhaustibility even in the very sacrifice of its highest types—*that* is what I called Dionysian, *that* is what I guessed to be the bridge to the psychology of the *tragic poet*. *Not* in order to be liberated from terror and pity, not in order to purge oneself of a dangerous affect by its vehement discharge ... but in order to be *oneself* the eternal joy of becoming, beyond all terror and pity—that joy which included even joy in destroying.[34]

From Nietzsche, we also understand eternal recurrence and another meaning in Mann's modern crime films: someone will always appear to challenge the stasis. Nietzsche suggests this person with the rhyme "Higher Men:"

> He should be praised for climbing; yet
> The other man comes always from a height
> And lives where praise can never get—
> Beyond your sight.[35]

Notes

1. Marc Augé, *Nonplaces: Introduction to an Anthropology of Supermodernity,* trans. John Howe (London: Verso, 1995), 77–78.

2. Ibid., 79.

3. Friedrich Nietzsche, *The Gay Science: With a Prelude in Rhymes and an Appendix of Songs,* trans. Walter Kaufmann (New York: Vintage, 1974), 227.

4. Robert Arnett, "The American City as Nonplace: Architecture and Narrative

in the Crime Films of Michael Mann," *Quarterly Review of Film and Video* 27, no. 1 (2010): 44–53.

5. Nietzsche, *The Gay Science,* 227.

6. Mark Rakatansky, "Spatial Narratives," *Harvard Architectural Review* 8 (1992): 102–21, http://www.haussite.net/haus.0/SCRIPT/ txt1999/05/TEXT1X.HTML, accessed January 25, 2012.

7. Friedrich Nietzsche, *Twilight of the Idols,* in *The Portable Nietzsche,* ed. and trans. Walter Kaufmann (New York: Penguin Books, 1976), "Skirmishes of an Untimely Man," 521.

8. Nietzsche, *The Gay Science,* 227, emphasis in original.

9. Mark Lamster, "Introduction," in *Architecture and Film,* ed. Mark Lamster (New York: Princeton Architectural Press, 2000), 1.

10. Steven Rybin, *The Cinema of Michael Mann* (Lanham, MD: Lexington Books, 2007), 76–77.

11. Mark Steensland, *Michael Mann* (Harpenden, UK: Pocket Essentials, 2002), 37, quoting Mann.

12. Steven Sanders, *Miami Vice* (Detroit: Wayne State University Press, 2010), 5–6.

13. Steven Sanders, "Sunshine Noir: Postmodernism and *Miami Vice,*" in *The Philosophy of Neo-Noir,* ed. Mark T. Conard (Lexington: University Press of Kentucky, 2009), 185.

14. "Return to the Scene of the Crime," special feature on disk 2 of the *Heat* DVD (Burbank, CA: Warner Home Video, 2005). Janice Polley and Gusmano Cesaretti, associate producer, visited many of the *Heat* locations in 2004. This special feature provides interesting details on how Mann manages a location for thematic effect.

15. The difference between the look of *Heat* and the look of Mann's earlier TV-movie version, *L.A. Takedown* (1989), is minimal. Many of the same spaces are depicted, but *Heat* at 172 minutes develops a more sophisticated use of space that the 92-minute *L.A. Takedown* can't and doesn't do. Vincent Hanna's home depicted in the opening of *L.A. Takedown* recalls Graham's home in *Manhunter.* As in *Heat,* many of the aerial establishing shots in *L.A. Takedown* emphasize the freeways and the grid pattern of downtown Los Angeles.

16. Mark E. Wildermuth, *Blood in the Moonlight: Michael Mann and Information Age Cinema* (Jefferson, NC: McFarland, 2005), 136–37.

17. Les Roberts, "'Welcome to Dreamland': From Place to Nonplace and Back Again in Pawel Pawlikowski's *Last Resort,*" *New Cinemas: Journal of Contemporary Film* 1, no. 2 (2002): 83.

18. Augé, *Nonplaces,* 103.

19. Nietzsche, *The Gay Science,* 174.

20. Ibid., 227.

21. Nietzsche, *Twilight,* 554, emphasis in original.

22. A variation of the "heat" advice occurs during the conversation between Neil and Vincent at the café.

23. Rybin, *The Cinema of Michael Mann,* 176.

24. Nietzsche, *Twilight,* 519.

25. Nietzsche, *The Gay Science,* 331.

26. Augé, *Nonplaces,* 103.

27. F. X. Feeney, *Michael Mann* (Cologne: Taschen, 2006), 67.

28. Rybin, *The Cinema of Michael Mann,* 28.

29. Jean-Baptiste Thoret, "The Aquarium Syndrome: On the Films of Michael Mann," trans. Anna Dzenis, *Senses of Cinema,* no. 19 (March–April 2002), Pandora Archive, http://pandora.nla.gov.au/pan/10772/20060909/www.sensesofcinema.com/contents/01/19/contents.html#mann, accessed May 16, 2008, but currently unavailable.

30. Ibid.

31. Nietzsche, *The Gay Science,* 282.

32. Ibid., 227, emphasis in original.

33. Nietzsche, *Twilight,* 521.

34. Ibid., 562–63, emphasis in original.

35. Nietzsche, *The Gay Science,* 67.

"AWAKENED TO CHAOS"

Outsiders in *The Jericho Mile* and *Thief*

R. Barton Palmer

Running in Circles

Recently released movies were an indispensable staple of prime-time broad-casting in the late 1960s. But once the networks discovered it was cheaper to produce their own features rather than pay increasingly expensive rent-als, telefilms became an even more forceful and enduring presence on the small screen. The popularity of such programming lasted for more than two decades, and even in the 1990s the telefilm revived, as cable companies such as Turner and HBO, rediscovering the same economic truth, began their own feature production, including a number of award-winning and very popular successes directed by experienced professionals, most notably per-haps John Frankenheimer. With small budgets (but often effective scripts), the made-for-TV movie has from the beginning offered the industry yet another advantage. An assured market makes possible substantial creative freedom. And so in the 1970s, telefilms provided interesting work for a num-ber of aspiring directors, including Daniel Petrie, Michael Crichton, Steven Spielberg, and, of particular interest to readers of this book, Michael Mann, whose movie *The Jericho Mile* (1979) was his first feature-length project.

Produced by ABC for its "Movie of the Week" slot and based on a script by Patrick J. Nolan (Mann collaborated on significant revisions), *The Jericho Mile* enjoyed not only a successful broadcast run, but, quite unusually, also a respectable theatrical release in the United Kingdom. Mann received positive reviews for his directing in the *New York Times,* the *Christian Science Moni-tor,* and even *Films & Filming* (a conservative industry journal not generally enthusiastic about small-screen features), and he and Nolan were awarded an Emmy for the screenplay. For Mann, the project proved an auspicious beginning in a number of ways, not the least of which was that *The Jericho Mile* gave him the opportunity to develop his personal inflection of a long-established Hollywood type: the solitary man who does not fit into society but lives instead by his own code, whose values he has acquired through difficult experience. His understanding of the world and his approach to living in it set him irrevocably apart from others. His solitude is no pathology, but a considered position whose rationale he can and does readily expound.

Going beyond long-standing industry traditions, Mann's outsider male reflects the intellectual currents of the era in which *The Jericho Mile* was made, in particular a fascination with then-popular conceptions of existentialism.[1] Often expressing a more generalized antiestablishment outlook, many films of the era feature attractive rebels against a social order portrayed as mindlessly restrictive or just plain stultifying. Consider the parking-meter-decapitating, hard-boiled-egg-eating misfit charmingly incarnated by Paul Newman in *Cool Hand Luke* (1967, Stuart Rosenberg), a film that channels countercultural rebelliousness on a soft target: the southern chain-gang prison farm, managed by ignorant rednecks and psychopathic state troopers. Other examples come readily to hand: the good/bad outlaws and mischievous con men incarnated by Newman and Robert Redford in *Butch Cassidy and the Sundance Kid* (1969, George Roy Hill) and *The Sting* (1973, George Roy Hill). Mann's outsiders, however, have been forced by circumstances to see deeply into the foundational hypocrisy of a culture in which the "war of all against all" prevails over the bonds of community that prove elusive, if not illusory. In that culture, the rule of law lacks a dependable connection to justice, giving individuals no rational choice but self-reliance. It is hardly surprising if they choose solitariness as a hedge against disaster, however difficult and bitter the denial or the severing of connections to others might prove. In its portrait of a convict who has learned these truths and chooses a life he lives for himself alone, *The Jericho Mile* offers the first sketch of the outsider that becomes a dominant presence in Mann's filmmaking. He explores this figure in greater depth and with much more poignancy in his next project and first theatrical feature, *Thief* (1981), based on the thinly fictionalized professional autobiography of John Seybold, a career thief writing under a pseudonym. Mann fashioned a tight screenplay from Seybold's rambling and annoyingly narcissistic account of his criminal career, instead infusing it with his own ideas. The film is in some sense a genre piece at a time when such neo-noir narratives about the criminal underworld were just starting to become an industry trend—especially if based on a "factual account," such as Martin Scorsese's *Goodfellas* (1990), an adaptation of Nicholas Pileggi's 1986 book *Wiseguy*. Much like *Goodfellas,* however, *Thief* is also clearly a director's film, an expanded reworking of ideas first broached in *The Jericho Mile* but now developed with the striking visual and aural effects that continue to be Mann's most recognizable signature.

Despite its origin in a script with more collectivist intentions, *The Jericho Mile* also strongly reflects Mann's fascination with those who live on the margins of society in a style they have formulated for themselves. In this case, the outsider figure, Larry "Rain" Murphy (Peter Strauss), is a specially talented runner, capable of an under-four-minute mile, or so the warden thinks when he arranges for coaching in hopes that Murphy might make the Olympic track squad and reflect some glory on the prison. Shot largely on location at Folsom Prison and with many of the incarcerated appearing more or less as themselves, *The Jericho Mile* engages authentically and in a generally liberal fashion with issues of justice, violence, and racial tensions in a national penal system that had come under intense scrutiny after the Attica riots and subsequent massacre in 1971. But the film focuses on a figure who, even in the company of men who are outcasts in some sense, remains an outsider unconcerned with the society of which, like them, he is an involuntary member. Most viewers would think Murphy wrongly imprisoned for the murder of his father, which he committed in defense of his sister, but the injustice of his confinement never becomes an issue in the film, which is otherwise only vaguely critical of "the system." Thoroughly in line with the conventions of the social problem telefilm (and the director's own political leanings), the tendentious rhetoric of *The Jericho Mile* was much praised by reviewers, but addressing social inequities is no more the film's main focus than the briefly developed, vaguely Marxist meditations on the alienation of labor that Mann inserts in *Thief.*

Dominated by a minimally stylized and unglamorous realism, the made-for-TV movie of the era regularly focused on social problems that were solved Hollywood style by the eventual triumph against the odds of sympathetic individuals who are trapped by circumstances not of their own making. It is difficult, in fact, to overemphasize the social conservatism of the telefilm, despite its intent to be attractively sensational or even shocking. No matter how outré the problem, such narratives routinely discovered a solution that confirmed the enduring value of established institutions, especially the family.[2] A characteristic and much acclaimed entrant to the series in 1984 was the provocatively titled *The Burning Bed,* directed by Robert Greenwald, then well on his way to becoming one of the most prolific and skillful practitioners of the form. Popular enough when broadcast to prompt a brief (if very unspectacular) theatrical release, *The Burning Bed* was based on a nonfiction best seller that recounts the plight of a young mother (a tour de force performance by Farrah Fawcett) who, suffering constant abuse from her husband, eventually sets him on fire after he brutally rapes her and then, rather foolishly, falls asleep. Charged with first-degree murder, the wife is exonerated when the jury, moved by her frightening tale of years of a violence that no police intervention could end, finds the homicide justifiable. In a bittersweet finale, she is reunited with her children, who are now safe from their father's violent rages. Utilizing the courtroom scenes to air and debate the relevant issues, including the right of women to nontraditional forms of self-defense, the filmmakers draw a clear moral: spousal abuse, especially in the form of marital rape, is a horrific and not uncommon problem that must be brought out of the closet. In fact, many credit *The Burning Bed* with bringing these issues to public attention and encouraging legal action and cultural change.[3]

To be sure, much like Greenwald's film, *The Jericho Mile* also engages with what we might call a structural social failure: the prison system's inability or unwillingness to prevent criminal gangs from controlling convict life through bribery, intimidation, and murder. Reflecting the protest spirit of Nolan's original screenplay, *The Jericho Mile* certainly dramatizes this issue, as Murphy's only close friend is murdered by the prison gang boss when he fails to go along with a drug-smuggling scheme. The narrative does detail how Murphy gets revenge of a sort for this outrage and otherwise challenges the gang's control of prison life. But the focus throughout is much more on Murphy's successful attempt to maintain his individuality in circumstances that would deprive him of it. In the film's conclusion, Mann emphasizes Murphy's assertion of self in an act of defiance with no larger meaning beyond what value he and convict onlookers in the prison yard decide to assign it. In speaking earlier with athletic commission officials, Murphy had refused to show remorse for the "crime" that had landed him in prison. As a result, he was barred from competing in the Olympic trials. Arranging to be timed, he decides to run his own race with only his fellow convicts as witnesses. The others realize Murphy is now staging the very competition from which he has been barred and cheer him on. He breaks the four-minute barrier and then hurls the timer beyond the walls, where it smashes into pieces.

If a perfect coda to Murphy's personal struggles, this finale fails to identify some newfound form of solidarity among prisoners prevented from being more than spectators to his act of defiance. Murphy contests society's refusal to accept who he genuinely is: someone who possesses the physical and mental talents required to perform a feat that others value. Importantly, it is the prison officials, not Murphy himself, who are at first eager to identify (and make use of) his abilities. (Running untimed and his effort hence not converted to a competitive value, he had initially asked for no such recognition.) Allowed limited space to be an individual, Murphy makes an individual gesture, devoting his exercise time to circling at increasingly rapid speed the track he has laid out. And this is the same gesture that, with more bravura and self-consciousness, he repeats at film's end. Murphy stands for himself, not as the representative or, worse yet, the leader of a group of inmates who otherwise have no special reason to protest. All of them have made accommodations to the hard facts of prison, as the film's opening sequence exemplifies through its anatomy of the various forms of yard-time recreation they pursue. This opening, though privileging Murphy more than any other convict, finds unity only through a dynamic montage and a pounding music soundtrack; it is a group shot of individuals orchestrating their own lives as best they can, brought together by the observable fact of their individuality in the face of a common and righteously repressive destiny.

In contrast to most conventionally plotted telefilms, the strength of this story is that it strings together events that literally go nowhere—that, in fact, have nowhere to go. The movement in place of the narrative correlates with Murphy's endless laps on a track he has laid out inside the prison walls. It is this rapidly traveled circular road to nowhere that becomes the film's most enduring image. Critic Steven Rybin, impressed by the power of that image, is correct in observing that Murphy is "the most solitary figure in the film." But when he concludes that Murphy is more "alienated than liberated," he judges him by the terms of a therapeutic culture whose lock-step approach to discovering the truth of the criminal character or personality the film resolutely ridicules.[4] Eager to effect Murphy's reform, the prison psychologist is never able to "solve" the problem of his self-marginalization, which, according to the therapist, is anger against his father. The simple reason he is unable to do so is that Murphy feels no anger, and so the talking cure goes nowhere. He killed the man for an eminently good reason, not from the emotion of the moment or some deep-seated hostility. From what mistaken or harmful view, one might ask, does Murphy need to be liberated? For Rybin, it is his self-contained persistence in living at the margins: "his loneliness is precisely his problem."[5] But the film carefully details that it is from his self-containment and refusal to be analyzed or normalized that Murphy draws his peculiar strength. His preoccupation with running makes him special, though that is not his intention, and it gives him a worth he can enjoy in itself and for himself even though he never (and this seems the point) determines precisely what that worth might be. In the end, by timing his mile and then hurling away the timer, Murphy demonstrates that he is unconcerned about what meaning or value others might find in what he does. As a matter of pride, he demonstrates that he can be a player in the game for which others have solicited him. But then he rejects their rejection. In any case, despite his exceptional talent, he is barred from participating more fully in society by his unwillingness to "reform." Scorned by the athletic establishment because he refuses to lie and embrace repentance, Murphy is confirmed in the rightness of his solitariness only by the events the film traces and over which, in the end, he asserts the limited control he can dispose of. He can say no, and he does.

The Jericho Mile, in short, could hardly diverge more dramatically from the reformist telos of the telefilm. Mann limns an attitude toward a harsh image of the world, not some path toward its remaking or deliverance. Reflecting Nolan's original vision, the film's title suggests that the prison walls might be made to tumble down by a symbolic gesture that defies unfair authority both within and without the prison. And yet nothing in the prison has changed at film's end. As Mann must have hoped, it is Murphy's unusual character and actions that instead command attention. Murphy is satisfied that justice has been served by his incarceration, even though he, still a young man, faces a life sentence with little chance for parole. He does not dispute killing his father, who could not otherwise be stopped from sexually abusing Murphy's younger sister. And yet these extenuating circumstances mean as little to him as they apparently do to the justice system. He does not offer them as an excuse, expecting no mercy for what, he confesses, was a coldly calculated act. Given the same circumstances, he sadly but resignedly affirms he would kill his father again. Absent some "change of heart," parole therefore seems beyond his reach. But Murphy never expresses any hope for exoneration, mercy, or special treatment. He asks only for the same privilege extended to every prisoner in Folsom: that he can use his time in the exercise yard as he sees fit and the rules allow. Otherwise, he surrenders himself to the system.

The other prisoners call him "Lickety-Split," which seems a sign of respect for his obvious accomplishments, and the name suits the irony of his situation: going faster and faster, but never going anywhere. In his cell, he remains devoted to his physical condition, stretching out his legs, and doing pull-ups on a pipe he keeps concealed in the cell's plumbing, an act that seems his only substantial rejection of prison rules. Murphy is, in a sense, training, but not for any event or competition. He will be what he is able to be in the very limited world to which his own actions have confined him. In this, he finds neither joy nor despair. The narrative that catches him up, only to abandon him later as an unworthy object, is not of his making. He is clearly no Joshua; Folsom is no Jericho, despite the false promise of deliverance in the film's title. This is what Murphy learns from this experience, and yet it is something he already knows. He had a glimpse of life's deepest ironies when the court condemned him for saving someone from unending abuse. In *The Burning Bed,* society, as represented by the jury, rewrites the law so that an evolving sense of justice might be better served. Rain Murphy can hope for no such salvific moment. He has only himself. There is no way back in from the outside, and it is precisely the immobility of his situation that the events traced by the film confirm. Like all of Mann's protagonists, Murphy is a man of his times, alive to their essential nature, which he had come to understand long before entering Folsom's walls.

The Era of the Outsider

"The Outsider is a man who has awakened to chaos," declares Colin Wilson in his famed 1956 study of the figure so dominant in postwar fiction and philosophy, written when the author was still in his early twenties and speaking to and for a generation then coming of age. Not for the outsider is the "comfortable, insulated world of the bourgeois." The average man believes, perhaps has to believe, that the "world is fundamentally an orderly place, with a disturbing element of the irrational, the terrifying, which his preoccupation with the present usually permits him to ignore." For reasons that are perhaps best summed up in the concept of temperament, the outsider has come alive to the truth that the world is "not rational, not orderly," and his irrepressible urge to communicate this "sense of anarchy" is not revolutionary in the ordinary sense. It springs from no desire to radicalize those who are comfortable with inhabiting an illusion whose untruth they sometimes glimpse. The outsider speaks out about the chaos he sees around him because he cannot escape the "distressing sense that truth must be told at all costs; otherwise there is no hope for the restoration of order." And yet he struggles under no illusions. The outsider acts from the simple belief that "chaos must be faced," perhaps even embraced; it does not matter if the hope for order is vain, if nothing can satisfy the collective need we have for a comfortable predictability in our dealings with the world and with each other.[6]

Wilson's book is an engagingly polemical synthesis of the ideas of others (including such usual suspects as Jean-Paul Sartre, Albert Camus, and T. E. Lawrence). A rare popular work of philosophy and cultural criticism, it attracted a wide readership in the United Kingdom and then throughout the Anglophone world to what was becoming known as "existentialism," though a number of its principal "exponents" did not embrace this label. *The Outsider* reflected, even as it furthered, the preoccupations of an era in which, so William Barrett enthusiastically proclaimed at the same time in *Irrational Man*, "existentialism, whether successfully or not, has attempted to gather all the elements of human reality into a total picture of man."[7] Like Wilson, Barrett was a successful popularizer of then-contemporary Continental thought in this tradition (*Irrational Man* introduced many American readers to existentialism). A missionary zeal is evident in his complaint that "the reaction of professional philosophers to existentialism was merely a symptom of their imprisonment in the narrowness of their own discipline." It had proven attractive to those outside the academy because "it seemed to have a connection with their lives." Neither writer had any use for logical positivism, then the dominant Anglo-American academic tradition. In Barrett's damning formulation, logical positivism concerns itself only with the "scientifically meaningful" and so brackets off "the whole surrounding area in which ordinary men live from day to day"; the result is that the dealings we have "with other men [are] consigned to the outer darkness of the 'meaningless.'"[8]

Existentialism, at least as it came to be widely understood in the Anglo-American world because of commentators such as Wilson and Barrett, is energized by its rejection of reassuring common sense, its promotion of the inherent freedom to self-fashion in the absence of transcendent meaning, and its embrace of physicality and the material. Through an interrogation and then rejection of the established order's central claims, it became in the postwar era very much a young man's philosophy. Its emphasis on individuals in control of what meanings their lives would have became the centerpiece of a European nouvelle vague, which rejected the political and cultural pieties of the older generation, whose authority had been discredited by the recent horror of world war. New waves of different kinds, in fact, would be the marks of an energetic and forward-looking global youth culture that would reshape the European intellectual and spiritual landscape and, in such movements as the sexual revolution and the establishment of a vibrant counterculture, would soon contribute to substantial change on the American scene as well.[9] Of course, the existential advocacy for turning human energies toward introspection and self-consciousness also identifies a connection to what Barrett finds "dark and questionable" in the Western tradition; his version of existentialism channels an "irrationality" whose opposition to positivism owes much to Christian notions of inherent evil as developed by such thinkers as Augustine, Kierkegaard, and Dostoevsky.[10]

Wilson ignores these problematic roots of the modern temper; for him, the outsider is a figure with a much shorter history, one that barely extends past the middle of the previous century. Wilson's chaos is secular, not metaphysical, a condition of the social order. His apolitical culturalism offers up a more heroic and enduring image: not someone who sees reason as a limiting force in the search for truth, but rather someone who does not ignore what is inconvenient and yearns for something better, even when he suspects it does not exist. Not for him Camus's often abstruse meditations about absurdity or Sartre's intricate arguments for the liberating embrace of nothingness. After the publication of *The Outsider* in 1956 (the book was sponsored by Victor Gollancz, the United Kingdom's most influential "engaged" publisher), Wilson became associated with the "angry young men," the signature literary movement of the period that coalesced after the staging in 1956 of John Osborne's *Look Back in Anger*, a drama that centers on the age's most famous outsider: the dissatisfied and self-destructive Jimmy Porter, who cannot keep from speaking out about the hypocrisies and inanities of postimperial Britain, a society of which he is only reluctantly a member, but from which he proves unable to separate himself.[11]

Osborne's rebel with no worthy cause moves through anger to resignation, and this is true as well for Wilson's outsider, a portrait inspired by his reading of Henri Barbusse's *L'Enfer* (Hell). *L'Enfer* is not a novel that, despite its huge success in France, had ever achieved much purchase in Anglo-American culture upon its publication almost fifty years earlier in 1908. And this is perhaps because Barbusse's unnamed protagonist is not a man of action. Largely confining himself to a hotel room, he somewhat implausibly observes through a crack in the wall a series of events that transpire next door; like a "mindscreen," these events correspond to his own preoccupations with disease, criminality, and sex of an unconventional sort. But Barbusse is interested in more than a Zolaesque sensationalism, though he has a talent for limning carnality and violence that connects him to a later generation of noirish novelists for whom the transgressive and its moral discontents are a principal subject—in the American tradition, James M. Cain, Horace McCoy, Patricia Highsmith, and Dorothy B. Hughes, chief among them. What Barbusse's outsider witnesses and what he discovers about his own proclivities convince him that he and his fellow humans are hypocrites because they live in the pretense that their actions are rational and moral when, instead, those actions in truth defy certain explanation. Though in the end the outsider remains apart from what he observes, he finds himself puzzled by urges that impel him to do or think what he had never intended doing or thinking. Initially afflicted by distaste and disgust, he comes to recognize in himself and in those he observes the essential absurdity of human nature, which is, in Wilson's useful formulation, that "the ape and the man exist in one body."[12]

Of course, this is hardly an original thought, but the special quality of Barbusse's outsider (and the reason that Wilson focuses on him) is that he persists more energetically than the rest of us in his perception that everydayness, including and especially social conventions about the normal, are illusions that can be swiftly swept aside by an eruption of the unanticipated, the irrational, the uncertain. One way or another, we all inhabit that hotel room with a privileged window on experience that should distress even as it enlightens us. However, it is only the outsiders in our midst who, in their embrace of the strangeness, have the power to make us see the world for what it is. What Wilson appropriately terms "the country of the blind" is inhabited by the untroubled majority who just don't get it: outsiders, then, constitute an elite—a heroic coterie who are devoted to the uncompromised truth and not afraid "to look in the direction where the uncertainty lies."[13] This radical individuality is hardly devoid of romantic overreaching, and it is devoted equally to the spurning of ordinary life and the self-creating embrace of meaninglessness. Wilson particularly channels the sunny pessimism of Albert Camus, who observes in *The Myth of Sisyphus* (1942): "Weariness comes at the end of the acts of a mechanical life, but at the same time it inaugurates the impulse of consciousness"; henceforth, "the worm is in man's heart,"[14] an "awaken[ing] to chaos" that is in some ways for ill.

And yet Camus also affirms that "there is no fate that cannot be surmounted by scorn."[15] This is a heroic thought fully consonant with the idea of dark, Homeric laughter that pervades Michael Mann's work (a telling example: when in *Collateral* [2004] the mortally wounded hit man Vincent [Tom Cruise] spends his last moments telling a wry anecdote). Camus's observation, in fact, would make an appropriate epigraph for Mann's oeuvre, with its ever-varying gallery of outsiders whose signal shared quality is their unshakable feeling of superiority to whatever happens to them, including and perhaps especially death. His protagonists are men defined, even ennobled, by scorn, a pattern that first takes shape in *The Jericho Mile*. Mann should not of course be pigeonholed. I do not mean to say that he keeps making the same film again and again. And yet his is in large part a cinema of Wilsonian outsiders who are "awakened to chaos" and, like Jeffrey Wigand (Russell Crowe) in the somewhat ironically titled *The Insider* (1999), find themselves compelled to speak as well as to live out the truth, even as they become protagonists or antagonists in narratives whose (often violent) action tests their commitment to integrity.

There is no little resemblance between Rain Murphy, who makes an inherently meaningless running in circles the determining value of the life that belongs to him, and Camus's Sisyphus, condemned by the gods for his presumptiveness to roll a huge boulder up a mountainside, from which it always rolls down again. Is unending, meaningless labor, with its taxing of but glorifying in the body, the most unendurable form of punishment? Or is ceaseless physical activity that has no point simply life reduced to its essentials? These are questions Murphy could ponder. What Camus says of Sisyphus Mann reduces in Murphy to a quintessential image: "His fate belongs to him. His rock is his thing . . . The absurd man says yes and his effort will henceforth be unceasing . . . the struggle itself toward the heights is enough to fill a man's heart."[16] The question to be asked, as Wilson sees it, is: "What will men *do* when they see things as they are?"[17] How will they live when they can no longer be carried along by the illusions of a "mechanical life," by what Camus identifies as that "incalculable feeling that deprives the mind of the sleep necessary to life?"[18] In what kind of story can the outsider play a part? This is the question posed and answered in Mann's first two features. An auspicious debut by many measures, these films announce that he is a philosophical filmmaker, an artist who, in Irving Singer's useful formulation, never "pontificates about eternal verities or the analytic niceties of academic philosophy."[19]

Like all talented and committed directors with a philosophical bent, Mann is passionately interested in telling visual stories and making cinema from them, and yet, in so doing, he also more or less consciously manages to "infuse [his] productions with a profound perception of, and concerted interest in, the human condition."[20] *The Jericho Mile* and *Thief* center on outsiders who do take action once they awaken to chaos. They become the subjects of narratives characterized by strong forward motion that sweeps them up, even while delivering them back, Sisyphus fashion, to where they started from. The restless motion of Mann's protagonists, however pointless in the end, distinguishes them from Barbusse's inactive observer, isolated for the most part in his room. There is nothing this man thinks should be done beyond embracing the nothingness outside the self. It is within the self that everything meaningful is to be found; introversion delivers him to stasis and contemplation.

Mann's cinema is resolutely external, built from dynamically edited shots of figures in action that is spectacularly staged and dependent on carefully authenticated detailing of performance and mise-en-scène. His outsiders are shown literally to be on the outside, free from physical constraints—the camera rarely glimpses them in interiors that force them to interact, at least cooperatively, with others. Though his films are never simply action cinema, they feature some of the lengthiest and most complexly staged action sequences in film history, such as the bank robbery in *Heat* (1995) or, on a more intimate scale, the final shoot-out in *Thief.* His characters are presented most often in unglamorized, seemingly casually framed medium shots, seldom in close-ups experiencing those private moments that are such a staple of modernist filmmaking. And yet, in the modernist vein, Mann's cinema focuses more on his characters than on his plots, which tend toward simplicity and predictability; he has little use for either suspense or surprise. As Christopher Howard observes, because Mann is devoted instead to the intensity and expressiveness of method acting, he attempts to "insert himself in the mindset of his characters," as his refocusing of *The Jericho Mile* on Rain Murphy makes clear. Howard, however, is right in maintaining that "his films are far from simply astutely observed character studies." In the manner of such art cinema directors as Alain Resnais and Robert Bresson, Mann's films communicate instead "a subtle sense of strange transcendental forces at work behind his human dramas,"[21] an effect that is achieved through striking visual style that effectively generalizes from the carefully depicted particularity of acting and mise-en-scène, aspects of the director's craft at which, by common critical consent, Mann excels.

Like Resnais's *Hiroshima, mon amour* and Bresson's *Pickpocket* (both

1959), Mann's first two films turn on moments of inner reorientation and clarification. For Mann, these moments are prompted but hardly determined by external events, whose power over the self is rejected. His cinema in this regard reflects in a general way the vaguely existentialist tone of many films of the so-called Hollywood Renaissance of the early 1970s, the work of such honored auteurs as Martin Scorsese, Francis Coppola, Hal Ashby, and Robert Altman. As Robert Kolker has observed of what he terms "the cinema of loneliness," these narratives often communicate a sense of "challenge and adventure" for their primarily male protagonists, but more forcefully "speak to a continual impotence in the world, an inability to change and to create change." He continues: "When they do depict action, it is invariably performed by lone heroes in an enormously destructive and antisocial manner. . . . When they preach harmony, it is through the useless conventions of domestic containment and male redemption."[22]

Mann's outsiders, in contrast, are neither lonely nor impotent. Containment is something they either contest, as in *The Jericho Mile*, or refuse entirely, as is the case in *Thief*. And redemption is something his outsiders deliver to themselves after a radically individual moment of recognition, an "awaken[ing] to chaos," as Colin Wilson puts it. In *Thief*, this moment is presented with more force and complexity than proved possible in *The Jericho Mile*. For this project, Mann was able to pen the script alone and otherwise make use of more substantial resources, including two talented "name" actors (James Caan and Tuesday Weld). The two films look (and sound) quite different, as one might expect considering their dissimilar contexts of production. But they tell what is in some important ways the same story.

"You Gotta Get to Where Nothin' Means Nothin'"

Perhaps it's just that *Thief* can tell more of the story, unburdened as it is by any pretension toward social commentary or political relevance—though, once again, it is a film that touches on civic and institutional corruption, limning a Hobbesian world in which the "war of all against all" prevails despite the persistent false front of bourgeois respectability. More clearly than in *The Jericho Mile,* which is limited by its exclusive focus on prison life, Mann demonstrates here that chaos is the fact of self-serving evil and of the legal system's concomitant failure to regulate with justice what men will do to satisfy their inevitable desire for wealth, self-sufficiency, and power. And yet the chaos is an underside that all concerned take great pains to mask, pretending to believe in something they know is a self-serving lie. At least for those in the know, society is founded on a collective agreement not to tell the emperor about his new clothes. To awaken to this chaos is to grasp and act on the evident truth that individuals cannot depend on institutions of either the official or underworld variety. In neither is there justice, in the elemental Aristotelian sense of equivalence between deed and reward, to be found. Everyone instead must make his own justice, rectify his own accounts, and embrace as necessary what Richard Slotkin calls the "righteous violence" that is one of the pillars of American individualism.[23] Mann obviously agrees with this perception and shares it with a number of filmmakers of this era, such as Don Siegel, whose *Dirty Harry* series (beginning in 1971) features a different kind of outsider, a cop devoted to rough justice who reflects then-current concerns with widespread law breaking and what to many at the time seemed a too permissive attitude toward the rights of the accused.

In a world of pervasive criminality, especially of the sophisticated, organized variety, the ethical border separating legitimate from illegal enterprise loses all meaning, or at least so Mann suggests in *Thief*. Ostensible success— the good life of family, home, and business lived under public scrutiny— can perhaps flow only from an exploitation of those opportunities for rapid advancement that are open to the talented, canny, and energetic lawbreaker such as *Thief*'s eponymous main character, Frank (James Caan), who is by day a successful and quite legitimate businessman, the owner of a used-car lot and a restaurant/bar. The film is set in a Chicago where organized crime controls a lucrative business: the robbery of high-value industrial goods such as diamonds, which are intended for resale by sophisticated fences to legitimate businesses. Such robbery may also further insurance fraud perpetrated on behalf of the "victims." These business arrangements depend on a corrupt police force that solicits a percentage of the proceeds in return for what one lieutenant calls "rounding off the corners" as well as on a justice system in which bribery (negotiated in open court through hand signals that are hardly difficult to decode) secures favorable decisions from judges on the take. The mob boss, Leo (Robert Prosky), is, like Frank, also heavily invested in legitimate enterprises; he makes his headquarters in an electroplating company that doubles as the blind for the orchestration of high-value property theft even as it provides an ideal site for the mastery of sophisticated technology and the obtaining of inside information about sites that are impregnable only to less-sophisticated thieves. What Leo manages is not a mob in the usual sense of the term, but something like a small corporation that even features a kind of pension plan, with the laundering of dirty money facilitated by investment in real estate around the country. Leo's operation depends on labor whose particular skills are in short supply and that can be secured only by contracts that feature attractive terms, including how the proceeds are to be divided. His operatives require sangfroid, strength, ingenuity, technical knowledge, and perseverance if they are to succeed without getting caught—a special and rare breed of self-reliant individual, likely indisposed by temperament to be intimidated, manipulated, or bamboozled, as the film demonstrates.

Frank is one such individual, having learned the tricks of the trade from a master thief, Okla (Willie Nelson), while serving a sentence for petty robbery that wound up totaling ten years after he killed another prisoner in self-defense. He has done well enough working as an independent contractor for a major fence, Joe Gags (Hal Frank), but does not know that there is a larger crime syndicate of which Gags is only a part. The film opens with what we learn is a typical caper, as Frank and his partner, Barry (James Belushi), carefully engineer a break-in at an office from whose safe full of diamonds Frank takes the most valuable after easily cracking it. These he turns over to Gags and, as is their custom, expects to collect his share of their proceeds in cash after the diamonds have been resold. Frank has cleared enough from such robberies to fund his legal businesses, afford whatever luxuries strike his fancy, and buy a home, which, until recently, he had shared with his wife, who divorced him when she discovered he was doing "scores" to augment their income.

Her desertion has shattered the picture he has of what his life should be. And Frank does in fact have a literal picture of that life—a piece of paper he keeps folded up in his wallet on which, while in prison, he pasted generic images, cut out from magazines, of a home, wife, and children. His aim is to put himself into that picture, an aim that has sustained him for years and to which he regularly turns for solace. Society owes him a leg up on success, he reasons, because a corrupt prison (run by "crews" of guards and convicts bent on the rape of younger inmates) forced him to commit acts of violence that were justified but (as in the case of Rain Murphy) judged as criminal by the system. Frank, however, does not imagine himself as a career criminal. When he feels he has taken back enough from what are victimless or nearly victimless crimes, he will simply become part of the law-abiding legitimacy that he recognizes is simply at bottom a bourgeois mythology sustained by collective hypocrisy. He has already picked out a partner for this new life: Jessie (Tuesday Weld), a waitress who works at the diner where he has breakfast (and conducts business with Joe Gags) and with whom he has been flirting for months, waiting only for his divorce to become final before romancing her. Frank is eager to remedy in this relationship what went wrong in the previous one. He wants the relationship with Jessie to be untainted by the unraveling of his marriage and, having sought out Okla's advice on the matter, is determined this time to tell her from the outset what he does to support a rather flashy lifestyle. Intentions, so he expects, will match up with results, a position for which he shows himself a very forceful advocate. Showing up two hours late for his first date with Jessie, he hustles the angry and now unwilling woman into his car (pushing away or intimidating bystanders who try to intervene). After explaining in sometimes lurid detail what his life has been, he persuades her to accept his version of a future they could share. Like Frank, Jessie has a somewhat sordid past; she connects quickly and firmly to his desire to find a better way for them both to live, accepting that his thievery will end when there is enough money.

But this vision of respectable ordinariness is not to be. Though Frank should know better, he has fallen into the trap of believing, as Colin Wilson puts it, that "the world is fundamentally an orderly place." Joe Gags does not show up for his meeting with Frank. He has offended those higher up in the criminal hierarchy and, as a result, been pushed out a twelfth-story window, hitting the ground with the substantial sum of cash owed to Frank still in his pocket. Finding out who was responsible, Frank comes looking for his money, connects to Leo, who pays him what he's owed and persuades him to work for him. With Joe Gags gone, Frank has little choice because he must have a reliable fence for his goods; a bonus is that Leo will provide him with set-ups (including inside information such as building plans) and protection from the police. Leo will be his father, so he says. And he proves true to his word: when Jessie and Frank are turned down by the state adoption agency because of his criminal past, Leo finds them a baby on the black market. Leo even arranges for Frank's friend Okla, who is dying of cancer, to be released from prison. His powers are considerable.

The first job engineered by Leo, among the most difficult Frank has ever attempted, proves a big success. When Frank goes to collect the $830,000 Leo owes him, however, he is given less than $100,000. The rest, Leo says, has been invested for him. Frank is unwilling to accept this arrangement and vows to collect what he's owed, telling Leo he'll "wear [his] ass for a hat" if he does not come across with the money. Leo was willing to pay up the first time when Frank was deprived of what he calls "the fruits of my labor," giving Frank the cash he took from Joe Gags. This time he is determined instead to reveal that the supposedly contractual nature of their relationship is a sham. Leo and his gang set an ambush at Frank's used-car lot, then kill Barry as an object lesson. Frank, pistol-whipped into unconsciousness, is apparently too valuable a property to be so disposed of and is given another chance. "I own you and your whole family," Leo says when Frank comes around. Frank, he commands, must "tighten up." Leo has underestimated him, however. Frank refuses the proffered lesson. Instead, he returns home, dons a bullet-proof vest, loads his pistol, and returns to Leo's house, where he shoots and kills his erstwhile boss as well as the boss's henchmen. The film ends with Frank walking back down the quiet suburban street where this seemingly incongruous violence has just occurred, a fitting microcosm of the society that *Thief* evokes and in which, it is now clear, Frank has no place.

So described, *Thief* seems little different from many Hollywood films of the past fifty years in which a charismatic and talented protagonist manages to exact a spectacular vengeance on those who have sought to dominate or destroy him. To be sure, Mann emphasizes this aspect of a project whose action sequences are carefully designed to produce expected generic thrills. For the final shoot-out, the director engaged a weapons expert, who instructed James Caan on how to find and kill an armed opponent hidden in the interior of the house. The suspenseful choreographed sequence that results is certainly unforgettable, and it is much of a piece with the detailed dramatizations of the two robberies, which concentrate on the expert use of heavy industrial tools, providing an ostensibly accurate textbook lesson about how the most apparently secure safes can be breached. But what makes *Thief* a director's film are the sequences that directly precede its explosive finale. As Frank on their first date tells Jessie the story of his life, he emphasizes a particular incident that seemed remarkable to him at the time. Attacked in his cell by a gang of guards and convicts intent on raping him, Frank defended himself with a great deal of success, inflicting substantial damage on his attackers before they subdued him. While recovering in the prison hospital, Frank learned that the attackers planned to kill him when he returned to the general population. Convinced there was nothing to do, he experienced a sudden movement of consciousness that removed the fear: it no longer mattered if he lived or died. Once he was out of the hospital, his erstwhile enemies left him alone, perhaps sensing the dangerousness of someone with nothing to lose. "You gotta get to where nothin' means nothin,'" he tells Jessie. Yet the Frank she meets is a man to whom some things mean everything, and one of those things, he has just declared, is her.

With the killing of Barry and Leo's threats, the need for complete detachment from others comes over Frank once more. This time when he takes the picture of his life from his wallet, he shreds it. Frank completes the job of trashing his dealership that the gang had already begun, setting fire to all the cars and buildings. Returning home, he tells Jessie to pack up herself and the baby; he provides them with money but sends them out of his life for good. No explanation or apology is offered. Perhaps Frank separates them out of concern for their safety, but the shredding of the picture seems to mean there is no going back. Once they are gone, he dynamites the house. Now once again a man with nothing and to whom nothing has any meaning beyond a desire for revenge and, if possible, self-preservation, he goes looking for Leo. Against the odds, he survives, but at the cost of destroying with his own hands everything he thought would make life worth living. Frank has worked hard to make a life that could be lived on the inside, but he finds he cannot abide the chaos of the "war of all against all." In that war, as he discovers, order (the world of contracts, promises, and relationships) proves an illusion that can be maintained only at a cost he has no intention of paying. Connections can be used against you. They threaten the free exercise of individuality, which in the final analysis Frank seems to think is the only value worth defending.

This self-concern hardly makes Frank an attractive figure, and it certainly sheds a different light on the picture he constructs of his future, with its reduction of a happy life to a shopping list of objects to be obtained by energy and force of personality. And yet, as it turns out, the dream can simply be ripped up and discarded. Frank's abrupt dismissal of Jessie and his child seems the most heartless of betrayals, a reenactment of the abandonment that Frank himself had suffered as a child. Refusing to be owned by Leo entails abandoning a comfortable lifestyle. For his part, Leo does not imagine that this is the choice Frank would make. After all, does it matter so much if Frank's talents are exploited and he cannot enjoy all the rightful fruits of his labor? It does to Frank, who chooses to remain an outsider. At film's end, he is confirmed in his solitariness—he is again in motion, but with nowhere to go, much like Rain Murphy, who never abandons his own self-chosen destiny of running endlessly in circles. In *Heat,* Mann revisits the story he tells in *Thief,* offering yet another version of the choice that a professional thief—here Neil McCauley (Robert De Niro)—must make between integrity (exacting vengeance on a man who betrayed him and his gang) and life with the woman he loves. McCauley can be true only to himself, a decision he pays for with his life. No Mann outsider can do otherwise, and the pattern is set from the very beginning of Mann's career.

Notes

1. In exploring Mann's connections to what I consider "popular existentialism" and the figure of the outsider, this study takes a very different approach from the detailed and quite useful survey of the same material by Vincent M. Gaine, *Existentialism and Social Engagement in the Films of Michael Mann* (London: Palgrave MacMillan, 2011).

2. An invaluable reference to the telefilm and the more than two thousand productions that aired by the middle 1980s is Alvin H. Marill's *Movies Made for Television: The Telefeature and the Mini-series, 1964–1986* (New York: New York Zoetrope, 1987).

3. See, for example, Louise Knott Ahern, "'The Burning Bed': A Turning Point in the Fight against Domestic Violence," http://www.lansingstatejournal.com/article/99999999/NEWS01/909270304/-Burning-Bed-turning-point-fight-against-domestic-violence, accessed July 21, 2012.

4. Steven Rybin, *The Cinema of Michael Mann* (Lanham, MD: Lexington Books, 2007), 29.

5. Ibid.

6. Colin Wilson, *The Outsider* (Boston: Houghton Mifflin, 1956), 15.

7. William Barrett, *Irrational Man* (Garden City, NY: Doubleday, 1958), 21.

8. Ibid., 9, 21.

9. For example, see Callum G. Brown, *The Death of Christian Britain* (New York: Routledge, 2009), which offers a detailed and quite persuasive argument that the secularization of Britain, though a long-term development, accelerated rapidly in the early 1960s under the influence of youth culture. For American developments, the classic account of the era is Todd Gitlin's *The Sixties: Years of Hope, Days of Rage* (New York: Bantam, 1987).

10. Barrett, *Irrational Man*, 22.

11. For a classic account of "the angry young men," of whom Colin Wilson was one of the most notable, see Kenneth Alsop, *The Angry Decade: A Survey of the Cultural Revolt of the Nineteen-Fifties* (London: Goodchild, 1985).

12. Wilson, *The Outsider*, 19.

13. Ibid., 15.

14. Albert Camus, *The Myth of Sisyphus*, trans. Justin O'Brien (New York: Random House, 1955), 10.

15. Ibid.

16. Ibid., 91.

17. Wilson, *The Outsider,* 19.

18. Camus, *The Myth of Sisyphus,* 5.

19. Irving Singer, *Three Philosophical Filmmakers: Hitchcock, Welles, Renoir* (Cambridge, MA: MIT Press, 2004), 3.

20. Ibid.

21. Christopher Howard, "Michael Mann," in *Contemporary North American Directors,* ed. Yoram Allon, Del Cullen, Hannah Patterson, and Nick James (London: Wallflower, 2000), 306.

22. Robert Kolker, *A Cinema of Loneliness* (New York: Oxford University Press, 2000), 10.

23. See Richard Slotkin, *Gunfighter Nation: Myth of the Frontier in Twentieth-Century America* (Norman: University of Oklahoma Press, 1998).

EXISTENTIAL MANN

Steven Sanders

Michael Mann is widely known as a cinematic stylist and visual artist of high accomplishment. This should not lead one to overlook the fact that the action, music, and conflict so prominent in his films are typically put in the service of ideas, as one can see by noting the prevalence of existential themes in his work. Mann's protagonists are typically alienated loners who find themselves in crises that call for decisive action—a metaphor in Mann's work for their attempts to break out of an existential impasse. As often as not, these crises are expressed through confrontations that propel them to violence and death, as, for example, in the finales of *Thief* (1981) and *Heat* (1995). In Mann's "existential urban tragedies," as film critic Scott Foundas calls them,[1] one finds a filmmaker whose cinema is strongly associated with identity, freedom, authenticity, and death—a fact that explains why his work is so highly regarded in France and Germany, where these themes have been addressed by existentialist novelists, dramatists, philosophers, and auteurs of the French New Wave. Of course, Mann is a filmmaker, not a philosopher, so it should come as no surprise that his existentialism is long on the kinetic and short on the metaphysical, a thematic through-line rather than a manifesto. Nevertheless, his film and television work resonates with themes that are faithful to the spirit of the action guide and outlook on life associated with the writings of Jean-Paul Sartre and Albert Camus, for example, if not the work of the more problematic existentialist thinkers such as Nietzsche, Kierkegaard, and Heidegger. The alienated protagonists of Mann's cinema take from existentialism not only a generalized sense of the contingency of things and the ways in which life can go unpredictably off course, but also a sense of engagement in the name of authenticity and individual freedom. In its embodiment of these themes, Mann's work is memorable for dramatizing the life-defining choices his characters must make and the ways these choices affect their fates. As Mann indicates in an interview with Graham Fuller in which they discuss *Heat,* but a statement applicable to so many of Mann's films, "The crime story/detective story is initially discrete, then it fuses with the personal stories in the fateful and sometimes doom-laden decisions each person has to make."[2] His films seem to say all too clearly that there is no conflict-free way to reset and restart one's life and simply begin all over again. And although existentialist philosophers may appear to be claiming that the slates on which our pasts have been written can simply be wiped clean by the exercise of our human freedom, Mann's work offers a corrective to the misconception that a "fresh start" is not only attainable, but easy.

If we confine our attention primarily to the fifteen-year period during which Mann directed his first two feature films, *Thief* and *The Keep* (1983), executive-produced the television series *Miami Vice* (1984–1989) and *Crime Story* (1986–1988), and directed what many regard as his masterwork, *Heat* (1995), we can already see this existential emphasis. Of course, these films are not the only texts that help us in our encounter with the existential Mann. There is also *The Jericho Mile* (1979), his Emmy-winning telefilm, as well as his most celebrated film, *The Insider* (1999), nominated for seven Academy Awards, including Best Picture, Best Adapted Screenplay, and Best Director. In the latter film, Jeffrey Wigand (Russell Crowe), a former research scientist for Brown & Williamson, is urged by TV producer Lowell Bergman (Al Pacino) to appear on the CBS show *60 Minutes* to discuss what he knows about the dangers of cigarettes and the methods by which tobacco companies increase the addictiveness of their product. As this fact-based drama unfolds, we are shown that by going public, Wigand will breach a confidentiality agreement he has with his former employer, and his choice to proceed with the disclosure invites severe reprisals that wreak havoc with his personal life. And there is *Collateral* (2002). "It is about the human experience," Mann tells Ian Nathan. "It is about the confrontations you find yourself in collapsed down to this night. All of what Vincent told himself of his life, his whole view of his existence. In that sense it is about existential matters."[3]

Existential Exit: *Thief*

In Mann's small but impressive body of films (and in the television series he has executive-produced, discussed later in this essay), his protagonists are men who must struggle against a backdrop of alienation and self-imposed isolation. Many of them—Frank (James Caan) in *Thief,* Neil McCauley (Robert De Niro) in *Heat,* Vincent (Tom Cruise) in *Collateral,* and more recently John Dillinger (Johnny Depp) in *Public Enemies* (2009)—are criminals, loners, or sociopaths whom Mann tries to depict in a fully dimensional, fully human way. Mann tells Scott Foundas, "Of course they're dimensional: They have mothers and fathers and kids. I knew a lot of these people, people like this. What do you have? You have a complete human being. The Tom Sizemore character [Michael Cheritto in *Heat*]: He has a nuclear family. He cares about his kids the same way you care about your kids. The big difference is that he doesn't care about *your* kids: He'll use one of your kids as a shield."[4] Mann is referring here to the robbery scene in *Heat* in which Cheritto grabs a child and holds her in front of him while he exchanges shots with police during his attempt to escape.

One of Mann's most revealing observations about his protagonists is his comments about *Heat's* McCauley. He says that a consequence of being inner directed and self-aware is "a certain solitariness" that is best expressed in McCauley's rule of having no attachments in his life that he cannot walk out on: "Don't let yourself get attached to anything you are not willing to walk out on in thirty seconds flat if you feel the heat around the corner."[5] This outlook had already been expressed in *Thief* in what is perhaps the most bleak of Mann's excursions in existential cinema.[6] Frank is a professional safecracker who steals jewels and works as an independent. "I am Joe the boss of my own body," he tells anyone who suggests that he should work for the mob. But when Frank urgently needs a large sum of money to finance his entry into the middle-class, noncriminal life he hopes to enjoy with his new love, Jessie (Tuesday Weld), he agrees to do a single high-paying job for Leo (Robert Prosky), a Chicago crime boss.

With this agreement, *Thief* ironizes the predicament of the existential protagonist who attempts to accelerate a bid for freedom and winds up even more fully entrapped. Frank's crisis begins after he carries out the arduous bank job in Los Angeles that Leo has set up for him. Frank believes the score will net him something on the order of $830,000 and the freedom to live the life he dreams of. He returns from California and goes to Leo's house to collect his cut and bid him adieu, but Leo has other plans for Frank. He tosses Frank an envelope. Frank can see at once that there is far less than he had bargained for. "What's this?" he asks Leo. "You're light. There can't be more than seventy, eighty, ninety here." Leo tells Frank that "this is the cash part" of the deal and that he has invested the balance of Frank's take in a package of shopping-mall acquisitions. "You've got equity with me in that," he proudly tells the agitated thief. "Plus, we've got a major score in Palm Beach in six weeks." When Frank tells Leo, "This is payday. It is over," Leo reminds Frank of the ways he has smoothed things over for him—the payoffs to corrupt cops he has made, his intervention to get Frank and Jessie a child when they could not obtain one through normal adoption channels, and so on—and asks, "Where is gratitude?" In a dramatic assertion of the code he lives by, Frank responds, "Where is my end? I can see that my money is still in your pocket. Which is from the yield of my labor. You are making big profits from my work, my risk, my sweat. But that is OK because I elected to make that deal. But now the deal is over. I want my end, and I am out." This appeal falls on deaf ears, so Frank, adverting to the weapon he is carrying, tells Leo, "My money in twenty-four hours, or you will wear your ass for a hat." This exchange occurs near the end of the film and condenses the antagonism between Frank, who realizes his dream has come to nothing but resolves to continue to fight to preserve his independence, and Leo in his unyielding refusal to acknowledge those, such as Frank, who would be independent contractors.

Frank's nightmare has only begun, though, because later that night Leo and his men attack him and kill his partner, Barry (James Belushi). Now Leo reads the riot act to Frank: he tells him that he "owns the paper" on his life. "You get paid what I say. You do what I say. I run you, there is no discussion. I want, you work until you are burned out, you are busted, or you're dead." Of course, this is something a character like Frank cannot accept, and he responds with a determination beyond anything Leo imagines. He sets out to destroy everything that makes him vulnerable to Leo's demand that he get back to work. He sends Jessie away with their infant, methodically dynamites his house and downtown tavern, and sets fire to his auto dealership—in effect, he destroys his dream, which he does symbolically by crumbling the picture-postcard collage of the perfect if perforce impossible life that he showed to Jessie when he first proposed that they become a couple. He now tosses this remnant of hope out the window and drives away as his auto dealership goes up in flames. Frank returns to Leo's house and kills him and two members of his crew in a violent twelve-minute finale virtually without dialogue, accompanied during its final five and a half minutes by a driving rock score performed by Tangerine Dream and aptly titled "Confrontation" by its composer Craig Safan.

As the wounded thief walks away from the carnage into the night, the camera moves slowly up through the trees, this final aerial shot an ambiguous depiction of his fate. This ending can be read as illustrative of a central Mann theme: the growing corporatization of criminal activity and, in consequence, the obsolescence of the independent criminal who tries to live by his own rules. Thus understood, it is an image of Frank's ultimate diminution—the onetime businessman cum highline thief who has lost everything *because of* his determination to live his own life and who will have to keep looking back over his shoulder as he awaits the moment of his capture by police or death at the hands of Chicago mobsters.

A second reading is suggested by Mann's fascination with a type who is sufficiently detached to remove himself from the scene at significant cost to others, which Frank does, sending Jessie and their son away and burning his businesses behind him. According to Vincent M. Gaine, "The bleak finale to the film makes the point that without social engagement, the existential guiding ethic is a barren way of life." Gaine asks with reference to *Thief*, "What sort of life does Frank have? His own, for sure, having severed all attachments, but . . . this is no life at all."[7] Gaine's insight is to see that an existential outlook and action guide do not make social engagement the supreme value—or even a very important one. But an existentialist would predictably reply that if social engagement and some sort of communality are to take priority over solitariness, rugged individualism, nonconformity, or the like, this ranking must be justified, at least to the agent. As a case in point, consider individualist maximizers—those who argue that they should take a course of action if and only if it maximizes *their own* self-interest (or satisfies their own rational preferences). They would point out that nonindividualist values such as social engagement, the wants and needs of the community, or even some sort of togetherness are not *their* ultimate or overriding values, perhaps insisting that without such a commitment, questions of social engagement might not even arise. Even Søren Kierkegaard, who famously said that "purity of heart is to will one thing," might recognize the appropriateness of the retort, "But *which* thing?" To this point we might add the observation, in good existentialist fashion, that not only eccentrics, criminals, and loners but also scientists, explorers, artists, and adventurers have been known to encounter a conflict between the personal and the social. When the two come apart, crises of authenticity require a choice between them, and this choice depends on a prior decision of principle over what values to adopt. As Sartre's famous example of the young man who comes to him for guidance about whether he should stay with his mother or leave her to fight in the French Resistance is meant to illustrate, no one can tell him what to do. This is a decision about which principles to adopt in the first place. Such decisions of principle require a choice, not the discovery of a given.

Of course, alternative readings of *Thief*'s ending may be indicative of an ambiguity created by design. Against the often cited assumption that Mann's male protagonists are defined by their work, it may be Mann's intent to show that they are defined by a commitment to a kind of personal excellence that renders them capable of the emotional detachment that is dramatized in *Thief, Heat,* and *Collateral.* As the various readings suggest, it may not be Mann's intent to leave us with a final, unambiguous picture of *Thief*'s existential man.

Miami Vice (1984–1989, 2006)

What makes the mid-1980s television series *Miami Vice* so remarkable, even now, is not just its setting with its color and light, architecture, music, and the ingenious way guest stars are cast against type, but how the show puts these elements together in the service of exploring basic existential themes: identity, commitment, authenticity, and existential choice. By foregrounding the constructed nature of the undercover police detective's identity, Mann found a parallel in Greater Miami itself with its cycles of boom, decline, decay, and redevelopment. This was the background for Mann and Anthony Yerkovich, already reimagining the city with its mid-1980s postmodern architecture and its aging art deco hotels along Ocean Drive on South Beach. Even the metaphorical titles of episodes such as "Heart of Darkness," "Baseballs of Death," "Back in the World," and "Yankee Dollar" indicated a new departure in episodic crime television. Although it is arguable that the mid-1980s had more than one paradigmatic crime series—*Hill Street Blues* (1981–1987), for example, has its partisans—*Miami Vice* had a memorable hold on the imagination and the following of an international audience.

The affluence and consumerism of the 1980s were part of the social and cultural frame of *Miami Vice,* so it should come as no surprise that the show's alleged style-over-substance look was taken as the genuine "voice of vice"—the first and only feature many critics and commentators remember about it. Without denying that the music track (composed and performed by Jan Hammer), song selections, and the freshness of the dialogue played crucial roles in making the show the phenomenon it was, pervasive the-

matic elements point to an emphasis on the existential predicament of protagonists who find themselves in increasingly precarious positions where
they must reaffirm their authenticity. At its most extreme, a kind of paranoia inhabits its principal characters owing to their need to maintain their
undercover identities. When Gina Calabrese (Saundra Santiago) asks Sonny
Crockett (Don Johnson) in the pilot, "Do you sometimes forget who you
are?" Crockett replies "Darlin', sometimes I *remember* who I am." Even the
most outlandish plotlines of its paranoid episodes are dramatized in ways
that lend themselves to a disconcerting realism, another Mann hallmark.

Sonny Crockett and Ricardo Tubbs (Philip Michael Thomas) express
1980s style in the way they initially represent two contrary types: the southern college jock turned cop and the habitué of the uptown New York nightclub scene.[8] Nevertheless, the philosophical aspect of their characters is in
evidence from the outset of the first season in "Heart of Darkness," an existentialist morality play about the challenge of living authentically and the
costs of the failure to do so. Working undercover as out-of-town porn theater owners looking to buy product, Crockett and Tubbs have been assigned
to bring down the operation of South Florida porn impresario Sam Kovics
(Paul Hecht). On the set of a porn film in the making, the buy is actually a
set-up for a prearranged bust to establish the pair's credentials as legitimate
buyers. The ruse works, and Crockett and Tubbs are sprung from jail in a
matter of hours by Kovics's right-hand man, Artie Rollins, who seems to be
running things in Kovics's absence.

Joseph Conrad's short novel *Heart of Darkness* is built up from the long-
deferred entrance of its villain, Kurtz. The appearance of Artie Rollins, also
delayed, builds enough suspense to suggest that something is not quite right
with the elusive second in command. In due course, Crockett and Tubbs discover that Artie Rollins is in reality Arthur Lawson (Ed O'Neill), an FBI agent
working undercover in the Kovics porn operation. Lawson is proficient in
his undercover role. In a violent sequence, he attacks a customer who is late
with a payment to Kovics, nearly killing him. Crockett and Tubbs learn that
over the past six weeks Lawson has cut himself off from the bureau, abandoned the wired apartment in which he had been set up, and moved into a
luxurious waterfront condo. Foreshadowing the episode's theme, no one is
shown observing his own reflection in the mirrors throughout the condo.

Artie has stopped filing reports and calling his wife. She is troubled and
ultimately uncomprehending, perhaps because she fears her husband is in
over his head. The situation has generated suspicion among his superiors

at the bureau that he is so caught up in the criminal enterprise he has infiltrated that he has gone over to the other side. Lawson is, indeed, a man in the middle, caught between a presumed upright life as a federal officer and a world of sex and money as well as criminal activity in which he participates as part of his investigation. His position is morally precarious: his aim is to gather enough evidence against Kovics to guarantee an airtight conviction, but while he is undercover, he does not want anyone to question his methods. "Are you trying to get me killed? I'm on an investigation here!" he shouts at Crockett and Tubbs after he learns that they are vice detectives. He tells the dismayed pair: "If I make a strategic decision to cut corners, to throw the book away, it's my decision, 'cause it's me out here and nobody else."

Crockett is determined to use Artie to bring down Kovics's operation, and much of the episode's power and appeal comes from trying to answer questions that arise about both Artie's reliability and Crockett's motivation to defend him. One way to interpret the episode is to see it in terms of people who have taken on roles and responsibilities that they are neither satisfied in assuming nor feel free to escape. Lawson gives himself over to the satisfaction of desires he has repressed, but he also feels an obligation to maintain his role as a respected member of law enforcement. By the episode's end, he realizes that his undercover intrigues have been attempts to give meaning to his life, a realization that he expresses when Crockett asks him what's going to happen with his wife. "I don't know if I can go back to my wife. It's like I've been riding an adrenalin high, all that money and all those women. And after a while, all of the things that came before, it got like a . . . it's like a . . . I don't know."

The changes that Arthur Lawson undergoes in the way he feels about his wife and what came before his entry into his undercover life are manifestations of existential anxiety. He seems unable either to reject or wholly to accept those drives and desires that are expressed through the persona of Artie Rollins. The rules, roles, relations, and commitments in terms of which Arthur Lawson has defined himself reach back into his past and are not easily forsaken, sustained as they are by the inertial forces of habit and convention, a point to which existentialists give special emphasis in their diagnosis of the human condition. These forces are now breaking up as Lawson comes to understand that he is free to choose how he should live. The realization of such existential freedom has given rise to dread over the choices he must make to define himself.

Crockett's compassion for Artie has its motivational source in a profound identification with the undercover agent. (As Tubbs, more clear-sighted in this matter than Crockett, tells his partner, "You don't see Artie. You see yourself.") This identification reflects his own ambivalence about the undercover life that he, Crockett, must live in his guise as Sonny Burnett. His role as an undercover detective has led to similar anxieties of identity, a sense of having his true identity subverted by the undercover role he must play that demands that he subordinate his true self to his alter ego. This undercover role is no nine-to-five masquerade; its demands encroach on his every waking hour because he must be prepared to act as Sonny Burnett at any moment. But the need to shift from those habits and dispositions he has built up over a lifetime to those he must feign as Burnett leads to a debilitating fragmentation of personality. Adapting a central argument that derives from Aristotle, we can say that this constant shifting from being disposed to do the things he would do as a representative of law enforcement to being disposed to do their polar opposites—the things required by his role as Burnett—is inimical to a stable personality and a healthy character.

A midnight drug deal between the principals goes haywire, and Crockett and Tubbs's covers are blown. Artie is ordered by Kovics (who is still unaware that Artie is an undercover agent) to kill the pair, but Artie instead comes to their rescue and in a gun battle proceeds to shoot Kovics and his bodyguard dead when they lock themselves inside Kovics's limo. Motivated by a flawed commitment to the ideals of law enforcement, Lawson knows that he has compromised his authentic self. His casting off of the bourgeois life of the law enforcement officer and his embrace of a fantasy life have been a flight from authenticity. As he is taken downtown for debriefing by FBI personnel, the overlapping music track of George Benson's "This Masquerade" extends into the next scene inside the Blue Dolphin Lounge, where Crockett and Tubbs are trying to unwind after the evening's harrowing events. The ensuing dialogue foregrounds and underscores the masquerade theme: the multiple roles that each of the central figures must play and the subverting of identity entailed by such masquerades. When Crockett says that for the past three days he's felt as if he's been staring at himself in one of those amusement park mirrors that warp everything out of whack, Tubbs tells him, "It's not a reflection of you, Sonny. It's the job. I don't see how you've been doing it as long as you have."

The association of the masquerade with disguising identity is obvious. Crockett and Tubbs are, of necessity, invested in fabrication, in the presentation of false selves that they must inhabit in order to survive in the den of sharks they penetrate in the course of their work. But Arthur Lawson's masquerade, his embrace of the fantasy life of Artie Rollins with its sexual enticements and excitement and its casting off of conventional morality, is something more: a flight from an identity that he had chosen but now can neither embrace nor disown. A disturbing coda consolidates the episode's bleak vision. Crockett and Tubbs are joined in the bar by police lieutenant Lou Rodriguez (Gregory Sierra), who tells them that he has just received a phone call from the federal agent who has been debriefing Lawson for the past three hours: "[Lawson] stepped out for a breather, made a call to his wife, went into the men's room, and hung himself." This news is delivered in reaction shots that conclude with Crockett in close-up, his eyes widening in shock, followed by a shot of Crockett, Tubbs, and Rodriguez that ends the episode in freeze frame as the haunting lyric of "This Masquerade" makes its ironic commentary on Lawson, who is so tormented by his own masquerade.

The 2006 *Miami Vice* feature film confounded the expectations of many fans of the television series, who believed that Mann would remake the television show without doing violence to its 1980s sensibility. Contrary to these expectations, the film does not reflect the sociopolitical contexts of 2006 the way that the television show reflected the cultural and political contexts of the mid-1980s. Inadvertently, perhaps, the film's main significance may lie in what it tells us about the importance of the TV series. Denying that he wished to pay homage to the TV series, Mann tells John Hiscock, "I'm not interested in nostalgia." He goes on to explain that "my intention was to characterize what a contemporary trafficking organization is like. In the post-modern world, what is trafficking? It's no longer one group of people in one location trafficking one product like cocaine. It's about networks that can move counterfeit pharmaceuticals, or pirated software out of China—you name it—all through the same extremely sophisticated channels."[9] In this respect, Mann succeeds in depicting the evolution of a wholly new model of criminal trafficking on a global scale.

Although Steven Rybin makes a convincing case that "*Miami Vice* looks and sounds nothing like its television predecessor,"[10] the film preserves key themes from the series, chief of which are the alienating effects of undercover police work and the need for existential choice on the part of the protagonists. Timothy Shary observes that Mann tends to revisit his own work in a spirit of what Shary calls "Kubrickian perfectionism."[11] Rybin also sees Mann's work as recapitulating certain themes and tropes: "As Mann's body of work has grown over the course of thirty years, his own oeuvre has begun to provide him in recent years with a grab bag of narrative tropes, psychological types, snippets of dialogue, and even pieces of music which are constantly reshaped into consistently distinctive aesthetic effects and thematic meanings in each subsequent film."[12]

It is also plausible to suppose that Mann wanted to make a contempo- rary film of *Miami Vice* so that he could utilize computerized special effects and high-definition digital cameras to achieve a style that was impossible in 1984 when the television series premiered. It is enough to witness the bravura moments in *Miami Vice* where high-definition photography is put in the service of style to appreciate the appeal this technology has for the filmmaker.

In the *Miami Vice* feature film, Mann and his director of photography, Dion Beebe, create aerial traveling shots and sweeping horizontal pans that display Miami at its bejeweled best. Mann's well-known command of detail and ability to choreograph action sequences with precision and verve are on full view in four sequences: the speedboat race, mentioned in the introduc- tion to this volume, that opens the director's cut of the film; an impulsive powerboat junket to Cuba where Sonny Crockett (Colin Farrell) and Isa- bella (Gong Li) have their first romantic moments; the rescue of Detective Trudy Joplin (Naomie Harris) from the trailer of the Aryan Brotherhood members who have abducted her; and the climactic shoot-out.

Mann sought to bring narratives with a political or psychological edge and an existentialist's awareness of the vicissitudes of life to the *Miami Vice* television series. In the feature film, he is as concerned thematically with the problematic nature of living authentically as he was in the series, and the film does a good job of illustrating the idea that events are inherently destabilizing and that in an unstable criminal environment actions are unpredictable. In the main plot device that Mann uses to set the film's action in motion, vice detectives Sonny Crockett and Ricardo Tubbs (Jamie Foxx) must infiltrate an international drug-trafficking organization to find out who leaked the identities of some murdered undercover FBI agents. This leads them to Jose Yero (John Ortiz), a middle manager in the organization who is charged with screening the detectives, posing as drug transportation specialists, before they meet the top man, Arcangel de Jesus Montoya (Luis Tosar). Montoya is a ruthless kingpin who hires Crockett and Tubbs to transport some drugs from South America to Miami. Mann's engagement with the patterns of contingency in which undercover work is inevitably enmeshed shows how variegated they can be. By tracing the steps Crockett and Tubbs must take to infiltrate a multibillion-dollar drug-trafficking operation, Mann adds drama to the inherently ambiguous situation they face when they try to internalize their fabricated identities and later, once the assignment is over, somehow to recover their authentic selves. Unfortunately, the film stints on Crockett and Tubbs as individuals, to say nothing of the relations between them, possibly because Mann believed that their backstories were so well inscribed in our collective memory that recapitulation was unnecessary. The resulting elliptical fashion in which the film treats moments of disclosure between them, so effectively dramatized in the television series, opens up a gap.

When Crockett begins an affair with Montoya's lover, Isabella, it is as if he is in flight from his authentic self, and this portion of the narrative is structured around the way Crockett is tempted by and temporarily succumbs to the temptations of vice in the form of giving himself over to Isabella. Nevertheless, it comes as a surprise that he cannot see at once how his cultivation of and subsequent romance with Isabella will end. It is disappointing to discover that Crockett may be the last character in the film to realize that a relationship with her would be impossible, which leads Tubbs to utter the film's best line when he tells his partner, "There's undercover, and there's '*Which way is up?*'"

Yero observes Crockett and Isabella together and tells Montoya they are romantically involved. Much of the rest of the film dwells on how this relationship, with its attendant peril for Isabella and Crockett, will play out. Montoya eventually abandons Isabella, and Yero brings her to a meet putatively where drugs and money are to be exchanged, but in reality where Crockett and Tubbs have been set up to be killed. Crockett, knowing that in order to put Isabella out of harm's way he must give up any hope of a future with her, spirits her away from the scene and takes her to a coastal safe house to wait until he can put her on a boat to her home in Cuba. With Crockett's decision not to give himself over completely to Isabella, the narrative achieves closure by showing how he ultimately resists the temptations of vice, a major theme of the television series as well.

This theme of the psychological toll of undercover law enforcement runs through the *Miami Vice* film. From its opening sequence inside a Miami nightclub, the film places Crockett and Tubbs against a dark and shadowy backdrop, as if to suggest a fatalistic atmosphere redolent of the noir style and point of view found in so many episodes of the *Vice* television series. And yet the theatrical film does not seem to work, either as a remake of the television series or on its own terms. R. Barton Palmer has suggested that this failure reveals something interesting about "the difference between feature and serialized treatments of the same material. [It] might have something to do with the difference between an episodic series (and the range of narrative forms, characters, and themes it can dispose of) and a feature film, which is much more restricted in scope." Palmer adduces the *Dragnet* film (1987, Tom Mankiewicz) as well as the *Sex and the City* feature films (2008 and 2010, Michael Patrick King) as further examples of excellent series made into feature films that were critical disappointments.[13]

Aeon Skoble, in response to this point, argues that if the *Miami Vice* film did not turn out particularly well, the source of the failure derives from a reception problem. He writes, "The problem isn't just feature versus serial—after all, 'Brother's Keeper' [the two-hour *Miami Vice* TV pilot] could stand alone as a good film—but [rather] the pastiche nature of the film. Part of what makes *Vice Vice* is its particular place in time. It's essentially tied to the 80s, as *Grease* is essentially tied to the 50s. Mann could have made a different film about undercover cops, but to redo *Vice* seems to be trying to recapture something."[14]

No doubt Palmer is correct to point out that "the dense narrativity and thematic complexity of the series are necessarily missing." This makes the film resemble an episode—temporally extended, to be sure, to fit the format of a feature film. In fact, as a number of critics noted at the time, the episode "Smuggler's Blues," written by Miguel Pinero, a poet and playwright who appeared as the drug lord Esteban Calderone in several *Vice* episodes in 1984, seems to have inspired the scene where Trudy is held hostage by white supremacists. Few of the thematic elements from the series were effectively exploited in the feature film and, judging from the comments one can find on various websites, this absence seems to have alienated many of its viewers.

Yet what remains to be observed is, as Skoble suggests, the failure of the casting to bear the burden of the collective memory of so many fans of the television series. Don Johnson and Philip Michael Thomas inhabited their roles as Sonny Crockett and Ricardo Tubbs in a way that seems to have escaped Colin Farrell and Jamie Foxx. This may have been inevitable, given the passage of time, and it may also have been a function of Mann's determination not to do a remake of the television series. For whatever reasons, Farrell and Foxx seem to be unable to sustain the burden of authenticity in a vehicle that had already established itself so firmly in viewers' minds.

In the end, what distinguished the television series from its feature-film counterpart may well have been how in the former Mann captured a place and its historic moment, an understanding of Miami as a city on the edge and a place whose disruptive elements could only be partially restrained but never eliminated. By the early 1980s, Miami was undergoing many of the dislocations produced by rapid multiculturization, crime, and racial unrest. In holding a camera up to Miami in that era, the series exposed the challenges that law enforcement had to confront. Its major achievement in this respect was to dramatize the points that undercover existence is deeply contaminated by the experience of fear, suspicion, betrayal, and paranoia; that there is more to criminal activity than drug trafficking; and that there are existential hazards to undercover detective work. As A. O. Scott observes, "In the history of cop dramas, *Miami Vice* remains an intriguing anomaly, a sleek postmodernist detour on the genre's march toward ever more emphatic realism."[15] By deemphasizing what Scott calls the "relentlessly procedural" aspects of crime detection,[16] *Miami Vice* was instrumental in rewriting the narrative of crime television, extending film noir to television, and restoring an existential thread to its thematic.[17]

Notes

1. Scott Foundas, "A Mann's Man's World," *L.A. Weekly,* July 26, 2006.

2. Graham Fuller, "Michael Mann—Hollywood Writer-Director-Producer," *Interview,* December 1, 1995.

3. Quoted in Ian Nathan, "Born to Break the Rules," *London Times,* September 16, 2004.

4. Foundas, "A Mann's Man's World."

5. Fuller, "Michael Mann." A variation of this maxim can be found in *Heat* during the café conversation between Neil and Vincent.

6. See Vincent M. Gaine, *Existentialism and Social Engagement in the Films of Michael Mann* (London: Palgrave Macmillan, 2011), 219.

7. Ibid., 219, 68.

8. See the pilot, "Brother's Keeper" (September 19, 1984), for the first of these images and the second-season opener, "The Prodigal Son" (September 27, 1985), for the second.

9. John Hiscock, "So You Think I'm Aggressive? Good," *Daily Telegraph* (London), July 21, 2006.

10. Steven Rybin, *The Cinema of Michael Mann* (Lanham, MD: Lexington, 2007), 196. Quotes referenced here and in note 12 are from the first edition of Rybin's book. An expanded edition has now been published with the title *Michael Mann: Crime Auteur* (Lanham, MD: Scarecrow Press, 2013).

11. Timothy Shary, "Which Way Is Up," *Sight & Sound* 16, no. 9 (September 2006): 17.

12. Rybin, *The Cinema of Michael Mann*, 189.

13. Quoted passages from R. Barton Palmer in this paragraph and elsewhere come from his correspondence with the author, June 25, 2012.

14. Quoted passages from Aeon J. Skoble in this paragraph come from his correspondence with the author, June 25, 2012.

15. A. O. Scott, "Michael Mann Loves His Work," *New York Times,* August 8, 2004.

16. Ibid.

17. I am grateful to Christeen Clemens for her many contributions to my appreciation of *Miami Vice.*

"Do You See?"

Reflecting on Evil in *Manhunter*

Aeon J. Skoble

> Whoever fights monsters should see to it that in the process he does not become a monster. And when you look long into an abyss, the abyss also looks into you.
>
> —Friedrich Nietzsche, *Beyond Good and Evil*

Michael Mann's 1986 film *Manhunter,* based on the Thomas Harris novel *Red Dragon,*[1] was one of the earliest cinematic explorations of the "profiling" approach to tracking serial killers. Profiling differs from traditional clue-based detective work in its focus on trying to understand the psyche of the criminal. Harris's 1981 novel was based on interviews with the FBI's Behavioral Science Unit, which was at the time relatively new. The film begins as Jack Crawford (Dennis Farina) tries to coax Will Graham (William Petersen) out of retirement to consult on a case. (The Crawford character is based on real-life FBI profiler John Douglas.) Graham had managed to apprehend serial killer Hannibal Lecktor[2] (Brian Cox), and Crawford believes Graham's insight and acumen will prove useful in catching a new serial killer, dubbed the "Tooth Fairy" because of the bite marks he leaves on his victims. The film *Manhunter* is often unjustly slighted by contrast with Jonathan Demme's *The Silence of the Lambs* (1991), also based on a Harris novel and featuring several of the same characters, but Mann's film is fascinating in its own right, both cinematically and philosophically. By using the work of FBI profiling, it affords viewers an opportunity to explore the conception of evil presented by the killers—both the Tooth Fairy, Francis Dollarhyde (Tom Noonan), and Lecktor himself—as well as by the FBI profiler Graham, whose methodology includes trying to think as the killers think. How is Graham able to do this? He is skittish about helping Crawford with the Tooth Fairy case, despite his success with Lecktor, because he sees his technique as potentially dangerous to himself, both physically and psychologically.

Graham is not an old man: he has retired from the FBI because his experiences with Lecktor three years earlier were traumatizing. There was physical trauma involved: we are told that Lecktor was able to severely wound Graham before being incapacitated. The tabloid reporter Freddy Lounds (Steven Lang) obtained entrance to Graham's hospital room and took photographs of the massive scarring, which he then published. But more significantly, Graham experienced psychological trauma—not so much in the sense that he was traumatized by Lecktor's attack, although that may have played a role, but because to apprehend Lecktor he had to "become" Lecktor, and that process damaged him. Graham explains this in his own words to try to help his son understand what happened:

> Will Graham: I tried to build feelings in my imagination like the killer had, so that I would know why he did what he did. Because that would help me find him. When I was sitting in Lecktor's office, I looked up, and I saw a book on his shelf. It had pictures of war wounds in it. And I knew it was him. So I went to a pay phone down the hall to call the police. And that's when he attacked me. You and Mom came to see me in the hospital, and that helped a lot. But after my body got OK, I still had his thoughts going around in my head. And I stopped talking to people. And a doctor friend of mind, Dr. Bloom, asked me to get some help. And I did. And after a while I felt better, and I was OK again.
> Kevin Graham: And the way he thought felt that bad?
> Will Graham: Kevin, they're the ugliest thoughts in the world.

One of the tag lines used in the film's marketing was "Enter the mind of a serial killer . . . you may never come back," and this is the phenomenon Graham explains to his young son. The point of "entering the mind of" the killer, the point of the profiling approach, is to gain insight into the killer's motivation and belief system so that it becomes possible to identify him or her.[3] The risk, though, as Graham notes, is that trying to think as the killer thinks can wreak havoc on the psyche.

Interestingly, the same year this film was released, an episode of Mann's television series *Miami Vice* (1984–1989) featured a remarkably similar plot. In "Shadow in the Dark," Detective Sonny Crockett (Don Johnson) tries to apprehend a ritualistic serial killer by reconstructing his mind-set, in the process incurring some psychological damage. Indeed, another detective was driven mad by attempting it. There is some dispute about Mann's auteur status with respect to *Miami Vice*—Can an executive producer have that kind of artistic vision and impose it on a series? Surely in many cases the answer is no, but in *Miami Vice* there is ample evidence of Mann's aesthetic sensibilities. The clearest way to see Mann's aesthetics all over *Miami Vice* is to compare the series to the film he made at the same time: *Manhunter*. The color contrast, the use of popular music, the hard-boiled dialogue—that there would even be an episode with a plot remarkably similar to *Manhunter*'s means it cannot be a coincidence. (To further underscore Mann's role in *Miami Vice*, one notes that several actors in *Manhunter* also appear in Mann's television dramas *Miami Vice* and *Crime Story* [1986–1988]: besides Kim Greist, this is also true of Dennis Farina, Steven Lang, Michael Talbott, Chris Elliot, Patricia Charbonneau, Michele Shay, and Bill Smitrovich.) In "Shadow in the Dark," the first detective who used profiling, who attempted to get inside the mind of the killer, lost himself and was ultimately unable to solve the case. Crockett is able to hang on, barely, and does apprehend the killer.[4]

In Graham's pursuit of Lecktor, the technique worked: he was able to get enough of a sense of Lecktor's thoughts and attitudes to be able to figure out that he was the killer, but having Lecktor's thoughts in his head also made Graham disturbed enough to need psychiatric care. It was this trauma, then, more than the physical trauma, that led to his retirement.

However, when Crawford is not able to glean any insight into this new serial killer, the "Tooth Fairy," he seeks out Graham. We do not know at the beginning of the film why Graham is reluctant to help or why he feels compelled to help despite his reluctance; we discover these things as the story unfolds. Graham's wife, Molly (Kim Greist), is furious with Crawford and concerned that Graham will "make himself sick" again. Graham is concerned also, but his commitment to preventing the slaughter of another family prevails.

The "Tooth Fairy"—we later learn that he refers to himself as the "Red Dragon"—obtains entrance to a family's home, kills all of them, and then manipulates the bodies. What he actually does is not shown on camera or even explicitly described, but Mann shows us quick glimpses of crime-scene photographs that suggest its violence and some sexual component. One thing we do know is that the killer puts shards of a shattered mirror in the victims' eyes so they can "watch" him doing whatever it is he is doing. The two families who have been murdered so far were attacked on nights with a full moon, so Crawford needs Graham to help profile the killer before the next full moon. Graham surveys the crime scenes and views home movies from the families. His first attempt to "enter the mind" of the killer is fruitful: seeing the young, beautiful wife on one of the videotapes, he wonders whether the killer might have found it frustrating to have to wear rubber gloves (despite their usefulness in avoiding fingerprints) when he touched her. There was some talcum powder on her thigh, but none in the room, so Graham realizes that the killer took off his gloves briefly so he could touch her. He calls for a fingerprint expert to examine the victims' fingernails, toenails, and corneas, and, sure enough, there are prints. Graham's discovery here is based on deductive reasoning yet informed by an insight from what he thinks is the killer's mind-set. In a conversation with a local detective, however, we discover that Graham is nowhere near close enough:

> Atlanta detective: I know a burglar is gonna fence what he stole because his motive is cash money. I know his motive, so I go to work on the fences. This guy, we don't even have motive.
> Graham: It's in his dreams.
> Atlanta detective: His motive?
> Graham: Yeah. His act fuels his fantasy.
> Atlanta detective: Which is . . . ?
> Graham: I don't know.

Graham realizes that it will be difficult to figure out just what the fantasy is, and he is in fact doubtful that he can do so. He cautions Crawford not to expect too much from him:

> Graham: You think I'm gonna see him standing in the street and say, "There he is"? That's Houdini you're thinking about. The Tooth Fairy's gonna go on until we get smart or we get lucky; he won't stop.
> Crawford: Why?
> Graham: He's got a genuine taste for it.
> Crawford: So you do know something about him.

Graham: Not enough. Think I'll go see Lecktor tomorrow.
Crawford (incredulous): Why?
Graham: Recover the mindset.

Although Graham has gained some insight into the killer's psychology, he doesn't know enough to know how the families are selected, which is the crucial piece of information they need in order to apprehend the killer. This will require a clearer understanding of the nature of the delusion. Graham used this technique to apprehend Lecktor and is hopeful that it will help again, despite his trepidation.[5]

Graham's first conversation with Lecktor does help somewhat, but it leaves Graham feeling physically ill. Lecktor uses the opportunity to taunt Graham, and he also decides to give Graham's home address to the Tooth Fairy, suggesting that he kill them all to save himself. After foiling this attempt, Graham later has a further conversation with Lecktor, which also helps him gain further insight. Graham comes to understand that the Tooth Fairy is motivated by transformation and by seeing, but he is still unsure of what they are directed toward. "You rearrange the dead families into an audience to see what you do. You think that what you do will make you into something different. You are becoming. What is it you think you're becoming? The answer is in the way you use the mirrors. What do the mirrors make you dream you're becoming?"[6]

Graham does not know this, but the audience gets more of a sense of the importance of seeing when the Tooth Fairy captures and tortures the tabloid reporter Lounds. As the Tooth Fairy shows Lounds what he does, he keeps asking, "Do you *see?*" He stresses that Lounds is a witness "to a great becoming," and his insistence that Lounds open his eyes refers to both the literal and the metaphorical. He wants him to see the films of the victims ("Open your eyes, or I'll staple your eyelids to your forehead") and to bear witness to the transformation. In most scenes at the killer's home, everything is brightly lit. (Ironically, his workplace is largely dark—the great becoming will presumably entail leaving his "regular" job behind.)

Lecktor suggests to Graham that killing feels good because it is an expression of power. God, he says, kills people all the time. He is trying to taunt Graham again, implying that his psychological problems are based on the conflict he has in feeling badly about the fact that it feels good to kill people. Despite the taunting, Graham is able to gain further understanding of the Tooth Fairy. Lecktor claims that "if one does what God does enough times, one will become as God is." For Graham, this is an essential piece of the puzzle. Revisiting one of the crime scenes, he is able to reconstruct more of the killer's thought processes, almost empathizing with him, coming to understand that the fantasy involves being loved and accepted by the families he kills. Graham talks to the victims in the persona of the killer: "I see me desired by you. Accepted. And loved. In the silver mirrors of your eyes." He is later able to articulate this understanding to Crawford: "He dreams about being wanted and desired, so he changes people into beings who want and desire him." When he realizes that seeing is so important, he figures out that the Tooth Fairy has seen the very home movies that Graham has been watching. This is the unifying thread that allows Graham to identify the killer as Francis Dollarhyde, a technician at the film-processing lab. Graham and Crawford, along with a SWAT team, track him down, and Graham kills Dollarhyde after a struggle. Later, we see Graham reunited with his family and evidently not in need of psychiatric care.

Strangely enough, as Graham and Crawford are learning about Dollarhyde, the audience sees Dollarhyde enter a relationship with a coworker, Reba (Joan Allen). Reba is blind, which at first glance might seem not to line up with Dollarhyde's need to be seen, but on further inspection makes sense: from his deranged perspective, Dollarhyde's victims had to be transformed into beings who wanted him, but Reba already does want him. For a moment, the audience is led to wonder whether Dollarhyde might be healed of his sociopathic nature through his finding of love and acceptance with Reba. But Dollarhyde is too unbalanced: he sees another coworker helping Reba, infers wrongly that she has rejected him (Dollarhyde), and so abducts her. He tells her that "Francis is gone for good"—only the Red Dragon remains. Just as Graham and Crawford find the house, Dollarhyde is on the verge of replacing Reba's sightless eyes with mirrors so that she too will "see" him with love and acceptance. Crawford urges Graham to wait for backup from the SWAT team, but Graham cannot let Dollarhyde harm Reba. To the sound of "In-A-Gadda-Da-Vida" by Iron Butterfly, Graham confronts Dollarhyde alone and gets his face slashed before finally shooting Dollarhyde. As the blood pours out of Dollarhyde's body, it forms a pattern like that of the Red Dragon painting he had modeled his transformation after.

Dollarhyde sees himself as becoming something great. He tells Lounds that Lounds is "privy to a great becoming" and should tremble. This statement echoes Lecktor's suggestion that killers like killing because it makes them feel powerful. On Lecktor's analysis, it's not so much that God is a serial killer as that serial killers are trying to become God. Dollarhyde, who, we are led to infer, has been abused and unloved, will transform himself into an object of love and awe. This motivation is wholly different from that of the aforementioned burglar trying to get money. Even some killers have more "straightforward" motives, such as money or revenge. In these cases, we express moral disapproval, but we understand what it means to be motivated by money or revenge. In a case like Dollarhyde, or Lecktor himself, we don't really even understand. As Graham notes, the motive is tied to a delusion, a fantasy we cannot wholly grasp. Graham's problem is that to understand it is to run the risk of being consumed by it. Lecktor remarks that Graham was able to catch him because "we're just alike"—he suspects Graham feels good about killing when he has had occasion to kill. Graham is hoping this is not the case, which is why he is skittish about the work. But he also feels a strong sense of duty to prevent more murders, which seems to indicate that Lecktor is mistaken. Graham is perhaps sufficiently grounded in the morality of our society that he doesn't allow the killers' fantasies to fully become his own.

One interpretation of Socrates's ethical theory is that to know the good is to do the good. That is, we are always acting in such a way as to promote what we *think* is right; the problem is that we are sometimes mistaken. If the mistake is minor, the wrongdoing will be minor, but what happens when the mistake is a large-scale delusion, as it seems to be for Lecktor and Dollarhyde? They will then see the world as existing to serve their delusion. Is this an "explanation of evil"? In one sense, of course it is: that is why Dollarhyde does what he does. But in another sense, it's no explanation at all—it only pushes the question back a level. How do people come to have such delusions or fantasies about the world? Even more troubling: How is Dollarhyde's "delusion" about the world different from, say, the delusion of the 9/11 terrorists that if they blew up the World Trade Center, they would receive eternal rewards in heaven? There's a way in which they're not different: both are typically characterized as evil. But one important difference is that no one but Dollarhyde believes he is becoming the great Red Dragon, whereas many people believe in the justice of blowing up buildings. In the latter case, it was people coming to share a worldview that led the terrorists to their course of action. This is the concern, the flip side, of the Socratic dictum. If we were to truly see the fantasy that is in their minds, we might come to accept it. After all, if we could see the fantasy with as much clarity as the killers do, how would we know which was which? This seems to be what Nietzsche is cautioning in the aphorism that serves as the epigraph to this essay: to gaze into the abyss is to risk incorporating its features in one's own psyche. This is what explains Graham's trepidation at the beginning of the film. The previous time he battled with a monster, he came close to becoming one. Lecktor's taunts play on this fear: that he and Graham are just alike. "You want the scent? Smell yourself." In this case, fortunately, Graham avoids becoming a monster.[7]

Notes

1. Lore has it that the studio made the decision not to call the film *Red Dragon* because it wanted to avoid association with the recently released Michael Cimino film *Year of the Dragon,* which did poorly at the box office, or perhaps to avoid associations with martial-arts films.

2. Although this character's name is spelled "Lecter" in the novel, it was rendered "Lecktor" in the film script, so it appears that way in this essay.

3. For greater insight into the nature and origins of the profiling approach, see John Douglas and Mark Olshaker, *Mindhunter: Inside the FBI's Elite Serial Crime Unit* (New York: Scribner, 1995).

4. For more on Mann's role in *Miami Vice,* see Steven Sanders, *Miami Vice* (Detroit: Wayne State University Press, 2010).

5. Brian Cox's portrayal of Lecktor tends to be underrated in comparison to Anthony Hopkins's more well-known interpretation of the character, but Cox is chilling and creepy in his own right and very effectively conveys the psychopathic killer. The 2002 film *Red Dragon,* directed by Brett Ratner, was less a remake of *Manhunter* than a refilming of the novel, primarily as a way to continue to use Anthony Hopkins as Lecter (although without Scott Glenn as Crawford). In general, this film was poorly received, certainly in contrast to *Silence of the Lambs.* In retrospect, viewed side by side with *Manhunter,* it doesn't compare well to Mann's work either. The scenes with Lecter and Graham in particular lack the same tense atmosphere as their counterparts in the earlier film.

6. The music in these scenes in particular, which is very similar to music used in scoring similar scenes in *Miami Vice,* provides further evidence of Mann's auteur role in *Miami Vice.* And much has been written on Mann's use of color; see, for example, Steven Rybin, *The Cinema of Michael Mann* (Lanham, MD: Lexington Books, 2007). Furthermore, the end credits of *Manhunter* even use the same font as the *Miami Vice* credits.

7. I am grateful to Steven Sanders for helpful comments on this essay.

MANN AND *ÜBERMENSCH*

Evil and Power in *Manhunter*

David Sterritt

Manhunter, the 1986 film adapted by writer-director Michael Mann from Thomas Harris's 1981 novel *Red Dragon,* introduced Hannibal Lecktor to the movies.[1] The cannibalistic psychiatrist—whose last name is spelled "Lecter" in other films and in the Harris novels, a detail to which we shall return— did not make his screen debut as a full-fledged antihero.[2] He is instead a supporting player in a saga centering primarily on Francis Dollarhyde, a similarly twisted killer, and Will Graham, a forensic investigator who consults with Lecktor during his efforts to end Dollarhyde's murderous career. William Petersen plays the detective and Tom Noonan plays Dollarhyde, his unhinged archenemy. For today's audiences, Lecter is definitively linked with Anthony Hopkins's signature performances in three films postdating *Manhunter,* starting with his Academy Award–winning portrayal in Jonathan Demme's *The Silence of the Lambs* in 1991 and continuing with Ridley Scott's *Hannibal* in 2001 and Brett Ratner's *Red Dragon* in 2002; but this does not detract from the nuanced excellence of Brian Cox's rendering in *Manhunter,* which prefigures his finely tuned interpretations of marginalized men in such unusual dramas as *L.I.E* (2001, Michael Cuesta), where he plays a secret pedophile, and *Red* (2008, Trygve Allister Diesen and Lucky McKee), where he sympathetically portrays a vengeful recluse.[3]

Manhunter stays reasonably close to the story line of Harris's novel. After tracking down and capturing Lecktor, at the cost of much injury to himself, Graham has retired to Florida with his wife, Molly (Kim Greist), and their son, Kevin (David Seaman), a youngster with only a vague idea of why his father withdrew from police work. Asked by his former boss, Jack Crawford (Dennis Farina), to lend assistance with a new serial-murder case,

Graham reluctantly agrees, knowing that he has a unique talent for teasing out the fantasies, motivations, and modi operandi of psychotic criminals. The new killer is Dollarhyde, who has slain two families so far. The police and the tabloids call him the "Tooth Fairy" because he leaves bite marks in the flesh of his victims, whom he arranges into hallucinatory tableaus after murdering them, in each case on a night of the full moon.

We eventually learn that Dollarhyde has a lifelong fixation on one of the four *Great Red Dragon* watercolors painted by the visionary poet and artist William Blake in the early nineteenth century. Inspired by a passage in the Book of Revelation, the series sets forth a biblical narrative wherein Satan, represented by the dragon, vainly plots to seize the yet unborn Jesus from Mary's arms as soon as she gives birth. Francis's favorite of the four paintings is *The Great Red Dragon and the Woman Clothed with the Sun,* the only one that gives approximately equal weight to the terrifying dragon and the consecrated mother-to-be.[4] Blake depicts Mary as a golden figure kneeling unafraid beneath the creature's hovering bulk; her transfigured face, angelic wings, and prayer-uplifted arms make a divine mockery of the dragon's hidden face, gaunt wings, downward-leaning arms, and excremental coloring. Seeing no mockery or irony in the image, however, Dollarhyde venerates the hate-filled beast, wanting not just to worship it, but literally to *become* it. This is why the dragon is tattooed on his torso, why he follows an intense bodybuilding regime, and why he commits his ritual murders. His psychosis stems from his tragically misshapen childhood, when he was terrorized by an abusive grandmother whose false teeth he now uses to bestow his trademark bites on those he kills. As a pathological biter, he greatly admires Hannibal Lecktor, who has employed his teeth in acts even more savage than Francis's own.

Intuiting some of Dollarhyde's aberrations early in the manhunt, Graham sets up a meeting with Lecktor, his detested foe. He knows that Lecktor despises him, but he hopes that a request for assistance will feed the former psychiatrist's narcissism enough to override his monumental self-absorption and elicit some kind of clue that could be useful in identifying the Tooth Fairy before he kills again. Subplots in the narrative involve psychologist Frederick Chilton (Benjamin Hendrickson), the pompous mental-institution chief who finds a fan letter from the Tooth Fairy in Lecktor's cell; tabloid reporter Freddy Lounds (Stephen Lang), whom Graham and Crawford use as bait for the Tooth Fairy, with appalling results; and Reba McClane (Joan Allen), a blind woman who befriends Dollarhyde at the film-processing lab where they both work. Piecing together seemingly disconnected observations and bits of evidence, Graham ultimately realizes that the Tooth Fairy chooses his victims by watching home movies they have sent to the lab for processing—a crucial insight that enables him to pin down the killer's identity and learn the address of his home. Arriving there just as Dollarhyde is preparing to murder Reba, he executes a Hollywood-hero crash through an enormous window, rescues Reba in the nick of time, and ends the Tooth Fairy's malevolent life.

Lecktor remains alive and well, however, and Mann forestalls potential moral objections to this outcome in the same way that Harris does. Like the novel, the film has three conspicuously reprehensible characters in addition to Hannibal the cannibal. One is Chilton, the feckless asylum chief; another is Lounds, the churlish journalist; and of course there is Dollarhyde, the out-of-control slayer. Their unholy fellowship, signaled by their alliterative first names—Frederick, Freddy, Francis—brings unpleasant consequences that more or less suit their offenses: Chilton is treated with disdain by cop and criminal alike; Lounds meets a hideous death; and Dollarhyde is defeated and killed despite his best efforts to escape detection and fulfill his misbegotten dream. Having satiated the audience's taste for righteous retribution by trouncing these three, Mann is free to leave Lecktor safe in the cell where we found him.

Mannhunter

Appropriately for a film about the search for a killer's identity, *Manhunter* pays close attention to nomenclature and orthography, making small but telling adjustments to the novel's usages. The most obvious alteration is the title change from *Red Dragon* to *Manhunter,* which appears to have made everyone unhappy except (uncredited) executive producer Dino De Laurentiis, who insisted on the change because, according to Mann's account, he feared repeating the failure of Michael Cimino's crime drama *Year of the Dragon,* a box-office disaster De Laurentiis had produced the previous year. Mann found the new title "inferior," and Cox deemed it "cheesy" and "bland."[5]

All of this notwithstanding, the new title lends a subtly self-reflexive quality to the film, punning as it does on the director's last name. By combining *man(n)* and *hunter,* it conjures up Mann-the-hunter, intently pursuing a suspenseful story and a trenchant commentary on modern life, and potentially stalked in return by some hunter-of-Mann that cannot harm him physically (it's only a movie) but may threaten him psychologically and spiritually, much as Graham is threatened by the serial-killer mentalities that he must reconstruct, identify with, and to some extent *share* in order to foretell future actions. In ways that are not so very different, the film-maker and the profiler assume the task of envisioning and comprehending thought processes that they (and we) would prefer to consider utterly alien to their (and our) own.

Another change is also noteworthy. Francis's surname is "Dolarhyde" in the book but "Dollarhyde" in Mann's movie. Although hints of dual personality *(Mr. Hyde)*, concealment *(hide)*, and thick, resistant skin *(hide)* are implicit in both spellings, the whiff of capitalism *(dollar)* is strengthened by the film's orthography, which underscores (by ironic inversion) the serial killer's participation in what sociologist Georges Bataille calls a "general economy" based not on utility and production, but on "unproductive expenditures" brought about by the loss, waste, death, sacrifice, and excess entailed by violence, war, games, spectacles, cultish ritual, rites of mourning, and "perverse sexual activity" that is "deflected from genital finality."[6] Bataille regards a person who is expended in the course of such activities—a victim, in plain language—as essentially "a surplus, taken from the mass of *useful* wealth . . . in order to be consumed profitlessly, and therefore utterly destroyed. Once chosen, he is the *accursed share,* destined for violent consumption."[7] Dollarhyde would never have heard of all this, but the hugely erudite Lecktor would surely have read Bataille during his voracious studies, and one can imagine his delight in coming upon a philosopher who shares his besotted fascination with death, waste, violence, games, and the rest, not to mention his indifference to "genital finality" on the rare occasions when sexuality enters his equations.[8] Anyone who writes off the hapless victims of the world with a phrase as romantic-religious as "accursed share" is automatically a friend of Hannibal's, and it is tempting to picture the convivial cannibal having the French philosopher for dinner with a nice Chianti and some fava beans. It would be a dinner date for the ages.

"Smell Yourself"

Lecktor would not have become an iconic villain of contemporary popular culture if he were just an enthusiastic killer with an unusually well-furnished mind. The secret to his remarkable success on page and screen lies in the way his mental functioning confounds traditional paradigms set forth by

Sigmund Freud and further expanded and revised by later psychoanalytic theorists, of whom Slavoj Žižek and his mentor Jacques Lacan are among the most influential today. It is easy to say that Lecktor, like Dollarhyde and Jame Gumb (Buffalo Bill), is perpetually stuck in the oral stage of infantile development, actualizing primordial fantasies of devouring the coveted mother, the dreaded father, and the resented sibling via spectacular acts of anthropophagy.[9] What flummoxes this id-driven model is the astonishing *self-control* that Lecktor displays in every aspect of his comportment and behavior, save only when he is destroying a victim or fighting off enemies. Although his words can burn like acid, they are usually couched in courtesy: "I'm glad you came," he says when Graham shows up to interview him. His slurs and insults can be as witty as they are penetrating: "He fumbles at your head," he says of Chilton's second-rate psychological testing, "like a fresh-man pulling at a panty girdle." He is exquisitely attuned to sensory stimuli, recognizing Graham by the scent of the "atrocious aftershave" Graham wore in court three years earlier—an apt maneuver, because he knows that Graham wants to reacquaint himself with the "old scent" of serial-killer evil.

Most startlingly, Lecktor exercises superhuman command over his mind and body. Chilton shows Graham an electrocardiogram tape and describes Lecktor's physical state at the very moment when he was savagely mutilating a caretaker who drew too close: "Here Lecktor's resting on the examining table getting an electrocardiogram. Complained of chest pains. Pulse seventy-two. Here he grabs the nurse's head and pulls her down to him. Here he's subdued by the attendant, and Lecktor's shoulder is dislocated. Do you notice the strange thing? His pulse never got over eighty-five. Even when he tore into her face." In another scene, Graham tells a colleague, "They tried sodium amytal [truth serum] on him three years ago to find where he buried a Princeton student. He gave them a recipe for potato-chip dip."

Lecktor's complete control of his autonomic nervous system makes him appear to be a semisupernatural figure. This begins to explain his enormous appeal for pop-culture audiences infatuated with superheroes and super-powers in movies, comic books, graphic novels, television shows, and every other available venue. But he is a supervillain, not a superhero, and unlike most of his mass-media counterparts—the Joker, say, or Lex Luthor or Green Goblin—there is no invulnerable Batman or Superman or Spider-Man to oppose him. Instead there are all-too-human professionals on the order of Jack Crawford and his crew, portrayed as well-trained public servants who reflect, in film scholar Philip L. Simpson's words, "a classically orthodox, populist mythology of American selfhood in rebellion against the posers and bureaucrats whose stewardship of cherished institutions is treasonously flawed."[10] Compared with the conventions and clichés of this mythology, the qualities of a quasi-superhuman figure such as Lecktor—blessed with preternatural self-control *and* a cheerful readiness to break every known rule of civilization—positively bristle with allure for consumers bored by the mechanical amusements ordinarily pumped out by America's under-nourished culture industry.

Lecktor's opponents are not without interest either, stuck though they are in standard crime-fiction paradigms. The extremities of iniquity represented by a Lecktor or a Dollarhyde can rouse professionals such as Graham and Crawford to "defy orthodoxy and flawed institutional procedure in the service of some greater good," Simpson accurately observes. At such moments, the crime fighters come to see that official wisdom, high-tech gear, and "narrowly defined academic knowledge" are of limited use against truly evil, truly irrational foes. Spurred on by this awareness, they strike out as more or less free agents, bypassing what Simpson calls "the distant machinery of due process" so as to probe the shadow zone of American individualism, where boundaries between order and chaos lose whatever tenuous stability they ever had.[11] Because the professionals' initiative stems from, as Simpson puts it, the same "fierce ideology of the asocial individual" that produces people such as Dollarhyde and Lecktor, we must conclude that the psycho and the psycho profiler are perilously similar beings.[12] This similarity poses great danger for Graham, who knows and fears his ability to put himself in the serial killer's bloody shoes; if he read Friedrich Nietzsche, he would surely remember the philosopher's maxim, "Whoever fights monsters should see to it that in the process he does not become a monster. And when you look long into an abyss, the abyss also looks into you."[13] Lecktor may have this warning in mind when he taunts Graham at the end of their first interview. "Do you know how you caught me?" he calls out as Graham scuttles anxiously toward the exit. "The reason you caught me, Will, is—we're just alike. You want the scent? Smell yourself."

The "Mad-Obscene Law"

Manhunter is not Hannibal Lecktor's story—Graham is the protagonist, and Dollarhyde is the primary villain—but Lecktor makes as powerful an impression as anyone in the picture despite his limited number of important scenes. On a philosophical level, in fact, he rather than Dollarhyde is Graham's true antagonist in the tale. Graham is an officer of the established law, dedicated to and governed by the statutory codes, ethical norms, and socially sanctioned mores that constitute the putatively benign superego of modern American life. In many respects, Lecktor is his polar inverse—a law unto himself, a radical transgressor, a mad doctor of disorder and misrule. In other ways, however, he is Graham's intimately related *converse,* dedicated to and governed by a distorted variant of the same psychic entity: the malignantly *corrupted* superego that enforces what Žižek calls the "obscene superego agency," the drastically transgressive "mad-obscene law which . . . derails the psychic equilibrium" and impels it toward "the 'impossible'/ traumatic/painful enjoyment" found only in liminal zones where neither the reality principle nor the pleasure principle prevails.[14] The terrifying conflicts at the heart of *Manhunter* are enacted on the visible plane of crime and police work, but they are generated and sustained on the dark, unconscious plane where aberration runs riot and evil is its own reward.

Dollarhyde's demons bear some resemblance to Lecktor's devils. Both men are plagued by megalomaniacal God complexes, for instance, as dialogue samples from two different scenes illustrate. Dollarhyde says to Lounds shortly before killing him, "Before me, you are a slug in the sun. You are privy to a great becoming, and you recognize nothing. You are an ant in the afterbirth. It is your nature to do only one thing correctly: tremble. But fear is not what you owe me, Lounds, you and the others. *You owe me awe."* Elsewhere in the story, Lecktor refers directly to God when cajoling Graham to admit taking secret pleasure from killing in the line of duty, saying to him, "God's terrific! He dropped a church roof on thirty-four of His worshippers in Texas last Wednesday night. Just as they were groveling through a hymn to His majesty. Don't you think that felt good? He wouldn't begrudge you two measly murders. . . . It feels good because if you do it as God does, enough times, you become as God is—*powerful."*[15] Both killers aim at being gods, wielding unlimited power and standing majestically above and outside the constricting laws of ordinary mortals. Like the devilish figure in Søren Kierkegaard's parable of the merman, each of them aspires to be "the single individual who as the particular is higher than the universal," and their respective notions of whence their superhuman strength derives—for Dollarhyde the Great Red Dragon, for Lecktor his own brain and body—speak to the parable's observation that the demonic has the "same property as the divine, that the individual can enter into an absolute relationship to it."[16]

The parallels between Dollarhyde and Lecktor cannot be pushed too far, however. For one thing, Dollarhyde is associated with images—that of the Great Red Dragon, of course, but also his self-image as an ugly man (he is acutely conscious of a facial scar from cleft-palate surgery) who can be romantically and sexually relaxed only with Reba, who cannot see him. His obsession with imagery leads him to place jagged mirror shards into his victims' dead eyes, using them as a means of reflecting himself to himself, a miserable way of extracting admiring gazes.[17] Lecktor, in contrast, is firmly linked with words. As a physician he practiced psychiatry, the most verbal branch of medicine, and as a prisoner he must communicate through speech, writing, and a book-based secret code rather than through action in the world; nowhere in Mann's *Manhunter* or Harris's *Red Dragon* does he make an artwork of blood and gore like the "snapshot from hell" that he creates while escaping from captivity in *The Silence of the Lambs*.[18] His surname underscores his connection with verbality: *lectus* derives from Latin *legere*, "to read," and is related to Greek *légein*, "to say, tell, speak, declare," as well as to *léxis*, "phrase, word," and *lógos*, "word, speech, thought, account."[19] He also uses his mouth to cannibalize entire bodies, whereas the less extravagant Dollarhyde merely kills and mutilates—biting off the victim's lips in the case of Freddy Lounds, as if to accentuate his hatred of the linguistic domain where Lecktor is at ease.

In another crucial difference, Dollarhyde is a foggy-minded predator who pursues his project of becoming more on impulse and instinct than on any kind of insight, however skewed and deranged, into the nature and plausibility of his impossible goals. In this he anticipates Jame Gumb (Ted Levine) in *The Silence of the Lambs*. By contrast, Lecktor is akin to Mason Verger, his mutilated former victim in the book and film *Hannibal*—a tireless, methodical schemer who plans his iniquitous deeds with exquisite care, exercising the brilliance of a savant and the patience of a lizard. Lecktor is an aesthetician of evil, a murder connoisseur, a cannibalism wonk who *thinks* about this stuff as he whiles away his solitary hours. His oubliette in the isolation ward is cramped and confining, but as the subsequent Harris novels make increasingly clear, his inner resources—his meticulously arranged memories, his learning in the arts and sciences, his inexhaustible creativity, his gift for inventing thought experiments, extravagant fantasies, and mental adventures—are spacious, far-reaching, and endlessly gratifying. Unquestioned confidence in his godlike strength and self-sufficiency is woven into the fabric of Lecktor's being, whereas Dollarhyde, who feels he is still becoming, must have the Great Red Dragon as his inspiration and role model.

"Mind-Forg'd Manacles"

The modern philosophers most interested in questions of becoming are Gilles Deleuze and Félix Guattari, most notably in *Anti-Oedipus* and *A Thousand Plateaus,* their two books on capitalism and schizophrenia. Viewing the human subject as integral to the same all-embracing "plane of immanence" that comprises the cosmos as a whole, they advocate a *schizoanalytic* mode of thinking that regards the unconscious as a locus of unbounded virtual energy, pulsating with positive desires that can either be diverted into static *being* or liberated into limitless *becoming* free of the entrenched paradigms and ideologies that hold the common run of us in thrall. Looked at through a schizoanalytic lens, borders of every kind—organic/inorganic, human/animal, male/female, and so on—are seen to be arbitrary and porous, existing only through the agency of sedimented forms, functions, preconceptions, and prejudices that block the infinite becoming we would otherwise experience. To participate fully in the inexhaustible cosmic flow, we must deterritorialize our locked-in mind-sets and reterritorialize them along new, emancipated lines of flight from the stifling principles and customs that normally constrict us.

Schizoanalysis evokes its conception of human materiality through the trope of the body without organs.[20] This phantasmal body is not the "organization of the organs called the organism."[21] It is a fluid, ungraspable, disorganized body of nonstratified desires and intensities that can undermine stability, subvert symbolic order, and fuel becoming in the most radical sense of the word.[22] "Reason is always a region carved out of the irrational," Deleuze has declared. "Underneath all reason lies delirium, and drift."[23] As sublimely positive qualities, delirium and drift are rife with possibilities for liberating our intrinsic desiring machines from cultural categories so they may become-animal, become-nonhuman, become-other-gender, become-whatever-we-may-wish.

Among the many metaphors that poets and philosophers have devised for the blockages, coagulations, impasses, and spiritual logjams of the ordinary human condition, few are more pithy and suggestive than "mind-forg'd manacles," coined by none other than William Blake around a decade before he painted the Great Red Dragon that Dollarhyde regards as his great red god.[24] Dollarhyde has forged a form-fitting set of mental manacles by granting the dragon absolute power over his thoughts and actions. Led by the absurd conviction that he is becoming a being more awesome and strong than any mortal, he grows steadily more trapped in a paralyzing web of delusion and paranoia, leaving enough clues as he commits his family murders for Graham to stop him after he has perpetrated only two. He dis-organizes the bodies of his victims effectively enough but remains so frightened of his own body that he uses someone else's teeth (his late grandma's false ones) to make the bite marks that have earned him his hated nickname. His life adds up to a sad parody of becoming in the schizoanalytic sense; despite his strenuous efforts to the contrary, he is less a great red dragon than a piteous tooth fairy.

If anyone in *Manhunter* is actually becoming, it is Lecktor, who has spent decades building his vast storehouse of scientific knowledge, cultural acumen, and creativity and who continues the process even in the solitude of his isolated prison cell. In addition to disorganizing his victims' bodies—so completely that he literally incorporates them into himself—he dazzlingly reterritorializes his own body by cultivating untold degrees of sensory awareness and physical discipline. The body without organs harbors dark possibilities, and Lecktor seems determined to experiment with them all. Calling him a "schizoanalyst" would be unfair to Deleuze and Guattari, so I offer a new term: Hannibal Lecktor is the world's first schizovivisectionist.

Enter the *Übermensch*

Mann has a longtime fascination with singular individuals who stand above and apart from the others in their milieu; think of Glaeken Trismegestus (Scott Glenn) in *The Keep* (1983), Hawkeye (Daniel Day-Lewis) in *The Last of the Mohicans* (1992), Jeffrey Wigand (Russell Crowe) in *The Insider* (1999), and Muhammad Ali (Will Smith) in *Ali* (2001), among others. Graham is comparable to those characters by virtue of his outstanding abilities and strong sense of morality, but Lecktor surpasses them all by dint of his *incomparable* abilities and unyielding *amorality*. He dwells categorically beyond good and evil, in Nietzsche's terms, and beyond freedom and dignity, to borrow B. F. Skinner's phrase.[25] Nietzsche preceded Deleuze and Guattari in the philosophy of becoming. "What does your conscience say?" he asks in *The Gay Science,* answering with one of his most famous aphorisms: "You shall become the person you are."[26] This applies easily to Dollarhyde, whose bogus becoming could never produce anything but the person he already is—to wit, a pathetic and deluded individual. Graham's situation is more complicated because the degree to which he harbors baleful tendencies and violent proclivities never becomes entirely clear, either to him or to us. If his career were to continue beyond the final credits of Mann's film, would he become more like Hannibal every time he plumbed the depths of a serial killer's crimes? This remains an open question.

Lecktor's case is the most interesting of the lot because *what he is* cannot be pinned down with the slightest degree of confidence, and *what he shall become* is downright impossible to figure out. But we are free to speculate along these lines, aided by our knowledge of three of his chief characteristics, all of which Nietzsche would have recognized: Lecktor is extraordinarily hedonistic, taking it as his privilege to seize, chew, and digest the flesh of any person he chooses to attack; he is extraordinarily ascetic, able to keep his composure for years on end in circumstances of involuntary solitude that would drive most of us as crazy as he was when he got there; and both his hedonism and his asceticism reveal the overwhelming presence of what Nietzsche terms the "will to power" at the deepest levels of his character. Lecktor has clearly cultivated his will from the early stages of his life, carefully and creatively transforming himself into a living work of art—a malign and wicked one, to be sure, but in his mind a splendid specimen of the incarnate will to power that Nietzsche calls the *Übermensch*.

Sometimes translated as "overman" or "superman," the term *Übermensch* is used to express an intricate and ambiguous concept, subject to many conflicting interpretations. But to the extent that Harris and Mann impute any kind of sociohistorical self-consciousness to Lecktor, they may well think of the overman as Hannibal the cannibal's ego ideal. The overman figures importantly in Nietzsche's magnum opus *Thus Spake Zarathustra*, wherein the eponymous teacher and prophet declares, "*I teach you the overman.* Man is something that shall be overcome." Zarathustra envisions the coming of a "great noon when man stands in the middle of his way between beast and overman and celebrates his way to the evening as his highest hope: for it is the way to a new morning." On that morning, humanity's knowledge will reach a pinnacle, thanks to the overman's ability to go "over and beyond" the cowardly ignorance of the present age. "*Dead are all the gods: now we want the overman to live*—on that great noon, let this be our last will," concludes Zarathustra, who insists that even the enemies of the overman must be powerful enough to merit his attention. "Verily, there is yet a future for evil too," he says in words that would surely make Dollarhyde's ears perk up. "The hottest south has not yet been discovered for man. . . . One day, however, bigger dragons will come into this world. For in order that the overman should not lack his dragon, the overdragon that is worthy of him, much hot sunshine must yet glow upon damp jungles."[27]

Discussing the intersection of aesthetics and politics in Nietzsche's thought, Daniel W. Conway observes that for Nietzsche the appreciation of beauty "furnishes the psychological basis for self-overcoming" and stresses that the chief transformative power of art pertains not to external works (books, paintings, etc.), but rather to the artist who makes them. "The artist always produces himself," Conway argues, "albeit unwittingly and inadvertently, as an embodiment of übermenschlich beauty, and thus as an object of erotic attraction."[28] When philosophers practice the art of experiment *(Versucherkunst)* or undertake ascetic trials, even to the point of self-inflicted cruelty, they demonstrate to themselves and others that they are robust enough for their struggles to have,[29] as Nietzsche writes in *Beyond Good and Evil,* "the effect of one more charm and incentive of life." And here is an explanation for the profound and enduring allure of tragedy. "What constitutes the painful voluptuousness of tragedy," Nietzsche contends, "is cruelty; what seems agreeable in so called tragic pity and at bottom in everything sublime . . . receives its sweetness solely from the admixture of cruelty."[30]

I am not proposing that Hannibal the cannibal be regarded as a de facto body or performance artist, notwithstanding his vague similarity to such avant-garde provocateurs as Rudolph Schwarzkogler, Chris Burden, Stelarc, and Marina Abramović, who are known for works entailing pain or damage to themselves rather than to others. Still less is Lecktor an *Übermensch,* however much he may call to mind a perverse version of that problematic figure. But it is hard to understand his lasting appeal for enormous numbers of readers and moviegoers without seeing a sophisticated aesthetic of cruelty at play in his narrative. *Manhunter,* the first movie about him, set the visual ground rules for the saga, building a somber and disquieting emotional tone by means of geometrically precise framing (cinematographer Dante Spinotti has pointed out the forbidding rigidity of the bars of Lecktor's cell, for example[31]) and the stylized lighting that has come to be regularly associated with Mann, here typified by shades of blue in scenes with Will and Molly Graham, contrasted by green and magenta when Dollarhyde or police officers dominate the shots. Mann injects the story of the cannibal, the Tooth Fairy, and the psycho profiler with precisely the right admixture of cruelty to bring them feverishly alive as hauntingly sad characters, if not the voluptuously tragic figures of whom Nietzsche speaks. The result is a horror–noir hybrid that proffers the "charm and incentive of life" even as it seethes with ghastly deeds.

Manhunter is quintessentially modern entertainment that draws its disturbing power from undertones of the primitive that we unconvincingly pretend we have outgrown. "No cruelty, no feast," wrote Nietzsche in a mood that is acidulous even for him: "that is what the oldest and longest period in human history teaches us."[32] The feast goes on vicariously in horror films, among which *Manhunter* stands with the most cunningly effective. Its narrative is steeped in suffering, and although Mann does not hesitate to hammer its terrors home in many scenes, he has the aesthetic sense to *insinuate* its chthonic aura at moments when subliminal expression is more suitable. I will close this discussion with the closing of the film, a seemingly serene tableau depicting Will, Molly, and Kevin Graham looking out over the sea adjacent to their home. It would be an idyllic image if we did not remember that this is where the story started, with Will wrenched out of retirement to embark on the same sort of traumatic course that sent him there in the first place—a fate that could easily strike again and again and again. If this possibility burdens Graham with ongoing anticipation and dread, he may be looking on the sea as the "invitation to die" that philosopher Gaston Bachelard movingly describes. Quotidian death is "the death of water," Bachelard writes. "Death associated with water is more dream-like than death associated with earth: the pain of water is infinite."[33] Such is the film's sad, sardonic reward for the manhunter who has crushed Dollarhyde and Lecktor so courageously.

Notes

1. *Red Dragon* is the first novel in a tetralogy by Thomas Harris. In order of publication, the novels are *Red Dragon* (New York: Dutton, 2000); *The Silence of the Lambs* (New York: St. Martin's Griffin, 1998); *Hannibal* (New York: Delacorte Press, 1999); and *Hannibal Rising* (New York: Dell, 2006).

2. Hannibal's surname is "Lecktor" in Mann's film but "Lecter" in all other treatments of the character, including Harris's four novels and the other movies based on them. Adding to the confusion, the Tooth Fairy's surname is "Dollarhyde" in *Manhunter* but "Dolarhyde" in the *Red Dragon* novel and in Brett Ratner's 2002 movie adaptation thereof. I use the *Manhunter* spellings (Lecktor, Dollarhyde) except when I specifically address one of the other works.

3. Ratner's film *Red Dragon* is a remake of *Manhunter,* but retaining the title of Harris's novel.

4. More confusion: Harris states in his novel that the painting Dolarhyde fetishizes is *The Great Red Dragon and the Woman Clothed with the Sun,* but the painting that Harris goes on to describe is *The Great Red Dragon and the Woman Clothed in Sun,* a similarly titled but quite different work in the series. Mann chooses to show the painting that Harris names *(Clothed **with** the Sun)* rather than the one that Harris describes *(Clothed **in** Sun),* perhaps because its content accords more precisely with that of the film's climax, in which Dollarhyde has the innocent Reba seemingly at his mercy. I discuss the painting that Mann employs *(Clothed with the Sun)* and ignore the other one.

5. Quotes from *Inside Manhunter: Interviews with Stars William Petersen, Brian Cox, Joan Allen, and Tom Noonan,* DVD supplement directed by David Gregory (Beverly Hills, CA: Anchor Bay Entertainment, 2001).

6. Georges Bataille, "The Notion of Expenditure," in *Visions of Excess: Selected Writings, 1927–1939,* trans. Allan Stoekl, with Carl R. Lovitt and Donald M. Leslie Jr. (Minneapolis: University of Minnesota Press, 1985), 118.

7. Georges Bataille, *The Accursed Share: An Essay on General Economy,* vol. 1: *Consumption,* trans. Robert Hurley (New York: Zone, 1991), 59.

8. Lecter has intimate ties to his foster mother in *Hannibal Rising,* and at the end of *Hannibal* he and his former nemesis Clarice Starling conjoin as a loving couple, but in both novels the sexual components of the relationships are left highly ambiguous.

9. In the fourth (and weakest) installment of Harris's tetralogy, *Hannibal Rising,* we learn more about Lecter's cannibalistic craving, which began during his childhood in Lithuania during World War II, when a group of starving deserters ate his beloved little sister.

10. Philip L. Simpson, *Psycho Paths: Tracking the Serial Killer through Contemporary American Film and Fiction* (Carbondale: Southern Illinois University Press, 2000), 72.

11. Simpson, *Psycho Paths,* 72–73. Perhaps the best-known movie protagonist to jump off the due-process ship is San Francisco police inspector Harry Callahan, played by Clint Eastwood in *Dirty Harry* (1971) and four sequels. Also of interest is the exploration of dark parallels between an aggressively sadistic serial killer and an incipiently sadistic homicide detective in the 1984 crime drama *Tightrope* (Richard Tuggle), which Eastwood stars in and coproduced.

12. Simpson, *Psycho Paths,* 72–73.

13. Friedrich Nietzsche, *Beyond Good and Evil: Prelude to a Philosophy of the Future,* trans. Helen Zimmern (New York: Vintage, 1989), 89.

14. Slavoj Žižek, *Enjoy Your Symptom! Jacques Lacan in Hollywood and Out* (New York: Routledge, 1992), 106, 182.

15. There is an oblique echo here of Charles Chaplin's dark comedy *Monsieur Verdoux* (1947), in which the title character (a serial killer) says, "Wars, conflict, it's all business. One murder makes a villain; millions, a hero. Numbers sanctify, my good fellow!"

16. Søren Kierkegaard, *Fear and Trembling: Dialectical Lyric by Johannes de Silentio*, trans. Alastair Hannay (London: Penguin Books, 2003), 122–23.

17. This is also an insipid parody of the "mirror stage" in Lacan's theory of development, the time when the infant gathers its first sense of personhood by observing a reflected image or equivalent of itself. See Jacques Lacan, "The Mirror Stage as Formative of the *I* Function as Revealed in Psychoanalytic Experience," in *Écrits: A Selection*, trans. Bruce Fink (New York: Norton, 2002), 3–9.

18. The quoted phrase comes from Ted Tally's screenplay for *The Silence of the Lambs*.

19. Hannibal's given name means "glory of Baal," deriving from Phoenician *hann*, meaning "glory" or "grace," and Semitic *baal*, meaning "lord" or "master." Although deities called "Baal" were widespread in ancient times, the usage most familiar in the Judeo-Christian tradition applies to local cult images condemned by the Hebrew Bible as false gods; the name also applies to the most powerful prince of hell (cf. Beelzebub) in Christian lore.

20. Deleuze and Guattari borrow the trope of the body without organs from a radio play by Antonin Artaud, *To Have Done with the Judgment of God*, trans. Helen Weaver, in *Antonin Artaud: Selected Writings*, ed. Susan Sontag (Berkeley: University of California Press, 1976).

21. Gilles Deleuze and Félix Guattari, *Anti-Oedipus: Capitalism and Schizophrenia*, trans. Robert Hurley, Mark Seem, and Helen R. Lane (Minneapolis: University of Minnesota Press, 1983), 8, 20.

22. Gilles Deleuze and Félix Guattari, *A Thousand Plateaus: Capitalism and Schizophrenia*, trans. Brian Massumi (Minneapolis: University of Minnesota Press, 1987), 158–59, 153.

23. Gilles Deleuze, "On Capitalism and Desire," in *Desert Islands and Other Texts: 1953–1974*, ed. David Lapoujade, trans. Michael Taormina (Los Angeles: Semiotext[e], 2004), 262.

24. The phrase comes from William Blake, "London," in *Songs of Innocence and of Experience: Showing the Two Contrary Sides of the Human Soul*, in *William Blake: The Complete Illuminated Books* (New York: Thames & Hudson, 2001), 410.

25. See Nietzsche, *Beyond Good and Evil*, and B. F. Skinner, *Beyond Freedom and Dignity* (Indianapolis, IN: Hackett, 2002).

26. Friedrich Nietzsche, *The Gay Science: With a Prelude in Rhymes and an Appendix of Songs*, trans. Walter Kaufmann (New York: Vintage, 1974), 219.

27. Friedrich Nietzsche, *Thus Spake Zarathustra: A Book for All and None*, trans. Walter Kaufmann (New York: Modern Library, 1995), 12, 78–79, 144.

28. Daniel W. Conway, "Love's Labor's Lost: The Philosopher's *Versucherkunst*," in *Nietzsche, Philosophy, and the Arts*, ed. Selim Kemal, Ivan Gaskell, and Daniel W. Conway (Cambridge, UK: Cambridge University Press, 1998), 297, 300, 302, 301.

29. Ibid., 301.

30. Nietzsche, *Beyond Good and Evil*, 112.

31. See "The Manhunter Look: A Conversation with Dante Spinotti," a special-feature video directed by David Gregory for Anchor Bay's 2001 DVD edition of *Manhunter*.

32. Friedrich Nietzsche, *On the Genealogy of Morality,* trans. Carol Diethe (Cambridge: Cambridge University Press, 2007), 43.

33. Gaston Bachelard, *Water and Dreams: An Essay on the Imagination of Matter,* trans. Edith R. Farrell (Dallas: Dallas Institute of Humanities and Culture, 1983), 55.

"Blood in the Moonlight"

Toward an Aesthetics of Horror in *The Keep* and *Manhunter*

Ivo Ritzer

> Have you ever seen blood in the moonlight, Will? It appears quite black.
> —Hannibal Lecktor, *Manhunter*

An auteur of visionary urban crime thrillers, beyond doubt. With movies such as *Thief* (1981), *Heat* (1995), *The Insider* (1999), *Collateral* (2004), *Miami Vice* (2006), and *Public Enemies* (2009), Michael Mann is widely known quite rightly as a masterful creator of elegiac gangster and cop movies. Hence, it may not be obvious that Mann has also put his mark on other genres. This essay analyzes a central aspect of Michael Mann's often neglected early work: the aesthetics of horror in *The Keep* (1983) and *Manhunter* (1986). Although these films create this aesthetic in different ways, they employ very similar strategies in presenting their scary events. Although *The Keep*'s narrative about a haunted castle in the Carpathians can be placed along Tzvetan Todorov's notion of the "fantastic-marvellous" that features supernatural powers threatening humans and therefore ends "with an acceptance of the supernatural,"[1] and although *Manhunter*'s serial-killer plot draws on manlike monsters in bringing the diabolical murderers Francis Dollarhyde (Tom Noonan) and Hannibal Lecktor (Brian Cox) to the screen, they both nevertheless confirm Mann's aesthetics of horror as an *aestheticization* of horror. In *The Keep* as well as in *Manhunter,* the frightening is transformed into the beautiful through the audiovisual means of mise-en-scène, montage, and sound. These stylized renditions of horror form the focus of this essay.

Horror Considered as One of the Fine Arts

[The] union of contraries, where the work required by the artistic idea and the originary power coincide, is the result of the long work of de-figuration that in the new work contradicts the expectations borne by the subject matter or the story, or that reviews, rereads, and rearranges the elements of old works. This process undoes the arrangements of fiction and of representational painting, and draws our attention instead to the painterly gesture and the adventures of matter lurking beneath the subject of figuration, to the glimmer of the epiphany and the splendor of pure reasonless being glowing just beneath the conflict of wills of the play or the novel.

—Jacques Rancière, *Film Fables*

Although *Manhunter* is a genre-bending hybrid of police procedural and serial-killer narrative, horror nonetheless lies at its core. The destructive powers of the psychopathic yet sovereign killers Dollarhyde and Lecktor draw on the viewer's primal fears of death and bodily infirmity. However, Mann introduces a complex difference between narration and narrated. Not until the showdown and final shoot-out involving manhunter Will Graham (William Petersen) and Dollarhyde is any act of violence shown on screen. What Mann shows instead are the results of Dollarhyde's dreadful deeds, which Dollarhyde happens to arrange like sculptures. He murders entire families, staging their corpses in tableaux and putting mirror shards over their eyes in order to watch himself. Dollarhyde is hereby equated with an artist who does aesthetic work, and this work itself results in aestheticized works of art. The whole film appears carefully stylized, embedding the killings in a context of beauty. It is all about poetic construction. In his characteristic manner, Mann sets *Manhunter* in the slick (post)modern United States, with its exquisite architecture and decorative interiors full of glass walls and metallic surfaces, further defined by meticulous shot design. Mann is not interested in an unobtrusive "realism"; in fact, his overly formative codes of narration dismiss any kind of transparency. On the level of the frame, he often composes his images as a kind of abstract still life with very little movement. Backgrounds rely on solid hues or achromatic surfaces, and whole sequences are frequently filtered with primary colors. The moments showing Graham at home with his wife, Molly (Kim Greist), are tinted blue, and Graham's meeting with Lecktor is filmed against the white wall of the prison cell, whereas green and magenta color Dollarhyde's scenes. As the cool glowing blues denote the reliable relationship between the spouses and the aseptic whiteness gets associated with the psychopathological connection of Graham and Lecktor that has something to do with death, the disquieting greens hint at Dollarhyde's dangerousness, which Graham tries to stem. In all cases, but especially the Graham–Molly scenes, Mann lets the colors convey mood and atmosphere, accepting or even underlining the fact that they have no direct diegetic motivation and so highlight the movie's stylization as a purposeful act of aestheticization. Style intrudes into the diegesis, shaping the fictional world according to an imperative of creative drive. Investing horrifying murders with these pointedly conventionalized compositions, Mann not only shows a serial killer with strong aesthetic occupations but also makes the movie itself an aestheticization of horror. *Manhunter* seeks to elicit responses of aesthetic acknowledgment because, for Mann, horror and beauty coexist. This coexistence can certainly be read as a statement on the quality of beauty as well as horror. Seen from this perspective, beauty lies in the eye of the beholder, and horror is not something out of its scope. This might sound surprising considering Western idealist traditions of aesthetic philosophy. Significantly, G. W. F. Hegel in his seminal "Lectures on Fine Art" bans horror from aesthetics, stating that "the purely negative is in itself dull and flat and therefore either leaves us empty or else repels us." For Hegel, horror therefore is inherently worthless and aesthetically impracticable "because nothing comes of it except what is purely negative, just destruction and misfortune, whereas genuine art should give us a view of an inner harmony."[2] What has to be handled by art, according to Hegel, is the true, the good, the beautiful, but never the ugly and horrific. Although aesthetics may be dominantly associated with beautifulness and horror with ugliness in the history of bourgeois thought, Mann demonstrates that aesthetic experience does not limit itself to a legitimized cultural tradition of pleasant artefacts in the service of reason and morals. By splitting aesthetics and ethics, he divides a culturally coded unity and conversely conflates traditional experiential opposites. This split is already envisaged in the thought of eighteenth-century German poet and philosopher Friedrich Schiller, who points out the relativity of crimes with regard to their aesthetic value. "A man who robs would always be an object to be rejected by the poet who wishes to present serious pictures," says Schiller. "But suppose this man is at the same time a murderer, he is even more to be condemned than before by the moral law. But in the aesthetic judgment he is raised one degree higher and made better adapted to figure in a work of art. Continuing to judge him from an aesthetic point of view, it may be added that he who abased himself by a vile action can to a certain extent be raised by a crime, and can be thus reinstated in our aesthetic estimation."[3] According to Schiller, a rift runs between the fields of law and art. What constitutes a crime in law may form a masterpiece in art. In his famous piece "On Murder Considered as One of the Fine Arts" (1827), British essayist Thomas De Quincey elaborates on this idea, arguing that "everything in this world has two handles. Murder, for instance, may be laid hold of by its moral handle . . . and that, I confess, is its weak side; or it may also be treated aesthetically, as the Germans call it—that is, in relation to good taste."[4] Another and perhaps the most openly unapologetic example of this line of aesthetic appreciation is W. H. Auden's 1948 essay "The Guilty Vicarage," in which he calls murder an "act of disruption by which innocence is lost" and the defining instant where "the aesthetic and the ethical are [put] in opposition."[5] How the foul can get rendered fair has also interested cultural theory in more recent times. What is of importance here is an interleaving of the production and the reception of horrifying actions. As Joel Black points out in his important scholarly study on "the aesthetics of murder," horror is highly capable of compelling "an aesthetic response in the viewer of awe, admiration, or bafflement." Therefore, Black deduces an artistic sensibility in the subject conducting horrific actions: "If an action evokes an aesthetic response, then it is logical to assume that this action—even if it is a murder—must have been the work of an artist."[6] Of course, not every murder compels such an aesthetic experience. But this distinction only reinforces the question why *Manhunter* so strongly does invoke aesthetic acknowledgment in the viewer. As a result of this acknowledgment, the viewer not only is prompted to reflect upon his understanding of horror and aesthetics but also is asked to analyze the connection between both concepts. Mann's aestheticization of horror suggests an alliance of otherwise demarcated phenomena and asks for an appreciation of what usually is not appreciated, but rather disapproved, deprecated, and even damned. As early as the beginning of *Manhunter,* this invitation to the viewer gets enhanced when Graham visits the house of the slaughtered Leeds family, its white walls "painted" red by blood. Graham attempts to recapitulate the killer's actions and examines this crime scene as if it were an abstract artwork. He records his observations in a tape-recorder and seems to verbally address the murderer himself.

Trying to get into the killer's psyche and to comprehend the killer's feelings in his own imagination, Graham starts a stream-of-consciousness dialogue/monologue with the murderer and, respectively, his own dark self, which seeks to reenact the crime. Eschewing any moral assessment, Graham calls the killer a "skillful" man and addresses the question why the crime scene looks how it looks. Steven Jay Schneider has therefore compared the detective to an art critic and the serial killer to an artist. According to Schneider, by valuing the murderer's work, Graham declares it an artwork and the murderer an artistic performer: "Dollarhyde turns killing into a theatrical, cinematic performance whose purpose is to (literally) transform himself into the Red Dragon, which is in his mind a composite of Blake the visionary artist (who believed that the imagination could change reality) and the Red Dragon. This becomes obvious in the complementary ritual by which he works out in front of a full-length mirror, literally reconstructing his body into a semblance of Blake's Michelangelesque figures. Dollarhyde is attempting to remake reality/himself through his performance of murder."[7] Instead of interpreting Dollarhyde's performance as a Lacanian instance of reliving the mirror phase, Schneider stresses the important fact that Dollarhyde's narcissism is less an expression of the killer's attempt to enter the oedipal stage by distinguishing himself as an autonomous being from his abusive mother's body[8] than Dollarhyde's search for transforming his corporal structure into an altogether different entity. He aims for physical effects on his victims' bodies, which in turn are meant to productively affect his own physique. In Mann's reading, the Red Dragon stands not for the culturally ordered Symbolic, but for part of the Real: an "imaginary Real" in Slavoj Žižek's sense of a "mysterious *je ne sais quoi*, the unfathomable 'something' that introduces a self-division into an ordinary object, so that the sublime dimension shines through it."[9] Dollarhyde's performance is directed to this elusive sphere, a nonsubstantial fictional area that nonetheless causes very substantial effects. And it is Mann's direction of the film that draws attention to this process by equating the aesthetics of horror with an aestheticization of horror.

This aestheticization comes to the fore very prominently and just about forces the viewer to take a stance on it because *Manhunter* is a movie explicitly concerned with the act of looking at a sensory experience involving questions of identification and power. At the most basal level, Dollarhyde is a murderer downright obsessed with the visual: working at a film-processing laboratory, recording his victims on videotape, posing in front of a mirror, and even watching himself in the shards of mirror he puts into his victims' dead eyes. But when Graham tries to reconstruct the killer's actions in his imagination, he also relies primarily on visual information mediated by television and videotapes, thus mirroring the murderer's own obsession with photographs and home movies of his victims. Both men use "machines of the visible"[10] to hunt down their prey. If Graham visits the crime scene or watches videotapes, he always looks at objects for clues. By emphasizing his directorial approach through visual stylization, Mann for his own part draws further attention to the importance of looking. The narration's stress on looking and Mann's aestheticization of these diegetic looks work together to question the audience's watching of the film. In this investigation of the viewer's gaze, Graham becomes an important mediating figure. Just as Graham runs into the danger of adopting the killer's murderous way of looking by visiting the crime scenes and watching the same home movies as Dollarhyde, the viewer is tempted to delight in the murderer's transcendent sovereignty. Considered from this angle, *Manhunter* may call out for a critique along the lines of sexual difference. Yet feminist film theory in its focus on the gazing male subject, which diminishes the female object to a pure "to-be-looked-at-ness"[11] either through reductionizing-scopophilic fetishization or voyeuristic-sadistic punishing, seems to come to its limits in grasping *Manhunter*. The film avoids fetishistic impulses as well as sadistic preferences by neither offering sequences of female nudity nor providing the viewer with eroticized violence directed against the female body. Not only is Dollarhyde clearly not a murderer of women in that he kills whole families, but his acts are rendered unusually devoid of sexual excitement. Mann mitigates the sexual connotations of Thomas Harris's novel and presents Dollarhyde with an artistic sensibility, so that he appears as somebody who needs to kill because of his superior aesthetic imagination. This understanding is further developed by Mann's own fondness of aestheticizing processes, thus constituting a pointed "projection of the artist's own subjectivity."[12] Mann equips Dollarhyde's horrific murders with the quality of art, and in so doing he not only renders the murderer an artist but also stylizes himself as a killer. However, contrary to the aestheticizing modus operandi of other highly stylized 1980s films such as William Friedkin's *Cruising* (1980), Dario Argento's *Tenebrae* (1982), and Donald Cammell's *White of the Eye* (1987),[13] Mann does not succumb to the fascination for flashy visuals. Rather, *Manhunter* needs to be read as a revealing essay on the significance of Mann's treatment of the aesthetics of horror as an aestheticization of horror.

Even the film's first sequence is telling on this issue. A person's nocturnal intrusion into the Leeds' house is shown via a handheld shaky video cam with spotlighted blurry electronic images (certainly not "in grainy 8mm"[14]). No diegetic sound is audible, no frame delimits the images, no reaction shots are given. "The camera records for itself"; that is, "the image itself appears to be a type of consciousness, one with which we merge in this voyeuristic simulacrum of invasion and terror."[15] In fact, Mann never clarifies the plain diegetic status of these shots. When is this happening? Who is this person visualizing her or his way up the stairs into the bedrooms? Mann mobilizes the subjective video shots not only to hint at, as Philip L. Simpson says, a "murderous use of technology in combination with the predatory male gaze,"[16] a gaze that belongs to Dollarhyde as well as to Graham and the viewer, but also to demonstrate an elemental difference between the textual and extratextual. Mann does not demarcate the subject of the gaze in attributing it unequivocally. Do we accompany Dollarhyde on the way to commit murder? Or do we see Graham imagining Dollarhyde on the way to commit murder? It is not so clear that we accompany "the grainy lens of Dolarhyde's [*sic*] movie camera"[17] at all. Only the fact that the viewer scans the frame analogue either with Dollarhyde's analyzing of the situation or with Graham's trying to reexperience this very analysis seems sure. Mann further complicates matters in modifying the video shots through the use of slow-motion images and finally cutting to black screen before the actual murder is to take place. His directing choices manipulate the visual in a way severely destabilizing the gaze. These shots already at the movie's beginning expose its deeply artificial quality: they show that they have been worked upon. Far from disguising his manipulations in the editing room as direct representations of the "real," Mann accentuates them, therefore undermining the images' status of immediacy. In addition to the use of the horror and serial-killer film's now rather firmly conventionalized tradition of point-of-view shots providing oscillating identifications between viewer and aggressor as well as viewer and investigator, Mann establishes a third subjectivity—his own as a director. What strikes me as important in this respect is not a return to the hypostatized "genius" of auteurism, but the fact that there is no longer a clear separation between diegetic and nondiegetic events. The first-person video camerawork achieves not only an identification between Graham, Dollarhyde, and the viewer but also collapses the distinction between Graham, Dollarhyde, the viewer, *and* Mann. It makes us participate in the killer's perspective yet further introduces Mann's own overly stylized presentation of the events through his aestheticizing devices. In this way, Mann may imply what Joel Black calls an artist's "identification with the criminal"—that is "his self-glorification as a transgressor."[18] Yet this seems to be the case only on a limited level, for Mann's self-conscious artistic choices evoke poetic effects that both heighten and distinguish the horror of Dollarhyde's actions. This putative disjuncture between subject matter and audiovisual stylization leads to an intensification of contradictory affects on the viewer. On the one hand, the killer seems to be encouraged by Mann's aestheticization, just as Mann appears to be incited by the killer's imagination. From this perspective, horror neither acts as a deterrent nor offers an affective surrogate but becomes an end itself. On the other hand, there are clear instances of difference between an affirmative and a discursive aestheticization of horror. The only sequence showing explicit acts of violence happens just before the final showdown between Graham and Dollarhyde. This shoot-out, accompanied by Iron Butterfly's epochal "In-A-Gadda-Da-Vida," notably fragments the violence depicted by means of abrupt zoom-ins, slow-motion and fast-motion camerawork, jump-cuts and skip-frames, as well as periodic repetition of images. The scene is less music-video-clip aesthetics than nightmarish rendition of destruction. Instead of a linear flow of time and a clear establishing of space, Mann introduces patterns of discontinuity and equivocation. The suggestion is not so much that Graham succeeds in killing the killer and thus deadening the dark part in his mind, but rather that he finally absorbs the killer's consciousness, transforming himself into a version of the Red Dragon, which must be carefully controlled from now on. This reading is sustained by the director's cut of *Manhunter,* which possesses an additional sequence that is of great importance regarding the implications of aestheticizing horror. We are seated behind the wheel inside a car that is driving through a violent storm. Thus, the viewer shares the driver's point of view but doesn't know who the driver is. He (she?) arrives at a remote house, where a young woman and her husband answer the doorbell. They are the people shown in Dollarhyde's films, his declared next victims. Then Mann gives us a nonfocalized "objective" shot showing that the person visiting the young family is none other than Graham. Being asked about his reasons for visiting them, Graham sluggishly replies, "I just wanted . . . to see you . . . that's all." His answer is totally and at the same time not at all convincing. It does not clarify whether Graham has come as the family's protector or is there because of his empathic closeness to the killer's mind. In any case, the emphasis on his desire to see the supposed victims brings the film to a close on a highly ambiguous note far from any "neoconservative happy ending."[19] Graham's psychic affinity with Dollarhyde suggests that he might be not only the family's savior, but also something very different: a revenant of the Red Dragon.

Glamour and Gloom of Horror

> The image has nothing to do with signification, meaning, as implied by the existence of the world, the effort of truth, the law and the brightness of the day. Not only is the image of an object not the meaning of that object and of no help in comprehending it, but it tends to withdraw from its meaning by maintaining it in the immobility of a resemblance that has nothing to resemble.
>
> —Maurice Blanchot, *The Gaze of Orpheus*

At the core of *The Keep,* a World War II set variation of the long-standing gothic haunted-house narrative, lies horror. And again Mann looks for its elements of beauty. But whereas the aestheticization of horror in *Manhunter* can be read in expressive, although ambiguous relation to the movie's themes, *The Keep* renders such a reading increasingly difficult, if not impossible. The film constantly draws attention to formal properties of Mann's painterly stylization, which becomes the main focus of the narration. F. Paul Wilson's eponymous novel is nothing more than a quarry of means for Mann. He takes only bits and fragments of it and almost completely leaves out central actions, such as the epic supernatural battle between Glaeken Trismegestus and Radu Molasar. Ahead of narrative logic lies Mann's interest in creating audiovisual landscapes of horror that have less a dramatic meaning than a performative concern. Only giving loosely causal motivations and sometimes completely abandoning an intelligible narrative structure, *The Keep* dwells in opaque imagery not meant to move the story forward. Instead of being oriented toward communicating content, the movie becomes absorbed in a poetically stylized "cinematic body"[20] characterized by the ecstatic materiality of its mediality. Doing away with a surface/depth dichotomy, Mann's aesthetics give the film an oneiric atmosphere that permeates all of its layers. The movie's opening proves remarkably programmatic in this respect. An authorial camera tilts from the clouds, raindrops clutter it as it pans along a forest. The long focal lenses obscure the shapes of trees and nature, abstracting and disorienting their forms. This obscuration is further reinforced by the pulsing ambient score by electronic musicians Tangerine Dream, which adds an artificial contrast to the presentation of elements (storm) and flora (wood). When the camera finally comes down to the ground, the important point is perhaps less the introduction of a motorized German army detachment that also forms an antithesis to nature, but the focus on Captain Klaus Woerman (Jürgen Prochnow). Initially he gets shown by an extreme close-up of his eyes, and it is not until several shots later and a wider framing that we notice that he is sitting behind the windshield of the leading army truck. After an enigmatic shot of the sky reflected in the water on the ground, which is almost too beautiful to be true, Mann returns several times to a close-up of Woerman's eyes constantly opening and closing. Woerman appears to be at least half asleep. His condition characterizes the movie: it moves in a kind of twilight zone between vigil and dream. The slow-motion images of the soldiers arriving at the deeply fogged Carpathian village and jumping from their trucks suggest a phantasmagoric atmosphere of mythical time outside history. As Mann eschews any shot providing a clear outline of the setting, the narrative appears to happen in an imprecise space coming from a scattered subconscious mind. Inside and outside melt into a hazy diegesis with always ambiguous status. The keep itself is also never shown fully in shots. With these techniques, Mann highlights Woerman's later insight regarding what drives people away from the castle: "Nightmares."

Unlike in *Manhunter*, in *The Keep* there is no longer any distance from the aestheticization of horror. The film features several violent set pieces, including memorable shots of horribly burned German soldiers, whose flesh is still smoldering after they have been attacked by the creature Radu Molasar (Michael Carter). Just like this creature's intangible body, which Steven Rybin calls a "sculpture in time,"[21] the film's cinematic body itself functions as an ethereal hallucination. *The Keep* is a movie extraordinarily stylized throughout, stirring up almost delirious effects: deep blue shafts of light flow through all the openings in the castle's walls, and its perpetually mist-layered interiors sink in dark areas of gray black. The keep's geometrical architecture is emphasized by symmetric compositions, which also frequently feature backlighting so as to abstract the protagonists to shadowy silhouettes. On top of this, heavy filters likewise lend the movie a pictorial design, further aestheticizing the gauntly events in the castle. Mann often sends his camera crawling through the narrow hallways, until the conflict between Glaeken Trismegestus (Scott Glenn) and Molasar finally culminates in a violent confrontation defined by canted camera angles and a great number of slow-motion shots highlighted by the mechanical throbbing of Tangerine Dream's synthesized score. In this total mobilization of image and sound, all references to discursive contexts outside the cinematic body are conclusively disavowed. The foreclosing of any symbolic-symptomatic readings comes to an apotheosis of aesthetics. All appears to be imagination, nothing to be imitation. Mann renounces representation in favor of creation. The audiovisual textures do not point beyond the screen at all; they do not stand for anything except themselves.

The Keep goes beyond informational-denotative and symbolic-connotative codes, working toward what Roland Barthes has called an "obtuse meaning." Whereas the informational shows actions and the symbolic provides these actions with meaning, the obtuse creates seemingly superfluous energies apart from the action itself. Both the informational code and the symbolic code are essential to conventional narration because the former shows the viewer what happens on the screen, and the latter ties it to the film's underlying dramatic structure. The obtuse meaning by contrast arises in contradiction to the demand for narrative cohesion: "The obtuse meaning is clearly counternarrative itself. Diffused, reversible, caught up in its own time, it can, if one follows it, establish only another script that is distinct from the shots, sequences and syntagmas. . . . You will not have another temporality, diegetic nor [sic] oneiric, you will have another film."[22] *The Keep* is such a film, very much contingent on the obtuse. Sight and sound act out an attraction to the terrifying setting and its atmosphere instead of being deferrals to a symbolic meaning to be interpreted. They do not stand for anything; they just look and sound aesthetically. What matters is their matter. So their effect consists in celebration over communication: they conduct style. This style can count as more of a physiological approach than a phenomenological consideration, never ontological but always performative. Mann's aestheticization of horror does not function as an expression of subjectivity; rather, every subjectivity is an effect of his stylized aesthetics. Beyond the control of narrative integration, the unleashed power of the images' and sounds' material sensuality provides a pleasure apart from discursive morality. It generates an audiovisual experience of self-sufficient beauty and evocative opacity while taking pleasure in the putative unpleasurable. Hereby, *The Keep* follows Barthes's "obtuse meaning" as well as a poetic principle outlined by Edgar Allan Poe. "It has been assumed, tacitly and avowedly, directly and indirectly, that the ultimate object of all Poetry is

Truth," writes Poe. "Every poem, it is said, should inculcate a moral; and by this moral is the poetical merit of the work to be adjudged." Whereas poetic dignity may ask for social relevance, aestheticization discovers, according to Poe, "that under the sun there exists nor *can* exist any work more thoroughly dignified, more supremely noble than this very poem, this poem *per se,* this poem which is a poem and nothing more, this poem written solely for the poem's sake."[23] Like Barthes's "obtuse meaning, Poe's poetic principle hints at a nonexpressive aesthetics. In this sense, *The Keep* is simply a horror movie filmed solely for the horror's sake. Its complete devotion to formal stylization suspends moral integration as Mann's aesthetics of horror follows only an aesthetic logic. There is no sense other than an aesthetic one that refuses any explanation.

The sole reference point and discursive object of *The Keep*, as an aestheticization of horror, are horror as an autonomous piece of art itself. It is a film not guided by a coding of absences but aimed at presenting horrifying images and sounds as events. These images and sounds are, following Michel Foucault's reflections on language, "neither substance, nor accident, nor quality, nor process." And yet they turn out to be perfectly material; an event "takes effect, becomes effect."[24] The performance of sights and sounds as events brings about a shattering of narrative continuity that gives rise to a concentration on the beauty of horror. Mann's aestheticization of the keep and the gruesome occurrences happening in it stop the narration, forcing it to be read as an articulate conglomeration of signs constituting material forces of sensation out of deterritorialized signifiers. Image and sound develop an immediacy of intensity beyond cognition and reflection. Mann's approach to filmmaking in *The Keep* thus follows the logic of what Gilles Deleuze and Félix Guattari call "planes of immanence" by analogy to Foucault's philosophy of the event: "Here, there are no longer any forms or developments of forms; nor are there subjects or the formation of subjects. There is no structure, any more than there is genesis. There are only relations of movement and rest, speed and slowness between unformed elements, or at least between elements that are relatively unformed, molecules, and particles of all kinds. There are only haecceities, affects, subjectless individuations that constitute collective assemblages."[25] Rather than serving a prior construct of narrative, Mann's audiovisual assemblages function autonomously. They are constitutive of a cinematic texture of dense viscosity that never forms a traditional whole of continuity and coherence, always referring back to the individual particle at work in transforming horrific events into beautiful compositions. Aestheticization in *The Keep* forms no organic totality of style and narrative but makes narrative look like the waste product of stylized forms. In contrast to the "redeeming value" of *Manhunter* in its discursive deconstruction of the power of the gaze, *The Keep* dwells in horrifying scenarios, offering nothing but the lust in horror: the "terrorization" of its protagonists with uncanny forces and the overwhelming of its audience with dreadfully gorgeous aesthetics. This presymbolic approach to fascination with horror may be at odds with Mann's later exceptionally pervasive contemplations of a postindustrial Information Age society leading up to *The Insider* and *Miami Vice,* but perhaps already finding an earlier culmination with *Manhunter.* However, it makes *The Keep* one of the most radically experimental horror films to date.

Notes

1. Tzvetan Todorov, *The Fantastic: A Structural Approach to a Literary Genre* (Ithaca, NY: Cornell University Press, 1975), 52.

2. Georg Wilhelm Friedrich Hegel, "The Beauty of Art or the Ideal," in *Hegel's Aesthetics: Lectures on Fine Art,* vol. 1 (Oxford: Oxford University Press, 1998), 222.

3. Friedrich Schiller, "Reflections on the Use of the Vulgar and the Lowly in Works of Art," in *Aesthetical and Philosophical Essays* (Middlesex, UK: Echo, 2006), 182.

4. Thomas De Quincey, "On Murder Considered as One of the Fine Arts," in *The Collected Writings of Thomas De Quincey,* vol. 13 (Edinburgh: Black, 1890), 13.

5. W. H. Auden, "The Guilty Vicarage," in *The Dyer's Hand, and Other Essays* (New York: Vintage, 1968), 153.

6. Joel Black, *The Aesthetics of Murder* (Baltimore: Johns Hopkins University Press, 1991), 39.

7. Steven Jay Schneider, "Murder as Art / The Art of Murder: Aestheticizing Violence in Modern Cinematic Horror," http://intensities.org/Essays/Schneider.pdf, accessed October 10, 2013; a shorter version (omitting the cited passage) appears in *Necronomicon: The Journal of Horror and Erotic Cinema, Book 4,* ed. Andy Black (London: Noir Press, 2001), 65–85.

8. On this reading, see Tony Williams, *Hearths of Darkness: The Family in the American Horror Film* (London: Associated University Presses, 1996), 255–59; Philip L. Simpson, *Psycho Paths: Tracking the Serial Killer through Contemporary American Film and Fiction* (Carbondale: Southern Illinois University Press, 2000), 97–122; Kendall R. Phillips, "Redeeming the Visual: Aesthetic Questions in Michael Mann's *Manhunter,*" *Literature/Film Quarterly* 31, no. 1 (2003): 10–16.

9. Slavoj Žižek, *On Belief* (London: Routledge, 2001), 82.

10. Jean-Louis Comolli, "Machines of the Visible," in *The Cinematic Apparatus,* ed. Teresa de Lauretis and Stephen Heath (New York: St. Martin's Press, 1980), 121–50.

11. Laura Mulvey, "Visual Pleasure and Narrative Cinema," in *Feminism and Film Theory,* ed. Constance Penley (New York: Routledge, 1988), 62.

12. Theodore Ziolkowski, "A Portrait of the Artist as a Criminal," in *Dimensions of the Modern Novel: German Texts and European Contexts* (Princeton, NJ: Princeton University Press, 1969), 290–91.

13. See Steven Jay Schneider, "Killing in Style: The Aestheticization of Violence in Donald Cammell's *White of the Eye,"* in *New Hollywood Violence,* ed. Steven Jay Schneider (Manchester, UK: Manchester University Press, 2004), 144–64.

14. Phillips, "Redeeming the Visual," 13.

15. Mark E. Wildermuth, *Blood in the Moonlight: Michael Mann and Information Age Cinema* (Jefferson, NC: McFarland, 2005), 94.

16. Simpson, *Psycho Paths,* 104.

17. Ibid., 103.

18. Black, *The Aesthetics of Murder,* 38.

19. Simpson, *Psycho Paths,* 112.

20. Steven Shaviro, *The Cinematic Body* (Minneapolis: University of Minnesota Press, 1993).

21. Steven Rybin, *The Cinema of Michael Mann* (Lanham, MD: Lexington Books, 2007), 62.

22. Roland Barthes, "The Third Meaning: Research Notes on Some Eisenstein Stills," in *Image, Music, Text* (London: Fontana Press, 1977), 66.

23. Edgar Allan Poe, "The Poetic Principle," in *The Works of Edgar Allan Poe,* vol. 5 (Middlesex, UK: Echo Library, 2007), 75.

24. Michel Foucault, "The Discourse on Language," in *The Archaeology of Knowledge* (New York: Pantheon, 1982), 215–37, 231.

25. Gilles Deleuze and Félix Guattari, *A Thousand Plateaus: Capitalism and Schizophrenia* (Minneapolis: University of Minnesota Press, 1987), 266.

STYLE, MEANING, AND MYTH IN PUBLIC ENEMIES

Steven Rybin

Michael Mann's films combine authentic realism with distinctive cinematic stylization. Mann emotionally immerses audiences in fully realized fictional worlds, including the historical worlds of *The Last of the Mohicans* (1992), *Ali* (2001), and Depression-era Chicago in *Public Enemies* (2009). At the same time, the style of these films always reminds the viewer that what is on the screen is not only an authentic re-creation, but also a Michael Mann film, an aesthetic object composed in a particular kind of way. This fascinating combination of emotional immersion and aesthetic exactitude has not escaped critical inquiry. As Anna Dzenis has astutely remarked, this director's work is in part "about a love for the texture of the medium, for its material, plastic qualities." And as she also points out, Mann's love for the medium is paralleled in the films' narratives by characters—such as Muhammad Ali (Will Smith) in *Ali* and *60 Minutes* producer Lowell Bergman (Al Pacino) in *The Insider* (1999)—who are aware of the power and vitality of imagery.[1]

The link between our emotional engagements with Mann's characters and our meaningful contemplation of his film style is emblemized by John Dillinger's (Johnny Depp) discovery of the power of images in the penultimate scene of *Public Enemies*. Dillinger, the infamous bank robber, spends the last evening of his life watching W. S. Van Dyke's 1934 crime film *Manhattan Melodrama*. After the film is over, he will be gunned down by Melvin Purvis (Christian Bale) and other FBI agents outside the movie theater. Mann shows us Dillinger watching a film in a theater, appreciating an aesthetic object called *Manhattan Melodrama* much like Mann's viewer appreciates *Public Enemies*. A film about the friendship between a hood named Blackie (Clark Gable) destined for the electric chair and his childhood friend, newly elected governor Jim Wade (William Powell), *Manhattan Melodrama* evokes something powerful for Depp's gangster. But what affects Dillinger so much in this scene? Mann's camera brings us close to Dillinger—indeed, so close that we perhaps feel as if we are watching *Manhattan Melodrama* right beside him. But the viewer is also put at a remove. Depp's Dillinger never explicitly confirms for us what he finds on that silver screen; after leaving the theater, it will be too late.

Strangely enough, the apparent ambiguity of Dillinger's fascination with Gable parallels some critics' responses to Mann's cinema. Even if it is clear that Mann's style has the function, on one level, of immersing us in the reality of his film worlds, *what* his style means (or *if* it is meaningful) is a question that often vexes the director's critics.[2] Any study of the philosophy of these films has to grapple with this vexed relationship between style and meaning in Mann. This grappling often takes the form of asking whether Mann's visual sense is achieved at the expense of substance. The first major invective launched against Mann in the context of American film criticism came from Vincent Canby, who unfavorably likened *Thief* (1981) to a mannered museum piece: "This neon-lit, night-time Chicago is pretty enough to be framed and hung on a wall, where, of course, good movies don't belong."[3] Although intended to convey distaste for Mann's painterly framing and use of color, Canby's words unintentionally capture something Mann's appreciators value. The viewer is immersed in the worlds of Mann's carefully researched films, but at the very same time the viewer also appreciates this style for its aesthetic, textural, and sensual qualities. Thus, no gap need exist between the substance of Mann's films and their style. The substance of his vision is linked to his style, his subject and content to his manner. This link between style and content is at its most interesting, I think, in the parallel between the viewer's search for meaning in Mann's style and his characters' search for authentic, existential self-definition. Indeed, this self-definition is something that Depp's Dillinger in *Public Enemies* appears to finally find by watching a gangster movie.

Several scholars have explored the relationship between the philosophy of existentialism and Mann's films. In his study of the television series *Miami Vice* (1984–1989), Steven Sanders suggests that the show illustrates the "absurdity of human existence, the dreadful weight of radical freedom, and the permanent possibility of death that sets a limit to one's aspirations and achievements" in part because it focuses on moral responsibility in the context of undercover police work.[4] For Vincent M. Gaine, Mann's characters have an "existential guiding ethic," a way of being that guides their trajectory through the world. As Gaine argues, these ways of being are either more or less socially engaged; there is always the danger that one's commitment to a code of conduct will result in isolation and a lack of social engagement.[5] What is interesting, for my purposes, is how Mann's characters embody existentialist contradictions similar to those contradictions at work in the critical response to the director's style. At once public in their personas and lines of work (as gangsters, journalists, scientists, boxing champions, serial killers, and daring frontiersmen), his characters are also often inwardly mysterious and brooding figures who do not always succeed in reconciling their ways of being and doing with the social world.[6] Even though they are guided by a certain code of conduct, their emotional and psychological interiority is not always immediately apparent to us precisely because we are joining them on a journey of self-realization and discovery. Much the same may be said of Mann's style. With the shape of his work at once a conduit for the stories he tells, there would also seem to be a kind of "surplus value" to it, a stylistic overfill that often leaves his commentators puzzled.[7]

Some Mann critics have hinted at this secret connection between Mann's style and the existential drive in his characters. As Richard Combs eloquently writes in a piece he describes as an "interim report" on the cinema of Michael Mann around the release of *Heat* (1995), Mann's films "may appear so indeterminately achieved, such inscrutable holding actions, precisely because they are in suspension, in between. Interim is the name of Mann's game—a game wherein the defining features of his films can be quite unfixed. The reason why so little is transacted in the meeting between Hanna and McCauley [in *Heat*], why cop and criminal can come together so easily, doesn't really have to do with the old noir theme of recognizing himself in the other. It's that the nature of both exists in the same spiritual flux, the psychic bath that is any Mann film."[8] Combs's language suggests that the meaning of Mann's style is anchored to his characters' struggles; Combs finds it difficult to disentangle character from style. Likewise, although evidence attests to the director's exacting research and attention to realism of setting, place, and, in his historical films, time period, Mann is not content merely to replicate reality. His style, like his characters, seems to be on the hunt for something, a search for meaning that is not simply attained via faithfulness to "representational" reality. As Combs goes on to say, it is "difficult to specify just what are the most significant stylistic features of Mann's films. Their most obvious or striking features might be in the process of becoming something else; their most significant features might be unrecognizable in the guise of something else."[9]

It is this elusive becoming, this "something else," that inspired Adrian Martin to cite Mann as one of the filmmakers who makes obsolete the distinction between traditional classical "realist" form and nonrepresentational aestheticism. As Martin writes, the two directives supporting Mann's style are to "quicken the scene, and thicken the scene—take it from quiet to noisy, manufacture a commotion of actions. It's a technique of layering, constantly adding layers and taking them away, adding and subtracting elements, dynamically, from moment to moment, almost frame to frame."[10] For Martin, this approach to filmmaking resists dichotomies between "form" on the one hand and "content" on the other. Mann instead achieves an inextricable mix of both, for as nonrepresentational elements (color, cutting, movement, sound, light) develop affective patterns that inflect our interpretation of character and plot, so too do narrative developments and character arcs return us to a further contemplation of the affects we have felt through style. Combs's and Martin's reflections on the meaning of Mann's films encourage us not to separate our immersion in the lives of Mann's characters from our appreciation of his style. As Mann's characters strive for meaning and authenticity in their existential endeavors, so too do viewers search for meaning in the experiences they have in contemplating the form of these films.

I have started with existentialism as a point of departure in order to build to a discussion of Dillinger's acceptance of the gangster myth as an authentic identity in the penultimate scene of *Public Enemies.* Just as Martin suggests that Mann's movies themselves move repeatedly toward a "big scene" that "builds and explodes," so too in this chapter I want to build slowly to the end of this film, for it has much to say about the special link between our experience of Mann's style and the drive for personal meaning at work in his characters.

In the opening sequence of *Public Enemies,* Mann introduces us to the Indiana State Penitentiary in Michigan City. Posing as a captured prisoner, with his friend "Red" Hamilton (Jason Clarke) disguised as a cop, Dillinger springs several of his friends from prison, forming the gang that will commit several of the film's thrillingly staged bank robberies. Cinematographer Dante Spinotti's high-definition digital camera captures not only the immediate reality of prison life, but also the particular details of Dillinger's daring scheme: prisoners march lockstep to the prison guard's orders; one prisoner, who has presumably disobeyed these orders, lies unconscious on the ground; several prisoners on the inside, Dillinger's friends, unpack carefully hidden guns from inside a series of boxes. A sense of immediacy in these moments comes through not only in the choice of a primarily handheld camera and Mann's impressive use of Illinois State Prison as a believable stand-in for the Indiana State Penitentiary, but also in the textural quality of the digital images. As Mann has suggested in an interview about his choice of using digital rather than film in shooting *Public Enemies,* "The strategy for how the story should tell itself was that you, as an audience, should feel you're in 1933 and 1934, and it's as detailed, real and complex an environment as 2009."[11] And Spinotti himself has commented on the possibilities of digital in filming period pieces: "We wanted the look of *Public Enemies* to have a high level of realism, not an overt period feel . . . Among the historical aspects . . . Michael and I talked about achieving an immediate feel."[12]

Mann's digital imagery, however, also pulls in another direction, one that somewhat paradoxically also reminds viewers that they are looking at an aesthetic object even as that object immerses them in the years 1933 and 1934. Although reflective of Mann's interest in a certain level of realism, *Public Enemies* does not look or feel like a documentary. It is at every step an *aesthetic* attempt to capture the "reality" of Dillinger's world. In addition to establishing many of the crucial, immediate details of the scene, for example, this prison break sequence also develops fascinating aesthetic patterns. In the images of the prisoners marching outside, our attention is drawn first not to the faces of the prisoners as individuals, but rather to the striped patterns on their uniforms. Mann's sensitive attention to the architecture at Illinois State Prison is also evident. The vertical columns of the interior wall echo the rigidity with which each member of the marching prisoners is made to walk. Finally, it is also the textural, dreamlike quality of the digital images themselves that is striking. Shots of the bright blue sky forming a horizon line above and beyond the prison avoid the "set in stone" classicism that Spinotti has associated with 35-mm filmmaking, tending instead toward a visual impressionism. A daring prison escape is depicted at precisely *this* time of day, when the clouds in the sky above the prison looked exactly like *this.* Such imagery simultaneously establishes a greater sense of immediacy— and, in terms of the characters, a sense that they are living on the screen before us—at the very same time as it fascinates through sheer film style.[13]

This combination of self-conscious aestheticism and painstaking realism is, in fact, central to the gangster film as a genre. Robert Warshow's influential essay on the gangster film, "The Gangster as Tragic Hero," offers us a reminder that the gangster cannot be understood apart from any sense of the gangster film as a self-conscious work of art: "Thus the importance of the gangster film, and the nature and intensity of its emotional and aesthetic impact, cannot be measured in terms of the place of the gangster himself or the importance of the problem of crime in American life. Those European movie-goers who think there is a gangster on every corner in New York are certainly deceived . . . What matters is that the experience of the gangster *as an experience of art* is universal to Americans. There is almost nothing we understand better or react to more readily or with quicker intelligence."[14] For Warshow, movie gangsters are not reflective of the "reality" of American life. They are instead mythological figures that express a desire for subversion. The gangster's reflection of audience desire has become a crucial idea in much scholarship on the gangster film written since the publication of Warshow's essay in 1948.[15] What is sometimes forgotten, however, is the importance Warshow afforded to the aesthetic nature of this experience. As he wrote (and the italics are his), it is only in "the experience of the gangster *as an experience of art*" that one finds the meaning of the viewers' confrontation with a figure they are not likely to come across in reality. Warshow understood the careful balance that classic gangster films struck between realistic detail (so that Europeans could be fooled into thinking such figures were in fact a common part of everyday American life) and almost mythological significance (a significance that was achieved through the gangster film as an experience of art, rendering mere criminal acts as the stuff of larger-than-life myth).

Seen in the context of Warshow's take on the gangster picture, then, Mann's combination of an almost documentary-like immediacy and a rigorous formalism makes sense. Many of his films reflect the special attraction criminal life holds for us, even if the desire to paint this criminal life realistically cannot be verified as realistic or authentic by most of his viewers, who lead lives much less glamorous and tumultuous than that of movie (or real-life) gangsters.

Curiously, however, the "experience of art" Mann offers us in *Public Enemies* is not concerned merely with presenting the gangster figure to us as an icon. Here, in fact, *Public Enemies* carves out its own unique departure from most gangster films. Mann's style immerses us in the present-tense world of the characters *before* they have become gangster icons. Depp's Dillinger is not simply *on* the screen: Dillinger becomes "Dillinger" as Mann's film unfolds. Depp—who, at the age of forty-six, nevertheless retains a youth-fulness that makes his performance as the twenty-nine-year-old Dillinger believable—guides us into the story of a gangster who at the beginning of the film is not quite yet a gangster, a notorious public figure who is nevertheless not quite yet notorious. This double-edged aspect to Depp's characterization not only forms the very substance of the film's take on the gangster figure but also shapes Dillinger's own existential confrontation with his mythical self-image in the film's penultimate sequence. Dillinger himself confronts the gangster as an "experience of art" at the end of the movie, a fascinating echo of the viewers' experience with Mann's film.

But even before Dillinger goes to the movies at the end of *Public Enemies,* we come to know him precisely through his desire to hold together both his public, mythical image and his personal identity. In his relationship with the hat-check girl Billie Frechette (Marion Cotillard), Dillinger's existential desire to articulate the meaning of his own life emerges. He tells Billie that he defines himself by what lies in the future—in other words, an existential identity that is yet to be shaped—and not by what lies in the past: "The only thing that's important is where somebody's going." Later, Dillinger success-fully persuades Billie to leave with him as he prepares his next bank heist, telling her she doesn't need to know about his past. Yet Depp's Dillinger also understands the importance of his public self-image to the very possibility of a future. In order to survive, he must blend in with the crowd.

Dillinger's sense of the gangster as a figure who must blend in also accounts for Depp's performance: whereas Brando in *The Godfather* (1972, Francis Ford Coppola) and Pacino in Brian De Palma's remake of *Scarface* (1983) define their gangster figures in broad, iconic strokes, Depp's Dill-inger may be the quietest, most soft-spoken gangster yet seen in movies. Even violent moments (such as Depp's striking of a bank teller as he stalls in opening a safe or his casual slamming of the wrist of an impatient man bothering Billie) register less as salient social transgressions than as signs of an internal disturbance. Like Depp's earlier Edward Scissorhands, his Dillinger is, in the words of Murray Pomerance, "not finished but only in the process of becoming."[16] And Mann's camera, which keeps close to Depp, is sensitive to the moment-by-moment nature of Dillinger's self-discovery.

Our understanding of Depp's Dillinger thus accrues piecemeal, like frag-ments of existential possibility not yet defined as an iconic gangster. Mann's Dillinger will become "Dillinger" only when he stares into the celluloid eyes of Clark Gable's hood in *Manhattan Melodrama* at the end of the film. This idea that Dillinger becomes "Dillinger" only at the end, rather than at the beginning, of Mann's movie is perhaps why some critics had trouble reconciling Depp with the role or, in other words, with our already articulated sense of who John Dillinger is. As David Denby writes, "The problem with casting a star as low-key and attractive as Johnny Depp is that you can't turn him into a man who is, at bottom, a loser."[17] But Depp's achievement is to invite the viewer to watch not a John Dillinger we can immediately grasp—the past-tense John Dillinger we know from history—but rather the present-tense Dillinger who is becoming and being in front of our eyes on the cinema screen.

In this sense, Depp's performance complements Mann's use of an impressionistic film style that generates a sense of presence and immediacy. The comments of Mann's collaborators provide evidence that Mann's stylistic choice to shoot *Public Enemies* on digital video was informed by the gradual, existential fluctuations of his characters' emotional and psychological states. As Mann's video colorist Stefan Sonnenfeld remarks, "Most times, [postproduction] is about balance or putting everything into a cohesive context . . . However, Michael Mann wanted to have juxtapositions and fluctuations—not balance. Not everything could be taken in 'context,' but the images would have a kinetic flow with contrast and color. In the sequence where Dillinger is transferred to prison, for example, we went frame by frame, some light, some dark—whatever supported the emotional context of the moment."[18] As Sonnenfeld suggests, in *Public Enemies* it is not the expressive significance of a *single* color in a given moment, but rather the "kinetic flow with contrast and color" that functions as an aesthetic correlation to Dillinger's own kinetic state of suspension over a variety of existential possibilities. Just as Depp's performance reveals different sides of Dillinger, so too is Mann's style sensitively attuned to the gradations of Dillinger's emotional and mental state of mind.

Mann's style, in other words, brings us close to the pulse of his characters. Sonnenfeld's citing of the sequence in which Dillinger is transferred to the Indiana prison is apt. As the sequence begins, the plane carrying Dillinger lands in Indiana under the cover of night, the blues and greens of the plane and its lights finding their analogs in the similar colors of the night sky, the grass, the buildings behind the plane, and the runway. These same cool shades of light and color inflect the close shots of Dillinger and his escorts inside the plane during a moment of quiet before the onrush of reporters and spectators. Up until this moment, Dillinger has avoided the public eye, sinking into invisibility even as J. Edgar Hoover's propaganda turns him into a notorious figure. The colors, which here work to blend the foreground figure of Dillinger with this background, complement that sense of invisibility, refusing to make Dillinger the only salient visual element in the frame. As Dillinger's plane lands, however, a cameraman lights flares that serve as a means of exposing the images of Dillinger the reporters capture with their cameras as he leaves the plane. The light shifts the scene's color to a sepia tone that evokes the palette of old photographs. To this Mann adds the stark black-and-white imagery of a shot intended as a re-creation of a newsreel image from the period. As Dillinger is escorted from the plane, the cool blues and greens of the first shots and the stark sepia of the later ones are replaced by the harsh orange brightness of the flares, which throw Dillinger, as a highly visible public figure, into strong visual relief.

These gradations in light and color subtly encapsulate a sense that prevails throughout the movie: we are watching not only a re-creation of a historical figure and a moment in history, but a figure slowly becoming the historical John Dillinger, one increasingly conscious of the public notoriety of his persona and his crimes. As the gradations in this scene attest, Depp's Dillinger is frequently suspended above two "Dillingers": the public enemy generated in publicity materials by Hoover and the FBI and the mythical yet private figure that the flesh-and-blood Dillinger would like to become. Throughout *Public Enemies,* Dillinger seems in control of his persona, cultivating a personal myth through the calling cards he leaves behind. In the first sequence of the film, prior to his prison escape, he brusquely informs a police guard to address him as "Mr. Dillinger"; after his bank robbery, he hands one of his hostages his hat, telling her it is something to remember him by (in the same sequence, one of his associates jokingly claims that he—the associate—is a scout for the movies); and after he pulls off a second prison escape, he sings a Woody Guthrie song, leaving his hostage with another memento of the experience. Here the gangster's own cultivation of his self-image accrues, moment by moment, in counterpoint to public perception and Hoover's manipulation of the media.

That Mann's Dillinger has achieved a degree of victory over the media's manipulation of his identity is clearly evoked in a sequence, after his second prison escape, in which he sees his own image on the film screen in a newsreel. As the lights in the theater are brought up, fellow audience members are instructed to report Dillinger to the authorities should they see him in the theater. Flanked on either side by his associates, Dillinger sinks into his seat, trying not to be noticed. No one spots him, and he smirks, content in the knowledge that the media's attempt to control his image has no power over his identity. For just as the media turn him into a "public enemy," the stuff of myth, Dillinger will himself harness this myth as an authentic articulation of self-knowledge.

Making meaning out of the flow of Mann's style thus brings the viewer closer to the existential journey taken by Dillinger himself. Many of the film's most striking moments do not show us who Dillinger "is," but what he may finally become: a gentleman criminal; protector of the public trust even as he robs banks; quietly violent, a powder keg about to go off when he is provoked; a daring gangster who puts innocence at risk in his pursuit of money. That Depp's Dillinger is all of these things and more is precisely the point because he is alive in front of us. Dillinger, though, finally finds his identity in the myth of the cinematic gangster in the film's penultimate scene.

But what ultimately makes *Public Enemies* special in Mann's oeuvre is that the director explicitly teases out, in a way only implicit in his earlier movies, the special bond between his film characters (ostensibly a part of the film's "realism," given that Depp's Dillinger is based on an actual historical figure) and his film aesthetic (which is interested, as Combs suggests, in the suggestive, affective, *experiential* meaning generated through style rather than in the transparent presentation of a reality that already exists). At the end of *Public Enemies,* Mann achieves a particularly special bond between his Dillinger and the movies themselves. Dillinger's experience of watching Clark Gable on the cinema screen fortifies his—and our—sense of the iconic gangster figure Dillinger becomes as the film arrives at its ending. But our sense of who Depp's Dillinger has become is linked not only to Dillinger's watching of *Manhattan Melodrama,* but also to Mann's refraction of that watching in his own imagery.

Prior to the theater scene, Purvis and his FBI agents learn through an informant that Dillinger will be attending a movie in the evening. They do not know if that movie is the one showing at the Marboro (a Shirley Temple picture) or the Biograph *(Manhattan Melodrama).* Texas Ranger Charlie Winstead (Stephen Lang), who has been brought onto the case as a field adviser, gruffly remarks through his cigarette that "John Dillinger ain't goin' to a Shirley Temple movie." However, by going to see the gangster film, Dillinger does more than fulfill the expectation of the police (and thus to a certain extent conform to their understanding of the iconic gangster he has become in the public eye). He also has a deeply personal experience through which he claims ownership of the myth of the screen gangster as an accurate articulation of his own self-identity.

After Dillinger takes his seat, Mann intercuts shots of the cops staging their ambush in front of the theater with shots of Dillinger watching *Manhattan Melodrama*. Dillinger, the surrounding audience, and the silver screen are initially framed all in one image; then Mann cuts to closer shots of Dillinger watching as scenes from Van Dyke's film unfold on the screen. Images from *Manhattan Melodrama* (of the opening credits, of Gable and Powell meeting before a Dempsey fight) are glimpsed from over Dillinger's shoulder, and then Mann's film cuts to a close-up of Dillinger himself, almost as if the cinema screen were looking back at him. In these first images in the sequence, the surrounding space of the theater is always present; other spectators are sitting near Dillinger, and all four sides of the screen on which *Manhattan Melodrama* is projected are visible.

But as the sequence proceeds, the spatial and aesthetic distance that separates Depp's Dillinger from the projected print of *Manhattan Melodrama* he watches seems to disappear. First, Mann begins to cut even closer: a shot of Depp smiling as he watches the film is matched with another over-the-shoulder shot of the screen itself. Some of the surrounding space is still visible (including the head of a spectator sitting in front of Dillinger), but now the bottom corners of the screen on which *Manhattan Melodrama* is projected are below the bottom of Mann's own frame. The screen itself (as Dillinger watches an image of Clark Gable gunning down a rival in a washroom) now seems *closer* to Dillinger, even though he has not moved an inch. As the scene cuts to shots of the cops outside, Mann continues to establish a great deal of suspense (a notable achievement because we already know what will happen from historical accounts). But his main focus continues to be on this increasingly intimate relationship between Dillinger and the silver screen. The intimacy between Dillinger and *Manhattan Melodrama* reaches its peak during two particular moments in Van Dyke's film. First, when the girlfriend (Myrna Loy) of Gable's hood, Blackie, announces with the words "Bye, Blackie," that she is leaving him, Mann first cuts to a close shot of Loy, who now seems to be literally hovering above Dillinger, as close to him as Cotillard's Billie was in the earlier scenes. Then a cut to a shot of Loy that engulfs Mann's own frame. Then when Gable refuses Powell's offer of a pardon in prison, choosing instead to meet the electric chair, he says: "Die the way you lived—all of a sudden. That's the way to go. Don't drag it out. Living like that doesn't mean a thing." After Gable utters these words, Mann cuts to the closest shot of Dillinger in the sequence, smiling as he assesses the value of Gable's words. Truly, these words embody for Blackie an existentially achieved self-definition with which Dillinger himself identifies.

In Mann's cutting and shooting (as well as in the complement of Elliot Goldenthal's stirring musical score, influenced in part by Hans Zimmer's "Journey to the Line" in Terrence Malick's 1998 war film *The Thin Red Line*), the space between Dillinger and *Manhattan Melodrama* dissolves. Dillinger's intense relationship with the silver screen is here also expressed through Mann's deft temporal rearrangement of imagery from Van Dyke's film. Those who have seen *Manhattan Melodrama* will know that the shots of Gable speaking to his fellow prisoner before being led to the electric chair actually precede the shot of Powell walking out of the prison in the original film. In Mann's editing, however, the shot of Gable speaking is seen last, as if to emphasize the extent to which Dillinger "reads against the grain" of the film's actual conclusion, holding on to the words Gable speaks even as the film on the screen ends with his dying in the electric chair. Mann also uses slow motion to convey the powerful sense in which Loy lingers over Dillinger's experience of the film. In particular, her words to Gable—"Bye, Blackie"—are clearly meant to evoke Dillinger's earlier moment with Billie as they danced to "Bye Bye, Blackbird" in the nightclub after their first meeting. Loy's departure from Gable's life, after all, parallels the permanent separation that will occur between Billie and Dillinger after he is gunned down by Purvis outside the theater.

But the most powerful moment in this sequence is still to come. As if to emphasize the special link between Loy and Billie, Mann shows us a shot, taken from over Dillinger's shoulder, of the screen, on which we see a montage of images of Loy from the film, all rearranged from their original temporal order (and thus not in the order of the actual images the real-life Dillinger would have literally seen). It is almost as if the Dillinger in Mann's film, in his very watching of *Manhattan Melodrama*, is wresting away his own personal narrative from the imagery we see in Dyke's film; and Mann, for his part, is *showing* us this rearrangement in his own images *as if* such a personal relationship to cinema could become corporeally manifest through mise-en-scène and cutting. In one magnificent moment, then, our own search for meaning in Mann's film style finds its direct parallel with Dillinger's search for meaning in the very textures of *Manhattan Melodrama*.

For a director whose work generally avoids cinephilic reference, this moment from *Public Enemies* is striking. The powerful sense in which *Manhattan Melodrama* becomes a part of Dillinger's own meaningful, existential self-definition evokes the power of movies to "step into our lives," as Christian Keathley puts it in his writing on cinephilia.[19] Just as cinephiles prize what François Truffaut once called "privileged moments" in the cinema, so too does Dillinger hold on to those moments from *Manhattan Melodrama* that enable him to articulate personal meaning. In such moments, our relatively more distanced view of films as aesthetic objects gives way to highly personal moments in which we feel that something we have seen on the screen has meaning that we, in turn, are driven to express. In the context of the gangster film, Dillinger's intensely cinephilic moment also suggests that the myth of the gangster has become real. Just as Robert Warshow once suggested that the gangster film achieves a certain realism only through a certain "experience of art," for Dillinger, too, art enables his authentic identification with a figure on the screen who appears real.

Mann's film comes close to romanticizing the gangster figure in the film's final sequence; we are as caught up with Mann's imagery as Depp's Dillinger is caught up with *Manhattan Melodrama*. Yet Dillinger's fascination with *Manhattan Melodrama* remains, for us, firmly within the purview of "the experience of art": even though Dillinger himself accepts the myth of the gangster as real, as a viable explanation for his own being, the viewers of *Public Enemies* are positioned to see this final stage in Dillinger's becoming as itself part of the aesthetic structure Mann has built. *Public Enemies* does not encourage us to see Gable as a parallel for Depp's Dillinger (the two, in fact, have little in common, an idea best understood through the distinction between Gable's highly expressive style and Depp's stoicism). Rather, Mann warns of the dangers of accepting the myth of the film gangster as real: just after Dillinger "finds himself" on the screen at the Biograph, he is shot down by Purvis and his men outside the theater. In other words, the gangster film can be productively meaningful only if it continues to be understood, as Warshow reminded us, within the frame of "the experience of art." When it becomes accepted as real (and as attractive), its dangers are clear—and more "real" than the myth itself. After all, the shooting of Dillinger is without question one of the most visceral and disturbing deaths in Mann's cinema as a combination of digital special effects and handheld camerawork show us the bullets ripping through Dillinger's body as he falls on the cement pavement.

Just as Dillinger arrives at this final stab at self-definition, he dies. The final images we see in *Public Enemies* are of Billie Frechette, in tears and alone in prison, as Winstead's cop shuts the door on her after telling her that Dillinger's final words were "bye bye, Blackbird." If Dillinger finds himself on the silver screen this fateful night, Mann's final sequence reminds us that he loses much else—as clear a statement of the costs of authentic self-definition as exists in Mann's films. Here the meaning the viewer finds in Mann's cinema and the meaning found by the characters part ways. Where Dillinger arrives at authentic self-identity only to face death, the journey through the director's style, for his viewers, is meaningfully alive and ongoing.

Notes

1. Anna Dzenis, "Michael Mann's Cinema of Images," *Screening the Past,* http://www.latrobe.edu.au/screeningthepast/firstrelease/fr0902/adfr14b.html, accessed January 19, 2011.

2. See, for example, Richard Combs, "Michael Mann: Becoming," *Film Comment* 32, no. 2 (March–April 1996): 10, where Combs remarks that Mann's style "frustrates interpretation."

3. Vincent Canby, "'Thief,' with Caan and Tuesday Weld," *New York Times,* March 27, 1981.

4. Steven Sanders, *Miami Vice* (Detroit: Wayne State University Press, 2010), 42.

5. Vincent M. Gaine, *Existentialism and Social Engagement in the Films of Michael Mann* (New York: Palgrave, 2011), 2.

6. This observation is one of the crucial insights of Gaine's study on Mann. As Gaine observes, "The existential individual must continue to inhabit their environment sensitively and understand the experiences that they undergo. A major experience . . . is the protagonist's engagement with others as, although existentialism requires understanding of one's environment, single-minded pursuit and maintenance of one's existential choice is shown to be potentially isolating" (ibid., 4).

7. Adrian Martin has suggested that film critics often treat film style as a kind of mannerist "surplus value" that is often not intrinsically connected to film content. He offers a corrective to this prejudice in his important essay "Mise-en-Scene Is Dead, or The Expressive, The Excessive, The Technical, and The Stylish," *Continuum: The Australian Journal of Media & Culture* 5, no. 2 (1990): 87–140.

8. Combs, "Michael Mann," 13.

9. Ibid.

10. Adrian Martin, "Delirious Enchantment," http://www.sensesofcinema.com/contents/00/5/delirious.html, accessed May 26, 2004.

11. Interviewed in D. Bonham, "The HD Insider," *HD Video Pro* 3, no. 4 (August 2009): 52.

12. Quoted in Jay Holben, "Big Guns," *American Cinematographer* 90, no. 7 (July 2009): 26.

13. Anna Dzenis has remarked on the impressionist aesthetic at work in some of Michael Mann's recent films. See Anna Dzenis, "Impressionist Extraordinaire: Michael Mann's *Ali*," *Senses of Cinema*, http://archive.sensesofcinema.com/contents/01/19/ali.html, accessed January 19, 2011.

14. Robert Warshow, "The Gangster as Tragic Hero" (1948), reprinted in *The Immediate Experience: Movies, Comics, Theatre, and Other Aspects of Popular Culture* (Cambridge, MA: Harvard University Press, 2001), 100, emphasis in original.

15. See, for example, Jack Shadoian, *Dreams and Dead Ends: The American Gangster Film*, 2nd ed. (Oxford: Oxford University Press, 2003), and Alain Silver and James Ursini, eds., *The Gangster Film Reader* (Pompton Plains, NJ: Limelight, 2007).

16. Murray Pomerance, *Johnny Depp Starts Here* (New Brunswick, NJ: Rutgers University Press, 2005), 44.

17. David Denby, "Tommy Guns and Toys," *The New Yorker*, July 6 and 13, 2009, 93.

18. Quoted in D. Bonham, "*Public Enemies*," *HD Video Pro* 3, no. 4 (August 2009): 53.

19. Christian Keathley, *Cinephilia, or the Wind in the Trees* (Bloomington: Indiana University Press, 2006), 152.

Interiorization in *Public Enemies*

Murray Pomerance

What is found within the *windowless* house is the true.
— Walter Benjamin, *Arcades Project*

Preamble: Inside Out

In Richard Fleischer's remarkable 1966 sci-fi/spy thriller *Fantastic Voyage,* a team of American scientists nestled in a submarine is reduced by special technology to atomic size, then injected into a defected Czech scientist in order that they might travel through his body, organ system by organ system, until they can reach his brain and discover the site of a blood clot that is preventing him from revealing an important military secret. Shot at Twentieth Century-Fox in color and CinemaScope, this film proved at the time a more than remarkable achievement in special effects since instead of matting the human figures into photographic blow-ups of various actual organ systems, a conventional and relatively inexpensive way to merge figures into an incompatible ground, art director Jack Martin Smith actually built gigantic replicas of the heart, the lungs, and other organic "settings" on the Fox soundstages so that, with fabulously suggestive lighting, cinematographer Ernest Laszlo could render the action of "tiny" people migrating among enormous alveoli, valves, and molecules of hemoglobin as though it were real. Even though the effects are unspectacular by early-twenty-first-century standards (a remake is apparently on the boards), the film remains fascinating today for a different reason.

The Czech scientist, "site" of the film in the most particular sense, is scarcely seen on the screen. The body that is principal to the action, in other words, is a space the interior of which the camera must discover so that the story may progress but is not of itself a telltale characteristic of a relevant environment, an object that others can see and manipulate or navigate around in the conventional way we use for seeing and being with other people. What this film is producing for its viewers, then, is a certain kind of proximate—indeed, intimate—perspective upon a significant other, an "inside view," and as a dramatic perspective or point from which storytelling can proceed this constitutes something decidedly strange in Western fiction, even if we consider the first-person narrative. Both optically and acoustically, the central character in a tale, whether it be the teller himself or some privileged character who has seized the teller's perduring attention, is rendered to the audience as a distinct form: a voice, a body, a committer of action, a victim, a mentality hard at work, a figure in repose. David Lean's *Dr. Zhivago* (1965) is told from the point of view, and using the voice, of a young female worker in the new Soviet state (Rita Tushingham), whom we actually meet on screen at key moments and whose voice and memory tell the story of someone she never quite fully knew. Michelangelo Antonioni's *La Notte* (1961) follows a dissolute and depressed pair, Marcello Mastroianni and Jeanne Moreau, as they go through a sad and revealing night together in Rome. François Truffaut's *Fahrenheit 451* (1966) sees the world through the eyes of its principal character, Montag (Oskar Werner), who is visually detailed on screen in virtually every scene of the film. The offscreen narrative presence that leads us through *L'année dernière à Marienbad* (1961, Alain Resnais) seems to attach itself to a château, the walls, the plasterwork, the window frames, then the grounds outside, then the people wandering in the grounds. In all these films and legion other examples, narrative is expressed about and through the agency of figures who have become figurations, so that the action of the story, the mathematics of the story, the motivation of the story, and the poetry of the story are all in a sense embodied for us to have and to see.

Fantastic Voyage works in a completely different way in that all of the agents we follow as they slosh their way along arteries and veins, into chambers of organs, and so on, are incidental to the tale. The point of the tale, the space of the tale, and the ultimate reality of the tale are lying anaesthetized on an operating table and visually, acoustically, and morally spread out around the actors and around our consciousness as a viewing audience. To some degree, although not with as wholehearted a commitment to this design principle, M. Night Shyamalan's *The Happening* (2008) reprises this outering derived from a forced interiorization: protagonists thrust into a natural setting combat the setting itself in the main story of the film, but there is a signal difference—our view of the setting is still objective and distinct, as though seen through the eyes of a character entirely removed from the action. There is very little of this external diagnosis in *Fantastic Voyage*. Mostly, after the dramatic injection scene, we are with the voyagers traveling inside the space that is both our topos and the focus of our desire.

The attachment we produce by going all the way in is in some important ways blinding and confusing. We see clearly enough, but not *what we need to see if we are to act with rationality, purpose, and method.* Attachment in its profound sense leads to feeling but not understanding. Tom Gunning notes one of the fascinating puzzles of modernity: how, for Baudelaire, the *intérieur* can become an exterior, how the myriad details of the bourgeois home can reflect and indicate the social world—often through the device of a kind of mirror or special window that would import an exterior view as a framed artistic surface *inside* the living space.[1] The *intérieur* is not wholly and uniformly a version of broadly conceived social space, however; in part, it is murky and historical, a trace of genealogy and lost experience and thus, essentially, a living but also hidden world.

The Gangster Ecstatic

Regarding the genre conventions of the gangster film, no one has particularly commented that its protagonist tends to stand *outside* himself—is, as it were, ecstatic—and that typically our view of him matches his own, being distanced, objective, measuring, and judgmental. I mean to suggest a very pointed orientation of gangster pictures as they are typically shot and edited—*Little Caesar* (1931, Mervyn LeRoy), *The Public Enemy* (1931, William A. Wellman), *Scarface* (1932, Howard Hawks), *High Sierra* (1941, Raoul Walsh), *Dillinger* (1945, Max Nosseck), *White Heat* (1949, Raoul Walsh), *The Godfather* (1972, Francis Ford Coppola), *Goodfellas* (1990, Martin Scorsese)—by which the gangster hero's state of mind is devoted almost exclusively to forces of law and order and to the way he is inevitably bound to appear from the point of view of such forces. The gangster knows himself to be "bad," for example, not out of an ethical leaning that is exclusively his but out of an ultimate convicted belief in the moral stance of the state; he knows the rules as reality, knows he has broken them, knows exactly how this is so, and knows what identity must befall him as a consequence. In other words, he is ashamed, and his shame riddles the characterization of him throughout the film, both as a preference for shadow—lurking, hid-ing, sneaking, planning, conspiring—and as a certain urgency that fills his actions to overflowing with spontaneity, malice, defensiveness, and pain. It is from the perspective of a police agent or jurisprudential force that the gangster recognizes himself, having adopted the critical framework and moral superstructure against which he fights. Because of this confliction, he is at war with himself; yet more importantly, the film's own point of view is consistently critical, no matter what forms and extent of sympathy it might seem to generate. The gangster as we apperceive him must go down, he will go down, he cannot but go down, and the motorizing question of the story is only when, where, by what exact fateful mechanism this will happen.

In his acts of violence and criminality, therefore, the gangster protago-nist consistently behaves just as police and law-abiding citizens—who know nothing of the inner life of thieves—would expect him to. He is surly not out of some inner characterological motivation as much as out of the screen-writer's need to rationalize his presence in congruence with the viewer's thoroughgoingly hungry disapproval. If the gangster is emotionally and physically appealing—Cagney, Bogart, Garfield, Pacino, Brando—we can love him even though we would never lower ourselves to do what he is doing. One frequent twist of plot has the gangster or criminal hero pressured or forced into his behavior by circumstances he cannot control, so that even he disapproves to some degree but cannot act on that disapproval: Farley Granger's Bowie in Nicholas Ray's *They Live by Night* (1949). Or he is forced by his own torments, sprung perhaps from the rank injustice of justice: Robert Mitchum's or Robert De Niro's Max Cady in *Cape Fear* (1962, J. Lee Thompson; 1991, Martin Scorsese). The screen gangster fights society, but in the end it is society that is making this film. Society sees him in negative light even if his glamour is undeniable.

Since the gangster protagonist is narratologically and optically appeal-ing, we do not take our eyes from him. Our vision is typically organized, then, around two views from the outside, two refusals to come into inti-mate space: we must get far enough away to watch him with acuity because he is so attractive; and we must be in a position to judge him because the thought of becoming what he is simply terrifies and alienates us, the bour-geois audience. He perdures for us as a freak, a creature worth continual observation, but is no object of love. (In this, he typifies many cinematic heroes.) His world and actions, as we see them, are organized against, and thus with complete consciousness of, an orderly system, and it is with and through order that we watch his story. His thoughts and understandings are continually alluded to on screen so that we, innocents to his labors, can grasp what he is about. Further, in the genre convention, in order that we may unmistakably witness his miscreance and therefore finally assent to his punishment or death, all his gangsterly activity is depicted in crisp, clear focus with good lighting (no matter that he is acting in the shadows of the underworld), clearly recorded sound, and a respectfully distant (and revealing) point of view.

He is both allure and difficulty, a diamond whose flaws we are counting through cinema's magnifying glass. The structure of watching the gangster is different entirely from what we find in *Fantastic Voyage,* where we can follow and understand only by going *into* the subject of the film. With the gangster hero, we usually stay out in the cold.

Targeting

Michael Mann's *Public Enemies* takes a very different approach. Here, together, are two films in one. First and more conventionally, there is the tale of Melvin Purvis (Christian Bale), a thirty-one-year-old, exceptionally promising Department of Justice field agent cum sharpshooter who easily brings down the notorious "Pretty Boy" Floyd and thus gains the twinkly admiration, not to say perfumed patronage, of J. Edgar Hoover (Billy Crudup). It is 1933, and Hoover is restructuring the Department of Justice's Bureau of Investigation after what Athan Theoharis points to as a "new sense of crisis" built upon the March 1, 1932, Lindbergh kidnapping and "the brazen criminal activity of a host of violent gangsters during the early 1930s" that "captured the attention of a fascinated public."[2] Hoover's poster boy, Purvis, "spent his youth as do most South Carolina boys in country towns—hunting and fishing and playing baseball," then grew into a man of whom his campus annual proclaimed that the law had "no more devoted and faithful student."[3] The sheepish agent is promoted by the gloating bureaucrat into leading the hunt for John Dillinger, bank robber extraordinaire, and it is in the context of this chase that Purvis's story takes shape for us as the gradual refinement, professionalization, and dehumanization of a hunter now brought into the fold of a complex bureaucratic organization. In the early 1930s, Progressives "placed their faith in 'experts' who would advance efficiency," and "Hoover was Progressive efficiency personified."[4] If we met Purvis as he raced after Floyd, a home-grown hunter seeking his prey in an orchard by blazing sunlight, the agent we follow as the film winds on has rationalized his locally gained talents, learned how to file and catalog his instincts, and become adept at interconnecting with skilled strangers—agents from afar imported to Illinois to lend more rarefied technical expertise to his marksmanship. Purvis's tale is thus one of modernization and urbanization, depending on the acquisition of grimly reductive reasoning, garrulous interpersonal skills, and dogged perseverance, which is to say the ability to envision, plan, and map the future.

Seen from Purvis's calculating point of view, Dillinger is not only exteriorized, reduced, and objectified but in fact miniaturized somewhat in the way that the doctors are in *Fantastic Voyage* because he becomes, figuratively if not actually, in shot after shot a tiny target in Purvis's nationally supported and technologically assisted sights. He is the prize that Purvis intends to catch, not so that he may have it, relish it, admire it, and display it but so that he may cash it in for a promotion to a position closer to Hoover's corrupt center of operations. In performing Purvis, Bale brings a coldness of manner that was perceivable even in his early work as the plucky Jamie in Steven Spielberg's *Empire of the Sun* (1987) and that developed through his crafting of the cunning and pathological Patrick Bateman in *American Psycho* (2000, Mary Harron), Sam in *Laurel Canyon* (2002, Lisa Cholodenko), the creepily gaunt and repressed Trevor Reznik in *The Machinist* (2004, Brad Anderson), the voluptuous lead in *Batman Begins* (2005, Christopher Nolan), and the desperately passionate Alfred Borden in *The Prestige* (2006, Christopher Nolan), not to mention buff John Connor in *Terminator Salvation* (2009, McG). Bale's Purvis is a man who allows himself to be made into a tool, who even relishes the conversion, as we can see by the eager gleam in his eye as he pursues Dillinger through the shabby hotel rooms, dusty roads, and dark streets of the narrative.

The Dillinger portrayed by Johnny Depp in this film, to the extent that he is Purvis's treasure, his "diamond," is thus akin, in a fundamental way, to the Johnny Depp whose career through the 1990s and 2000s seduced the affections and consciousness of a vast international audience, a Depp so perfect for being spotted, targeted, pursued, and coolly desired as to have been worth a huge investment so that he would agree to incarnate Dillinger here. As a performer, Depp has attracted notable and profuse publicity, in part because of his complex allure (a good part of which is romantic, at least for the females ages thirteen to seventy-three in his audience), but also because he has gained a certain (perhaps now fading) notoriety as a rule breaker, independent spirit, and enemy of the state. He draws at the box office in a more than substantial way, upping the take for films that without him would have little hope of serious earnings: *Public Enemies,* for example, formally a straightforward gangster pic, netted a very respectable $25 million on its opening weekend and has by now brought in almost $215 million worldwide in total. We have, for almost twenty years now, scarcely allowed Depp out of our visual range and have attempted to probe the secrets of his personal life with lusty energy. Purvis, then, symbolizes and typifies any one of Depp's myriad fans in his incessantly hopeful race after Dillinger. The persistence of his gaze, the gross objectification through which it converts Dillinger/Depp's personhood and commitment into little more than movement and illumination, and, supremely, the obsessive desire on Purvis's part to possess, control, and devour Dillinger/Depp all sum to a mirroring of our own fascination and will to control.

Although Dillinger is attractive, even magnetic, for Purvis in the way that prey must be, the wily thief never becomes alluring, intriguing, desirable, curious, personable, haunting, or otherwise affective for him. He could be a prized mechanical object in a shooting gallery for all the concern and emotional investment the agent makes in spotting him and hunting him down and for all the pleasure the agent shows when, gaining ground, he finally gets the upper hand over Dillinger by arresting the robber's girlfriend, Billie Frechette (Marion Cotillard). Melvin Purvis becomes a paragon of achievement orientation, the telltale virtue of the organization man.[5] And to the extent that the film is framed from Purvis's perspective or from Hoover's, Dillinger is less a person than an accomplishment.

Undiscoverable

It is perhaps a telltale characteristic of Purvis that he does not seem to breathe and, more importantly, that the film does not seem to breathe with him in his activity. He moves as though with breath held, a suspension that is a project and a presentiment. We isolate and capture him in his project of isolation and capture, but he is stilled, posed, aggrandized. Thus, in a vital way he has himself been mechanized, and Mann renders the bargain Purvis makes with Hoover as a Faustian sellout.

Dillinger makes for another story altogether ("Johnny was not near as bad as was painted," his sister and father said after he was killed[6]), and the film as it concerns him makes for a second film. Contravening the genre convention altogether, Mann uses his camera to approach, touch, and penetrate the world of this devoted bank robber and popular hero of his time. The camera, in fact, is often handheld when it nears Dillinger, so that we have the sense of hovering near a star in a crowd of admirers and curious hangers-on, much as we might have in trying to get a glimpse of Depp. In moments, the camera cannot catch up or swoops too close, so that we lose focus. When we enter Dillinger's private spaces—his hideouts, his hotel rooms—we have a distinct sense of not being alone with him, but instead of having accessed a "privacy" that is shared by close comrades who come and go from the frame in such a way as to disorient us and keep us off balance. If Purvis is obsessively focused on Dillinger, Dillinger has virtually no knowledge of, interest in, or attentiveness to Purvis or any other agent of the law. He moves from instinct and the impetus of desire and situated logic, not in reflection of the orientations and boundaries laid out from outside and above. We catch him in midconversation or in intimacies that are not wholly comprehensible. Although he is exceptionally canny and observant of his surround—Erving Goffman notes that individuals tend to "mediate" between "placidly attending to easily managed matters at hand" and being "fully mobilized, a fury of intent, alarmed," getting ready "to attack or to stalk or to flee"[7]—we do not see him as a man who aims a calculated and focused gaze at the world or who is nothing but a treasure to be gawked at and desired by others. He is instead an animal always energized by need and feeling, who moves through space not in order to arrive at a destination but in order to have a definite rhythm, that of anticipating and realizing the feeling and movement of being alive. "He was kind of the ultimate existentialist, figuratively," Depp told an interviewer.[8] Dillinger's breathing and embodied experience dominates our perception of him. He is sexual, cupidinous, generous, hungry, meditative, vengeful, eager, and—to a degree that seems to befit his present conditions, whatever they are—trustful. Whatever logic it is that grounds his being, we do not have access to it. He remains a force we wish to watch and be close to, and the central operation of the film insomuch as it addresses Dillinger himself is a joining, a penetrating, an unyielding struggle to be near.

Whereas the film's treatment of Purvis concentrates on positioning, preparing, and planning, its treatment of Dillinger resides in constant fluid movement and procedure. We frequently watch Dillinger from a position of unanticipated proximity and through the agency of that handheld camera that places us in action inside Dillinger's space. This technical alignment of

Dillinger the character with Depp the star produces an experience in which we constantly grasp at fugitive visions, fragments of his lived life, any remnant we can see with a reasonable focus and then hold on to. The situations tend to be in full play by the time we catch up with them, so that the film becomes striking for its generalized omission of preparatory or establishing dialogue. We find out what is happening by going along for the ride—this operating mode drawn out to a frightening limit, indeed, in our very first introduction to the characters and the filmmaker's way of showing them because the ride, basically thrilling, is also mortal. Dillinger and his associates are breaking into a prison in order to free some of their comrades, but even this fact is far from salient as we first see some men in long coats and hats striding across the huge perimeter toward the wall. The breakout goes badly—one might say "not according to plan," except that there is no evidence of a solid plan—and as the gang flees in an automobile, one of the newly freed prisoners is badly wounded. He clings to the running board of the vehicle, his fingers interlaced with Dillinger's until it is evident that our hero is holding on to nothing but dead weight. Dillinger lets go his hand as the car speeds away, and the body, lost now to the forward movement in which we share, seems to glide away into history along the dusty ground. Now Dillinger erupts upon the henchman who, shooting a guard back in the prison, had prompted the gunfight that resulted in this death. In a flash, he has thrown open another door of the car, not running at full speed, and thrown the man onto the road as so much unwanted baggage. In a matter of seconds, then, we see the full gamut of Dillinger's emotional range—from tender and compassionate fidelity to a wounded friend near death to vengeful anger and murderous brusqueness.

Depp's handling of Dillinger's emotional range is somewhat unique, however. Whereas in his performance of the same character in the 1945 *Dillinger*, Lawrence Tierney had presented a cool mask that covered every feature of Dillinger's feeling, a mask that finally said, in effect, anesthesia, aphasia, and affective neutrality, what Depp does is to infuse himself utterly in the emotional spasm of any moment. This commitment results in a stuttering chain of depictions, unbridged one to another, in which the character's attitude develops out of the situational moment and is played to the full with no regard for secrecy, masking, containment, or camouflage from the observing world. If we try to understand Depp's Dillinger, we find only our capacity to be sympathetic to his unending presence, his momentary being in the world. The fragments we see are phrased with utter authenticity, but without preparation or resolution. Given the arbitrariness of Mann's camera positions, his sense of continuing motion, the sliding and gliding of the characters into and out of the frame, the lingo and expressively vocalized sonorities, the speed, Dillinger's inventiveness as he makes do with whatever resources lie to hand, and Depp's charming engagement in character variably from moment to moment, the effect of the film is to bring us through the fourth wall and into the action world itself, always hunting to see more, retain more, while understanding passes us by.

It need hardly be said that Johnny Depp's presence in the film was Mann's greatest asset, potentially and actually, at the box office; far greater, for example, than the substantiality of John Dillinger as subject or the fact that many scenes would be shot on real locations or the fact that such luminaries of the screen (by 2009) as Cotillard, Bale, and Giovanni Ribisi would join the cast. Depp by the late 2000s had become a universal megastar of such proportions that any flimsy pretext for a tale could subtend a major publicity extravaganza in newspapers and, more potently, magazines. Even as the locus of a biography, he had managed to remain more or less a mystery,[9] with the cumulative effect that audiences across cultures, languages, religions, and histories wanted to access his image, probe it for connection, and in some way bring themselves up against the "reality" that it promised. Joining a crew of which Depp was the "leader" was therefore an entirely desirable project for viewers of the film, and it was canny on Mann's part to use the handheld camera as a way of moving close to, around, with, and beside him in a characterization that was, in and of itself, only arbitrary and indistinct. As with much of this actor's work on screen, only a thin tissue separates character from actor. Dillinger is Deppish. And the hunt for Dillinger thus mirrors viewers' own passions and program in hunting for the essence of Depp. What is remarkable about *Public Enemies* beyond this, however, is the nature of our experience as we approach Dillinger, enter his private territory, witness his relationships, and suffer his fate.

In two different ways we fail to find revelations about either Depp or Dillinger. First, no aspect of character is presented as would surprise our expectations or received view. Dillinger behaves as a common man against the imposing and domineering forces of an always more encroaching federal bureaucracy in law enforcement, in banking, in social regulation. But there is no idiosyncratic motive for his moves or pattern to the organization of his daily routines. He addresses what presents itself, but he does not seem to have a plan for finding experience, nor must he, given that Mann's intent is to contrast this Dillinger with a Purvis who is all plans and anticipations, a Purvis whose collar is always neat and whose hair is always in place. Dillinger flies free, then, but his freedom is in some ways incomprehensible. Second, the figure of the man passes close to the camera, is devoured by the camera, is encircled by the camera—all without our ever having a tranquil portrait of him on which, slowly meditating, we might deduce his qualities and tones. The singular putative exception—a scene where he saunters into a police station while the inhabitants are gathered together in a corner over a broadcast of a baseball game; where he paces slowly around the huge empty room, with its filing cabinets and desks all bathed in pallid green afternoon sunlight; where he stares at posters on the wall depicting not only himself but also his closest friends and associates; and where he pauses to ask the policemen in a friendly voice what the score is, and they answer him, not a single one of them guessing his identity—is really only an essay on Dillinger's mask, Dillinger's secret and public face, the wall that no will to knowledge can penetrate. If the audience responds to this scene with a little levity because Dillinger is teasing his enemies and we are on his side watching him do it, the truth remains that the canny malevolence he harbors but hides here is as unavailable to us as his charm is present. The scene is a riddle, not a picture of the true man.

Our approach to Dillinger, then, our movement inside his private sphere, produces a sort of visual and experiential debility. In sudden flashes he is distinct in front of us, but without context, or else we feel close to only part of him, or we sense the grace of his movement without quite plumbing his form. He is, perhaps, not unlike Walter Benjamin's "windowless room," in which if we get the real truth there, it is also probable that we are in a kind of darkness. He participates in the "dialectic of flânerie," as Benjamin describes it: "on one side, the man who feels himself viewed by all and sundry as a true suspect and, on the other side, the man who is utterly undiscoverable."[10] There is, too, a pervasive sense of nostalgia about Dillinger, as though our every glimpse of him takes us too quickly forward to a foreordained future, while also opening to us vistas of a shining and lost past: "Often these inner spaces harbor antiquated trades, even those that are thoroughly up to date will acquire in them something obsolete. They are the site of information bureaus and detective agencies, which there, in the gloomy light of the upper galleries, follow the trail of the past. In hairdressers' windows, you can see the last women with long hair."[11] We can easily think of Dillinger's trade as antiquated—it is impossible to conceive of Purvis and Hoover without doing so—and of his manner and method as being obsolete for his times, obsolete and thus charming. That Dillinger could be thought a detective agency or information bureau is hardly a stunning possibility because only with access to a flow of vital information could he engage himself as he does. Following the trail of the past is the constitution of his every present move, and his past is one that Hoover and his minions intend to render obscure and void, whence our feeling of loyalty to Dillinger. As to the women with long hair, they are surrounding him, their hair perhaps a clue to their intentions.

Benjamin goes on—he is discussing collecting—to remark that "the object is detached from all its original functions in order to enter into the closest conceivable relation to things of the same kind."[12] Nothing less is the fate of Dillinger in the care of the FBI, made up of collectors par excellence, who have classed him as only another of their "public enemies," phantoms who mobilize a certain dully mechanical address. Creating the category "public enemies," writes Rhodri Jeffreys-Jones, was "akin to the Wild West technique of posters proclaiming, 'Wanted: Dead or Alive.'"[13] Detected and then caught, Dillinger will be neutralized, historicized, categorized, analyzed, but always abstracted and reduced from his personhood; the same fate will befall the superior Purvis, but a crowd will not gather to look him up in the library; and he is part of this film only so that Mann can demonstrate the social mechanism and its penchant for contempt. As we see from our position of extreme proximity, Dillinger and his incarnator here are equally idiosyncratic, unitary, distinct, incomparable, ineffably pure, indescribably personable. The irony of the film's title is that the Dillinger we meet is only a "public enemy" when viewed from Purvis's perspective, a perspective that the camera's eager (and hot) attention to Dillinger's private life makes reductive, marginal, and silly.

Nature

I quote Walter Benjamin in the context of this analysis of Michael Mann, Johnny Depp, John Dillinger, and contemporary action cinema because in the end *Public Enemies* is a film about nothing other than modernity. The press of J. Edgar Hoover's fledgling, dilettante bureaucracy upon what had been a relatively *heimliche* and agrarian preoccupation for Dillinger; the use of tools (such as the Tommy gun—"a machine gun for the home"[14]) and invocation of expertise (the FBI field teams); the urbanization emphasized by Hoover's presence in Washington, DC, and Dillinger's final escapade in

Chicago; the importance of communications systems in finding and cornering Dillinger; and, most importantly, the transformative reduction of integrated personalities to types, roles, occupations, and codable characteristics, as it were the explicit transformation of the human experience to a set of glyphs: all signal a modern venture. Dillinger hides out with some cronies at a cabin in the Wisconsin woods (the attack at Little Bohemia, April 1934), where the FBI comes upon him in the middle of the night: the flashes of gunfire through the trees as Dillinger flees—lightning white, blinding—and the amplified sound of the gunfire, which seems to explode just at the meatus of the listening ear so that one recoils with shivers as one attends, not only indicate violence, the forces of justice, and male aggression but provide striking emblematization of modern technology, focused in the multiplied gunshots and staccato rhythm of the scene. The darkness sliced with jolts of illumination suggests strobing, as in motion-picture projection. And through all this, the killer agents operate without any human interest or passion, without the least fascination for their targets. Although we see, for instance, that they are men, it is clear that they are also not angry or enthused warriors as much as agents of a system, operatives, tools themselves. And the agents' targets, brushing past us in the dark undergrowth, are so many animals in flight, racing through Mann's shots for their lives. The forest setting idealizes the tone of the scene: urbanized and systematized forces of control invading and "redeveloping" a bucolic, pastoral landscape.

Hoover and his imperious designs must be understood as essentially bourgeois in that the Federal Bureau of Investigation, as he has conceived and promoted it, aims at order, control, and self-aggrandizement. Benjamin comments on how the bourgeois individual "sets store by the transformation of nature into the interior": "In 1839, a ball is held at the British embassy. Two hundred rose bushes are ordered. 'The garden,' so runs an eye-witness account, 'was covered by an awning and had the feel of a drawing room. But what a drawing room! The fragrant, well-stocked flower beds had turned into enormous *jardinières,* the graveled walks had disappeared under sumptuous carpets, and in place of the cast-iron benches we found sofas covered in damask and silk'"[15]—also a description, of course, of how the undesigned "garden" of the sound stage or location is transformed through cinematic production into the "interior" of the set. This importation of nature bespeaks an interior that is filled with "outside" views, judgmental views, appreciative and calculating views that measure, compare, justify, and promote. Dillinger has become one of the rose bushes Purvis is gathering to help furnish and decorate the drawing room that is Hoover's showplace, with all the green growth in *jardinières* and all the wildness clipped, shaped, and tamed. (The scene in which Dillinger invades the agents' headquarters is telling, with its WANTED posters covering the bulletin boards and neatly capturing, framing, defining, and reducing the targets we have already met in their "natural" state.) Nature—Dillinger's nature—is being repositioned *inside,* not in the ultimate privacy that is any man's real being but in a public place and for show. He is becoming a specimen for the FBI's museum. Benjamin also reads Balzac: "Do your utmost . . . to remain unknown" because the administrative apparatus "ere long will have every acre of land, down to the smallest holdings . . . , laid down on the broad sheets of a survey—a giant's task, by command of a giant."[16]

Affiliation

In the collection of the Musée des Beaux-Arts d'Orléans hangs Hugues Fourau's canvas *Tête décapitée de Fieschi* (Fieschi's Decapitated Head). Here before the painter's eye—also before the astonished viewer's—and incorporated in a bust is the aggregation of muscular contractions, skin tones, and physiognomic proportions that in a choir speak—speak if not a condition and a challenge, then an explanation, or so nineteenth-century theorists would have had it. Fieschi had been put to death in 1836 for his attempted regicide of Louis-Philippe. He was now on view, if not in whole, then in the telling part, the head that would reveal his former proclivities and desires, his capabilities and designs. (We may recall that Johnny Depp, in all his screen appearances, has been concentrated for us by virtue of his head, not his body.) This is the positivist dream of explaining reality, now appositioned to the evocative and productive special torso, the active torso, that is the head; Alphonse Berthillon operationalized this thought through his catalog of portraits.[17] Guy Davenport observes that Edgar Allen Poe's Roderick Usher is a "man of abnormally acute senses, sensitivity, and sensibilities. He has no body; he is all head. His morbidity subtracted and his sharpness of eye and analytical genius directed toward the common good, Usher becomes César Auguste Dupin, who became Sherlock Holmes"—ironically pinpointing the identity of criminal and investigative desires as wellsprings of "sensitivity" and "sensibility," urgency and devotion.[18]

The cataloging and collimating of Dillinger—the concentrating blades of legal attentiveness were methodically closing in on his persona, specifically his head—had proceeded in the press through his string of bank robberies in late 1933 and the first half of 1934. The Merchants' National Bank of South Bend, Indiana, was robbed of $28,439 on July 1 by "a bandit quintet with John Dillinger reported to be in command," who "engaged in gun battles with a detective, two officers and a jeweler as they fled."[19] The *Washington Post* reported, indeed, that Dillinger was "struck by gunfire" during that escape,[20] this happenstance hardly a major drawback for the outlaw because, as the *New York Times* reported three days later, quoting an unnamed ex-convict, he was already "suffering from a permanent injury so serious that he no longer drives an automobile."[21] If he had trouble moving, he managed nevertheless to be omnipresent: he was "reported seen" on July 3 in Whitinsville, Massachusetts.[22] The next day, Floyd Privett of the Muncie, Indiana, police force saw him driving with two companions through the busiest downtown intersection of the city.[23] On July 8, he was ostensibly back on the East Coast, where a motorist in Palmer, Massachusetts, noted that "the desperado whizzed by his car on a highway" in a vehicle with three other men inside and bearing Missouri or Michigan plates, "followed by another machine containing four men."[24] On July 10, the *New York Times* reported sheriff's deputies on the trail of a "gang of gunmen possibly including John Dillinger" in Fond Du Lac, Wisconsin.[25] By the third week of July, Dillinger was roaming with a $15,000 bounty on his head,[26] enough to stimulate the East Chicago police, moved by the suspicion he had killed one of their own, to tip off the FBI that he was in town.

The actual takedown, one of the ignominious moments in American cultural history, occurred at 10:40 PM on the night of July 22, 1934, on the pavement outside the Biograph Theater at 2433 Lincoln Avenue in North Chicago. Dillinger had gone into the theater to watch W. S. Van Dyke's *Manhattan Melodrama* (1934), a heart-pounding tale of two childhood buddies who grow up to be a kingpin of crime and a district attorney, respectively, one of whom must take responsibility for sending the other, his fondest chum, to the electric chair. "Die the way you lived—all of a sudden. That's the way to go. Don't drag it out," Clark Gable manfully intones on screen (at which Depp's Dillinger, seen in full head shot, lifts the corner of his mouth in a sweet, comprehending smile). According to police and press reports, "The end of the greatest manhunt in contemporary criminal annals came in the swift tempo in which the notorious outlaw had lived." Dillinger "ran into [a] cordon of officers" who had been waiting outside with excruciating patience for more than two hours. "He reached quickly into his pocket and the guns roared."[27] "He saw me give a signal to my men to close in," Melvin Purvis said to the *New York Times*. "He became alarmed and reached into a belt and was drawing the .38-calibre pistol he carried concealed when two of the agents let him have it. . . . Dillinger was lying prone before he was able to get the gun out and I took it from him."[28] He was shot twice, one bullet penetrating his head and another his chest. Subsequent reportage intensified the cachet of law enforcement authorities and their prowess in locating and terminating Dillinger by revealing that the "desperado," something of a chameleon, had "treated his fingers with acid which blurred out some identifying loops and whorls"[29] and had changed his hairstyle, neither of which fooled the astute and sharp-eyed Purvis. Attorney General Homer Stille Cummings smugly pronounced the kill "exceedingly gratifying as well as reassuring" and noted that the slaying of Dillinger "reflected great credit on the Chicago office of the division of investigation."[30] The *New York Times* sanctimoniously opined, "Dillinger's active professional life was short. It covered only a little more than ten months. Punishment was not long in coming."[31]

Given this rather one-sided—and official—view of the culminating events of Dillinger's career, it is worth paying strict attention to the way Michael Mann fictionalizes these happenings in the climax of his film, especially because the production team expended considerable labor to achieve a sense of verisimilitude in the film, notably in the selection of certain authentic locations (certain, but not all—the scene at the Congress Hotel in Tucson, Arizona, was not actually filmed there). Mann's approach, I have been arguing, has consistently been to bring us close to Dillinger—indeed, to escort us into Dillinger's private world: his feeling and his sensibilities, not merely his space. It can hardly be surprising, then, if in describing the action at the Biograph Mann decided to take a view more in sympathy with Dillinger than with those who hunted him down, a view that can be typified as "unconventionally sentimental" and that is certainly *interior* to Dillinger's state of being.[32] Thus, a view similar to Mann's vision of a somewhat contradictory perspective on the Dillinger slaying is provided by one Edgar L. Allenmand. A garage mechanic positioned directly across the road from Dillinger as he stepped southeast from the theater, Allenmand saw something the newspapers did not by and large report:

> Everything seemed calm and peaceful. There were not many people around and little traffic. I had a clear, unobstructed view of the sidewalk on the opposite side.

Suddenly I saw a tall man fire two shots in quick succession. He seemed to be standing almost beside the man who was shot. The wounded man fell to the alley [a few steps down the street from the Biograph] without uttering a sound.[33]

In other words: (1) no cordon of officers; (2) no attempt on Dillinger's part to find or use a gun; and (3) lethal shots fired from extremely close range.

In the film, we are positioned in front of Dillinger and tracking backward as he makes his way down the sidewalk of Lincoln Avenue (several blocks of which had been closed down by the production, a resident noted, and "redone in 1930 style: laid down streetcar tracks, re-fronted all the stores, and every evening thirty black sedans rolled off trucks and parked up and down both sides. . . . [Mann] had the set-up in place for a month—the local merchants made big $$"[34]). Our attention has already been drawn to the fact that it is a warm night by a banner—COOLED BY REFRIGERATION— dangling from the theater's marquee (air conditioning was born in Chicago, meat capital of America, and Balaban & Katz, the movie theater impresarios, were important innovators of the process for exhibition venues[35]). Dillinger is meditating as he paces, self-conscious, uncomfortable, perhaps too aware. The Biograph's marquee is receding in the distance, and men and women are flocking past, heading in the opposite direction. A man (one of a trio of specialist sharpshooters Purvis had called in and who failed spectacularly at Little Bohemia) finally slides up behind Dillinger, points his pistol—a pistol, not a Tommy gun, because "the police never took to the Thompson gun with the same enthusiasm as the gangsters"[36] and because, possessing position and authority, they have no need for that "greatest aid to bigger and better business the criminal has discovered in this generation"[37]—and fires twice, the sound strangely thudding and echoing as if in some cavernous chamber. Dillinger has groped for a gun, but his arm has been jostled by one of the passers-by, and he has no hope of even raising it. One bullet comes through his cheek just below the eye, a second emerges from his chest. *Bullets from behind.* A look of astonishment on his features as he falls forward into the camera, dark blood gushing from his head. The man labeled J. Edgar Hoover's "Public Enemy No. 1" is thus shown in Mann's vision to merit the singular treatment of being executed summarily by agents of the government in lieu of standing trial and being subjected to a verdict. (Mark L. Robbins, superintendent of the Police Identification Bureau in Tucson and the man responsible for Dillinger's capture there in January of that year, had in early July 1934 warned police officers "not to try to capture Dillinger alive" even though he had done so himself.)[38] An Associated Press reflection on July 24, that "John Dillinger accepted the fact that his days were numbered and he died the way he wanted to," is thus both a kind of confirmation of this extraordinarily abrupt move to judgment on the part of the FBI and a legitimation post hoc. "If I go to trial I'm a goner, by the electric chair," Dillinger is reported to have told reporters in Tucson months earlier.[39]

It is the head shot upon which Mann concentrates: the shot *to* the head, but also the shot *of* the head—summary execution, but also the publicity item that helps actors (such as Johnny Depp) get their jobs. With Dillinger prostrate on the pavement, the camera drops down to focus straightaway upon his face, blood streaming out darkly in the night. This exact defacement is symbolic and poignant, indeed pious, given the cultural centrality since the nineteenth century of our attention to the head as *the* indicator of self, purpose, and action. Both Dillinger and Depp, joined in an instant—a fake instant, to be sure, constructed only of makeup and SFX technology, but at the same time an instant of our experience—lose their heads. As part of its coverage of the slaying of Dillinger, the *New York Times* published a head-and-shoulders portrait of him on July 23, 1934, with the caption "KILLED BY POLICE IN CHICAGO. John Dillinger"; he is seen in three-quarter view from the side, his eyes looking up inquisitively as he sits with jacket slumped over his neck and dapper necktie neat as a pin.[40] His lips are pressed together "pensively," his chin as cleft as Kirk Douglas's. We have every reason to think, as did readers of the time, that this was a purposive, directed, unstoppable, relentless man driven by forces even he did not understand. Again, a supremely external view.

Cinema, for all its possible proximities, is endless distance. It never really takes us in but only shows what something looks like. Yet, with all Mann's contrivances, we seem nevertheless to approach this figure, to achieve an *intimate distance,* contradiction, and truth. In the final sequence, our own observing heads, gawking in the theater, are linked with Dillinger's. We "put our heads together."

Seen in detail, the film's end is all head shots. Dillinger is bespectacled in his trance with *Manhattan Melodrama* (a story of his life). Purvis is on the street, in his white fedora, sweating, gazing, waiting, anxious, worried Dillinger went to another theater, worried his agents will mess things up. The agents outside, hiding, twitching, one by one dully focused and hopelessly purposed on a project beyond their means. Now on the street, as celli, trombones, double basses intone a molto lento dirge, Dillinger, having left the theater, is moving forward in and out of light, commercial light, neon, a jaunty boater on his head, his lips grim. Now, dogging his footsteps, we see the back of his head, the complete locus of agency but without the mystifying expression of the face. He turns and glares directly at us watching—in fact, the camera sweeping into his face. This is, at once, Dillinger knowing that his time is up, that the hounds are here, and Depp confronting his international audience, who can never get enough of his heady self. Cold brown eyes, reflection in his eyeglass lenses, the pencil moustache enunciating and at the same time annihilating Depp's presence as animator of all this. Then the head and hatefully frowning face of his executioner, sharp lips pursed, gun aimed at the supreme target. The kill shots. And for some inexplicable reason, Mann offers a third shot, one that emerges near Dillinger's heart. The man is down now, his head filling the screen, his face little more than a riverbed for the gushing stream that is emerging from his cheek, his eyes and mouth are open, receptive, mute in death or near death. A tiny authorial gesture: the camera moves slightly to reframe, but with a *handheld* jiggle, as if to sign the film. A reaction shot of Purvis, head and shoulders, catching his breath with eyes agog and the banner "ICED FRESH AIR" behind him. Back to Dillinger, who is whispering under gravity.

"We have discarded the classical herm," writes Davenport, "a bust on a shaft where genitalia were included as integral to the person. We accept the full body in sculpture, or the bust." But the detached head is "symbol of what we think we are or what we're up to" (Johnny Depp's genitalia are *never* included as integral to his person).[41] Dillinger's killer takes his hat off, kneels down. Macroclose shot of Depp's mouth and nose, blood streaming down. But the head of the killer, blond, pink-faced, pale blue eyes staring coldly down at the ground, now obtrudes from above and takes over the shot. Whatever the inmost privacy Dillinger in his final breath expresses, it becomes fully a part of this feelingless soldier's personal file.

"What'd he say?" asks Purvis.

"I couldn't hear," the agent lies. And now he goes to the jail to confront Dillinger's girl and give her the lover's last words, if they really are that, if he really is passing along the spirit of the dead instead of lying once again, to keep it buried for himself, germ perhaps of a new inner life that is here conceived and will someday take an unprecedented form.

Notes

1. Tom Gunning, "The Exterior as Intérieur: Benjamin's Optical Detective," *boundary 2* 30, no. 1 (2003): 105–30.

2. Athan G. Theoharis, *The FBI & American Democracy: A Brief Critical History* (Lawrence: University Press of Kansas, 2004), 39–40.

3. "Dillinger's Nemesis a Small-Town Boy," *New York Times*, July 24, 1934.

4. Theoharis, *The FBI & American Democracy*, 55–56, 73.

5. William Hollingsworth Whyte, *The Organization Man* (New York: Simon and Schuster, 1956).

6. Quoted in an untitled article, *New York Times*, July 23, 1934.

7. Erving Goffman, *Relations in Public: Microstudies of the Public Order* (New York: Basic Books, 1971).

8. Earl Dittman, "The Johnny Depp Interview: On Dillinger, Mad Hatter, & Capt Jack," *Top—Digital Journal*, http://www.digitaljournal.com/article/275336, accessed June 8, 2010.

9. Murray Pomerance, *Johnny Depp Starts Here* (New Brunswick, NJ: Rutgers University Press, 2005).

10. Walter Benjamin and Rolf Tiedemann, *The Arcades Project*, trans. Howard Eiland and Kevin McLaughlin (Cambridge, MA: Harvard University Press, 1999), 420.

11. Ibid., 204.

12. Ibid.

13. Rhodri Jeffreys-Jones, *The FBI: A History* (New Haven, CT: Yale University Press, 2007), 90.

14. William J. Helmer, *The Gun That Made the Twenties Roar* (New York: Macmillan, 1969), 77; John Ellis, *The Social History of the Machine Gun* (New York: Pantheon Books, 1975), 151.

15. Benjamin and Tiedemann, *The Arcades Project*, 220.

16. Benjamin and Tiedemann, *The Arcades Project*, 225, citing Régis Messac, *Le "detective novel" et l'infuence de la pensée scientifique* (Paris: Champion, 1929), 461, which cites Balzac.

17. Tom Gunning, "Tracing the Individual Body: Photography, Detectives, and Early Cinema," in *Cinema and the Invention of Modern Life*, ed. Leo Charney and Vanessa R. Schwartz (Berkeley: University of California Press, 1995), 15–45.

18. Guy Davenport, *Objects on a Table: Harmonious Disarray in Art and Literature* (Washington, DC: Counterpoint, 1998), 47.

19. "Dillinger Raids Bank in South Bend, Ind., Reported Shot; Officer Slain, Loot $28,000," *New York Times*, July 1, 1934.

20. "Dillinger Shot as Gang Kills One, Wounds 4 in Holdup," *Washington Post*, July 1, 1934.

21. "Reports Dillinger Crippled by Injury," *New York Times*, July 5, 1934.

22. "Midwest Continues Hunt," *New York Times,* July 3, 1934.

23. "Dillinger and Pair Sighted in Indiana," *Washington Post,* July 4, 1934.

24. "Dillinger Is 'Seen' in Massachusetts," *Washington Post,* July 8, 1934.

25. "Dillinger Hunted near Fond Du Lac," *New York Times,* July 10, 1934.

26. "Dillinger Reward $15,000," *New York Times,* July 23, 1934.

27. "Slaying Detailed by Federal Chief," *New York Times,* July 23, 1934.

28. Quoted in "Dillinger Slain in Chicago; Shot Dead by Federal Men in Front of Movie Theatre," *New York Times,* July 23, 1934.

29. "Outlaw Blurred Tips of Fingers," *New York Times,* July 23, 1934.

30. "Cummings Says Slaying of Dillinger Is 'Gratifying as Well as Reassuring,'" *New York Times,* July 23, 1934.

31. "Crime and Punishment," *New York Times,* July 24, 1934.

32. Howard Saul Becker, "Introduction," in *The Other Side: Perspectives on Deviance,* ed. Howard Saul Becker (New York: Free Press, 1964), 5.

33. "Saw Outlaw Shot and Drop in Alley," *New York Times,* July 23, 1934.

34. David Edelberg, in discussion with the author, July 5, 2010.

35. Douglas Gomery and David Bordwell, *Shared Pleasures: A History of Movie Presentation in the United States* (Madison: University of Wisconsin Press, 1992), 54.

36. Ellis, *The Social History of the Machine Gun,* 155.

37. John Kobler, *Capone* (London: Coronet, 1973), 91, quoted in Ellis, *The Social History of the Machine Gun,* 152.

38. "Captor of Dillinger Visits Police Here," *New York Times,* July 1, 1934.

39. "Dillinger Forecast End as a Way He Wanted to Go," *New York Times,* July 24, 1934.

40. "Slaying Detailed by Federal Chief," *New York Times,* July 23, 1934.

41. Davenport, *Objects on a Table,* 50.

Works Consulted

Becker, Howard Saul, ed. *The Other Side: Perspectives on Deviance.* New York: Free Press, 1964.

Benjamin, Walter, and Rolf Tiedemann. *The Arcades Project.* Translated by Howard Eiland and Kevin McLaughlin. Cambridge, MA: Harvard University Press, 1999.

"Captor of Dillinger Visits Police Here." *New York Times,* July 1, 1934.

"Crime and Punishment." *New York Times,* July 24, 1934.

"Cummings Says Slaying of Dillinger Is 'Gratifying as Well as Reassuring.'" *New York Times,* July 23, 1934.

Davenport, Guy. *Objects on a Table: Harmonious Disarray in Art and Literature.* Washington DC: Counterpoint, 1998.

"Dillinger and Pair Sighted in Indiana." *Washington Post,* July 4, 1934.

"Dillinger Caught on Fireman's Tip." *New York Times,* January 26, 1934.

"Dillinger Forecast End as a Way He Wanted to Go." *New York Times,* July 24, 1934.

"Dillinger Hunted Near Fond Du Lac." *New York Times,* July 10, 1934.

"Dillinger Is 'Seen' in Massachusetts." *Washington Post,* July 8, 1934.

"Dillinger Is Surrounded in a Forest in Wisconsin; National Guard Called." *New York Times,* April 23, 1934.

"Dillinger Raids Bank in South Bend, Ind., Reported Shot; Officer Slain, Loot $28,000." *New York Times,* July 1, 1934.

"Dillinger Reward $15,000." *New York Times,* July 23, 1934.

"Dillinger Shot as Gang Kills One, Wounds 4 in Holdup." *Washington Post,* July 1, 1934.

"Dillinger Slain in Chicago; Shot Dead by Federal Men in Front of Movie Theatre." *New York Times,* July 23, 1934.

"Dillinger Victim's Pals Gave Tip for Capture." *New York Times,* July 23, 1934.

"Dillinger's Nemesis a Small-Town Boy." *New York Times,* July 24, 1934.

Dittman, Earl. "The Johnny Depp Interview: On Dillinger, Mad Hatter, & Capt Jack." *Top—Digital Journal,* http://www.digitaljournal.com/article/275336. Accessed June 8, 2010.

Ellis, John. *The Social History of the Machine Gun.* New York: Pantheon Books, 1975.

Goffman, Erving. *Relations in Public: Microstudies of the Public Order.* New York: Basic Books, 1971.

Gomery, Douglas, and David Bordwell. *Shared Pleasures: A History of Movie Presentation in the United States.* Madison: University of Wisconsin Press, 1992.

Gunning, Tom. "The Exterior as Intérieur: Benjamin's Optical Detective." *boundary 2* 30, no. 1 (2003): 105–30.

———. "Tracing the Individual Body: Photography, Detectives, and Early Cinema." In *Cinema and the Invention of Modern Life,* ed. Leo Charney and Vanessa R. Schwartz, 15–45. Berkeley: University of California Press, 1995.

Helmer, William J. *The Gun That Made the Twenties Roar.* New York: Macmillan, 1969.

Jeffreys-Jones, Rhodri. *The FBI: A History.* New Haven, CT: Yale University Press, 2007.

Kobler, John. *Capone.* London: Coronet, 1973.

Messac, Régis. *Le "detective novel" et l'infuence de la pensée scientifique.* Paris: H. Champion, 1929.

"Midwest Continues Hunt." *New York Times,* July 3, 1934.

"Outlaw Blurred Tips of Fingers." *New York Times,* July 23, 1934.

Pomerance, Murray. *Johnny Depp Starts Here.* New Brunswick, NJ: Rutgers University Press, 2005.

"Reports Dillinger Crippled by Injury." *New York Times,* July 5, 1934.

"Saw Outlaw Shot and Drop in Alley." *New York Times,* July 23, 1934.

"Slaying Detailed by Federal Chief." *New York Times,* July 23, 1934.

Theoharis, Athan G. *The FBI & American Democracy: A Brief Critical History.* Lawrence: University Press of Kansas, 2004.

Whyte, William Hollingsworth. *The Organization Man.* New York: Simon and Schuster, 1956.

Mannerism

Neoclassical Style in the Films of Michael Mann

Tom Paulus and Vito Adriaensens

In *The Cinema Effect,* Sean Cubitt discusses what he calls the "neoclassical film" of the postwar period as being characterized by the "spatialization of time." This spatialization is achieved through cinematic techniques such as the freeze frame, slow motion, and camera movement. The latter, especially the Steadicam variety, is typical of a "Hollywood baroque," in which "both narrative and stylistics have been subordinated to the exploration of the world of the film."[1] In the Hollywood baroque, film has become a medium of movement instead of a time-based medium, replacing a focus on the exposure of story with an exploration of time as raw material. Essentially, Cubitt is saying nothing new here. In 1934, Erwin Panofsky had already remarked that cinema's dynamic elements—such as a moving camera, slow and fast motion, and the use of extreme lenses—can be defined as a "dynamization of space and, accordingly, spatialization of time"; Panofsky even called this insight "self-evident to the point of triviality."[2] More important here, however, is the relationship that is established between neoclassical cinema and a renewal of the aesthetics of the baroque. The conception of a cinematic (neo)baroque was first given critical currency by Angela Ndalianis, who in her influential book *Neo-baroque Aesthetics and Contemporary Entertainment* identifies neobaroque aesthetics with the immersive nature of new effect-ridden cinematic spectacle, which engulfs the audience in cinematic displays in ways recalling the scopic regimes of the seventeenth-century baroque spectacle of trompe l'oeil.[3] The dynamic compositional arrangements of the neobaroque open up the frame, Ndalianis argues, decentering the classically ordered space of perspectival optics. Rendered in more distinctly cinematic terms, this means that instead of the self-effacing realism, or "invisible" style, identified with classical Hollywood, we get the open

system of seemingly infinitely mobile tracking and zooming shots of contemporary effects cinema. Cultural theorist Scott Bukatman has called this
mélange of delirium, immersion, and kinesis "kaleidoscopic perception."[4]
As an immersive, borderless spectacle, neobaroque cinema grounds its narration in simplistic Manichaean scenarios that are then elaborated through
a similar amplification of narrational technique. Neobaroque narratives are
networked and essentially serial in that they are both fragmentary and open
to sequels or elaboration in subsidiary media.[5]

In a recent essay, Cubitt revisits the idea of a cinematic neobaroque
as a spatial aesthetic, tying it closer to post-structuralist conceptions and
postmodernism in general by focusing on its "proliferation of signs." He
also stresses the grotesque, irrational, and occult elements in the baroque
to discuss the new Hollywood supernatural thriller. At the same time, he
takes as a central question, albeit timidly, the newness of the form: How different is contemporary Hollywood cinema from cinematic classicism? With
Ndalianis, he argues that the (neo)baroque should not be seen in binary
opposition to classicism, but as the result of a cultural dynamics whose
histories are braided together.[6] This position resonates with that taken by
David Bordwell, who, coming from a film historical angle, argues that the
contemporary Hollywood cinema, far from being postclassical, differs from
its classical variant only in degree: "Far from rejecting traditional continuity
in the name of fragmentation and incoherence, the new style amounts to an
intensification of established techniques. Intensified continuity is traditional
continuity amped up, raised to a higher pitch of emphasis." The four dimensions of such "intensified continuity" that Bordwell identifies are decreased
shot length, decreased shot scale, bipolar extremes of lens lengths, and the
constantly prowling camera. Although this style did not "crystallize all at
once, the 1960s mark a crucial transition."[7] Cubitt similarly situates "neoclassical cinema" and the return of baroque elements in the New American
cinema of the late 1960s and 1970s. The first neoclassical film he discusses
in *The Cinema Effect* is Sam Peckinpah's *The Wild Bunch* (1969), a movie
typified by rapid editing, crash-zoom effects, and slow-motion violence.
Most of the contemporary Hollywood movies he treats under the rubric
of the neobaroque are related explicitly to the New Hollywood cinema of
De Palma, Scorsese, Altman, Lucas, Spielberg, and Coppola. He cites the
latter's *Apocalypse Now* (1979) next to *The Matrix* (1999, Andy Wachowski
and Lana Wachowski) and *Casino* (1995, Martin Scorsese) as a primary
instance of "near-Zen metaphysics built on the emptiness of the commod-

ity."[8] Like much of Cubitt's writing, this sounds like Jean Baudrillard, who famously attributed to *Apocalypse Now*—a film he called "a technological and psychedelic fantasy, the war as a succession of special effects"—the "same immoderation, the same excess of means" with which Americans wage war.[9] As a thoroughly baroque movie, *Apocalypse Now* certainly displays many characteristics of neobaroque aesthetics cited by Cubitt, tying "staggering, awe-inspiring spectacle" to "conspicuous waste."[10] Narratively, Coppola's movie is both fragmentary (Serge Daney compares its structure to the succession of numbers in a musical[11]) and serial—an unfinished film, it was later restored to its original form by making it shorter than the release version. *Apocalypse Now* is Michael Mann's favorite film; he placed it at the top in the 2002 *Sight and Sound* poll of the greatest films ever made; other movies in Mann's top ten include Peckinpah's *The Wild Bunch* and Scorsese's *Raging Bull* (1980).[12]

Mannered and Mannerism

David Bordwell's perspective on Michael Mann, a filmmaker he has praised for handling the schemas of intensified continuity in imaginative ways,[13] is that his most recent films, especially his most ambitious foray into digital shooting, *Public Enemies* (2009), have become belabored: "Investing wholly in a new look, he belabors even the simplest action through staccato cutting; getting people in and out of cars should not take such effort. Action scenes occasionally succumb to the jittery camera."[14] Accelerating cutting rates, prowling or shaking handheld camerawork, and the loss of spatial unity and action continuity are what Bordwell finds regrettable about the "intensification" of classical strategies of visual storytelling. Such conspicuously "stylish style," he suggests, may have distracted talented filmmakers such as Mann from their basic craft. Throughout his writings on intensified continuity, Bordwell has been quite critical of its most showy contemporary applications, speaking out against movies that have generally been celebrated for their technical flamboyancy and innovation, such as the *Bourne* movies directed by Paul Greengrass[15] and Scorsese's *The Departed* (2006). What bothers Bordwell most about these films and about Mann's recent efforts is their application of outré technique and their self-conscious flourishes and overt narration. When he calls Mann's cinema "belabored," he is using a synonym for a term he employs more regularly to describe this type of hyper- or supercinema: *mannered*. In fact, he makes explicit the parallel to mannerism in Italian painting of the sixteenth century, preferring *maniera* as a description of contemporary Hollywood aesthetics over the much more fashionable *neobaroque* and quoting several authorities on mannerism in art, such as Werner Weisbach ("Mannerism exists when forms that originally had a precise meaning and expressive value are taken over and carried to extremes, so that they appear affected, artificial, empty, degenerate"), Heinrich Wölfflin ("It wants to carry us away with the force of its impact, immediate and overwhelming; it gives us not a generally enhanced vitality, but excitement, ecstasy, intoxication"), and Arnold Hauser ("A completely self-conscious style, which bases its forms not so much on the particular object as on the art of the preceding epoch").[16] What is striking about these quotations, save perhaps the one from Hauser, is the sense of disparagement that is attached to the term *mannerism,* a disparagement Bordwell appears to share. But perhaps Bordwell's conclusion that the substantive analogy between mannerism and intensified continuity probably shouldn't be taken too strictly was inspired by the sense that "mannered" and "mannerist" do not always mean the same thing.[17] As Hauser points out, "Mannerism belongs to the terminology of the art historian and defines a type; the mannered is a matter of aesthetic judgment, i.e., is part of the terminology of the critic. Admittedly there is a considerable area of overlap, but there is no necessary connection between the two. There is certainly a tendency in mannerist artists towards a mannered way of expression, but there is no compulsion in them to sacrifice their individuality to a formula and to appear forced and bizarre."[18]

So the first question we need to raise is to what extent Mann's variation on intensified continuity is "mannered" and to what extent he is "mannerist." Before we do this, however, we need to make sure that we are clear on Bordwell's aesthetic position. Although he regrets a loss of basic craft in today's filmmakers and mourns the apparent loss of certain resources of classical filmmaking, such as ensemble staging, he does not characterize intensified continuity as anticlassical per se. This is where his argument comes in that intensified continuity is not a rupture with tradition, but a heightening of traditional means to engage the viewer's attention and involvement. It is not a break with the normative, but an elaboration or a variant upon it, and it is there that we find what is perhaps the most distinct area of overlap with the most inspiring art historical engagements concerning mannerism, such as that by Hauser, who suggests that a "proper understanding of mannerism can be obtained only if it is regarded as the product of tension between classicism and anti-classicism, naturalism and formalism . . . traditionalism and innovation, conventionalism and revolt against conformism."[19] We can also distinguish ourselves here from the conceptions of neobaroque, in which, despite a more nuanced engagement with Bordwell's ideas on classicism, a more dramatic break seems to be assumed than the one posited by either Hauser or Bordwell.

Michael Mann has almost always persisted in underplaying, if not wholly negating, the presence of a prominent visual flair in favor of what he describes as a form of realism. It is this paradox that is at the core of his work. An exemplary anecdote comes from the shooting of the film *Heat* (1995), in which Mann and his cinematographer Dante Spinotti opted to shoot the iconic scene on the terrace between Neil McCauley (Robert De Niro) and Eady (Amy Brenneman) against a green screen so that they could later add the nighttime cityscape and still retain perfect sharpness on both planes of action. One would imagine that, for all intents and purposes, this scene would be shot in the studio, but with a peculiar sense of authenticity Mann insisted that the green screen be set up at the actual location.[20] Nick James similarly points out that "of all the ambivalences that make *Heat* such a high-wire act, none is more extreme than the contrast between Mann's desire for a hard factual basis to his films and the gleaming, hyper-real end result."[21]

James's use of the terms *gleaming* and *hyperreal* could hardly be more apt to describe the visual dynamics of a Michael Mann film, but what exactly are the elements that make up the glossy finish of a heightened form of aesthetics that Bordwell likes to label "stylish style," and how do these elements evolve in Mann's work? In *Thief* (1981), the hosed-down city streets of nocturnal Chicago catch the reflections of the bright streetlights to the sound of Tangerine Dream synths. The film is a sleek product of its time and follows the line set out by director William Friedkin, who debuted Tangerine Dream to great effect in *Sorcerer* (1977) and whose *The French Connection* (1971) provides a grittier and less processed predecessor to Mann's crime gem, which in turn preludes *Heat* (1995), *Collateral* (2004), and *Miami Vice* (2006). Like Friedkin, Mann uses many long-lensed shots and invests in a daytime look that has the overexposed feel of natural lighting. Stylized slow motion, nightly neo-noir color and lighting schemes, and a steady camera, fueled by an emotional soundtrack, make all the difference, however, in what Mann himself dubbed "a very stylized street movie (that is) nevertheless stylized realism."[22] Mann's "stylized realism" is another's neobaroque, and we see from the start of Mann's career how his style adheres closely to

Cubitt's qualification of neobaroque aesthetics as grounded in a spatialization of time.

Mann seemed to venture further into neobaroque aesthetics, more specifically its introduction of the occult in the immanent and paganism,[23] with his 1983 horror film *The Keep*. The *Chicagoan* described the film as "very dreamy, very magical, and intensely emotional."[24] Tangerine Dream was once more enlisted to provide the emotional underscoring, and Mann made the fog machine work overtime and manipulated the audience with a mostly low-key aesthetic in which the titular keep is penetrated by foggy shafts of light and presented to us by slowly roving dolly shots in an updated wide-screen format. Fashionable slow motion, abundant lens flare, tight compositions, high-key daytime exteriors, long lenses, varied low- and high-angle shots, and a freeze-frame tableau ending further heighten the spectator's experience of the Nazi-invaded village and its occult keep. Mann is always intent on actively and aggressively seducing the audience and wants to manipulate feelings "for the same reasons that composers write symphonies."[25] In favor of carefully thought-out compositions, *The Keep* does not show a clear predominance of close shots or rapid editing. In accordance with Bordwell's concept of intensified continuity, it does, however, contain extreme differences in focal lens length—with Mann's eternal proclivity for the long lens—and lots of engaging camera movements. Interestingly, one can take Mann's oeuvre and watch it evolve right alongside Bordwell's concept. In his films, Mann thus decreases both shot length and scale while at the same time emphasizing loose camera movement, extreme lens lengths, and, above all, color and lighting.

Mann objects to equating his aggressive seduction of the audience with style, however, for when Gavin Smith told him that his "hijacking [of] the viewer's nervous system so completely that it becomes . . . emotionally overwhelming" boils down to stylistic choices on the part of the filmmaker, Mann protested: "It's not style . . . it's the intensity of the experience, the power of film to make you dream. . . . Style gets you seven minutes of attention, that's it."[26] The director's apparent fear of being perceived as a mere formalist goes hand in hand with his ongoing emphasis on diligent preparation that is meant to inject his narrative with a sense of believability or truth, but as Christopher Sharrett rightly notes, Mann's "sense of the world is manifest precisely in the realisation of style."[27] In Michael Mann's next film after *The Keep, Manhunter* (1986), the hostile and twisted reality that is inhabited by both serial killer Francis Dollarhyde (Tom Noonan) and detective Will Graham (William Petersen) comes at us straight away in the form of a fluorescent green opening title. Their realm is shaped by the use of outlandish and unnatural color patterns and filters; acute low-angle, short-lensed shots that distort the image; long-lensed shots that severely flatten the image; ruminative tableau vivant compositions that result in a final freeze frame; dreamlike slow motion and special effects to approximate the inner workings of their minds; and impeccable Steadicam and dolly shots that ooze an eerie sense of calculated calm. Tangerine Dream's musical reveries have given way to an equally ominous soundscape by Michel Rubini. Mann legitimizes the film's outlandish visual nature by striving for an expressionist reading that is meant to connect with the characters' intellectual and emotional world.[28]

In stark contrast to *Manhunter* stands Mann's adaptation of the James Fenimore Cooper classic *The Last of the Mohicans* (1992). After directing *Manhunter* and producing the television series *Miami Vice* (1984–1989), Mann had suffered some critical backlash accusing him of being "mannered." *New York Times* critic Walter Goodman pointed toward a "taste for overkill" that pulls attention "away from the story to the odd camera angles, the fancy lighting, the crashing music," and Richard Combs, writing for the *Monthly Film Bulletin,* called Mann out on glossing his subject matter to the extent of making it "more resonant at the surface than it can ever be underneath."[29] This critique pushed Mann into eschewing the style debate and investing heavily in a discourse centered on real-life details; he stated that he is not a stylist because "style is simply gratuitous form with no content."[30] As Sharrett has hinted, however, the irony is that Mann's heightened attention to detail contributes to the work's classification as mannerist. A rather conservative adaptation of the Cooper classic *The Last of the Mohicans* therefore seemed to be the perfect response to these accusations. Disregarding the dynamic Steadicam shots following Hawkeye (Daniel Day-Lewis) through the forest, *Mohicans* is moderately classical in style, especially given the fact that Mann obsessively pursued historical detail. The director and his cinematographer Dante Spinotti chose to preserve the natural beauty of the wilderness in *Mohicans* by keeping the landscapes modest, using "broad strokes of light."[31] It would not be the last time that Mann banked on adaptation, either, for *Heat, The Insider* (1999), *Ali* (2001), and *Public Enemies* all capitalize on being mired in "real life."

It has been made clear that Mann's wedding of form and content would hardly qualify as documentary realism by any touchstone. Mann has always been adamant, however, about pursuing psychological character design in order to establish a believable diegetic environment. From *Heat* onward, the intensity of the protagonists that inhabit his universe is brought about increasingly by an emphasis on faster cutting, tight close-ups, long lenses, and a highly expressive use of both color and lighting. Character, in other words, becomes effect. In *Heat,* tightly compressed long-lens shots force the characters to interact closely with both each other and the Los Angeles cityscape. Mann's use of digital compositing and color grading was key in achieving the almost abstract nature of both minutely composed close shots and contemplative tableaux vivants.[32] Cinematographer Dante Spinotti described the calculated accuracy of the visual process as "being in front of a Caravaggio scene and changing it into a Kandinsky painting."[33] Spinotti similarly shaped the desaturated world of whistleblower Jeffrey Wigand (Russell Crowe) in *The Insider,* where bright shafts of light serve to overexpose and invade the protagonist's private life, but also to shroud him in shadows to stress his alienation. Ben McCann succinctly states that Mann and Spinotti's gorgeous character representation presents the audience with "detached . . . professionals who move through beautifully composed environments."[34]

So too did Mann set out to make his take on boxing legend *Ali* both authentic and contemporary. Cinematographer Emmanuel Lubezki explained that *Ali* was shot with multiple cameras and is "99 percent Steadicam and handheld work" to give it a sense of spontaneity.[35] The roaming cameras and long-lens shots that compress several planes of action into densely readable shots are combined with a heavy reliance on overexposure—light generally pours through every available window—and color grading that, in spite of Lubezki and Mann's best intentions, does serve to add a nostalgic period feel. Furthermore, Mann's first foray into the world of high definition betrays that he's a stickler for aesthetics; despite the textural noise that accompanied this stylistic rupture, Mann and Lubezki decided to integrate the footage into the film because, as Lubezki put it, "sometimes you have to accept anomalies like noise in order to get a beautiful image."[36] Almost all the aforementioned stylistic traits support Bordwell's understanding of intensified continuity and at times serve as an excellent example of how a variety of amplified options can serve the narrative in a refreshingly interesting way. Bordwell's beef with contemporary stylistic strategies, however, lies with directors who revel in an amplified display of technique that functions both to highlight plot points of an otherwise uninspired narrative and to complicate actions that do not need complication.[37]

Collateral is perhaps one of Mann's most restrained exercises, both at the level of narrative construction and characterization and in terms of visual style. The straightforward narrative that unfurls between hit man Vincent (Tom Cruise) and taxi driver Max (Jamie Foxx) against the nighttime backdrop of Los Angeles is set in a low-key environment that is dominated by cold blue, green, and gray hues—only at times offset by the warm yellows and oranges of streetlights—that emphasize Vincent's cold professionalism and denote the impending sense of doom that pervades the atmosphere.[38] The film switches between long-lens close-ups and extreme close-ups of the two main characters, on the one hand, and long shots of the sprawling city, on the other, but is not excessively fast cut. Steady dolly movement and slow pans and tilts guide us through the protagonists' dangerous world once we leave the car. As a counterpoint to *Collateral,* it seems, Mann next helmed a no-holds-barred action film by reimagining *Miami Vice* for the big screen. The film is as fast cut as they come, packed with almost nothing but intense medium close-ups and close-ups, frantic handheld camera work, and a hard, low-key, high-contrast aesthetic that clashes with the soft, controlled feel of *Collateral.*[39] The frenetic editing of *Vice* causes normal actions to become complicated and action sequences to lose a sense of unity through overlapping shots and handheld camera work. As such, one might perceive *Vice* as belabored or mannered in a way that distracts the viewer from basic narrative comprehension.

Underlying Mann's turn to digital shooting from *Ali* on are two basic contradictions, the second following from the first. Chroniclers of postclassical cinema such as Sean Cubitt see digital effects, cinematography, and editing as introducing a new viewer–spectacle relationship. Borrowing from Jay David Bolter and Richard Grusin's conception of "hypermediacy," and realigning postcinema with a preclassical "cinema of attractions,"[40] Cubitt argues that postcinema's primary delight lies in the illusory perception of illusion. That is to say, it lies in the illusion of a world beyond the medium, an illusion that at the same time turns back to its mediation: "The spectator has a double vision, pleased to be connoisseurs of effects and their generation, but equally delighted to be suckers for the duration, enjoying both spectacular technique and the spectacle itself, illusion and the machinery of illusion."[41] In Mann's case, digital cinema is not employed primarily to spectacular ends, but, again, as a means toward the enhancement of reality. We will not, for now, develop the implications of this conception but merely point to the incongruent nature of Mann's association between the digital and realist aesthetic from the point of view of Cubitt's theorization of the hyperreal. On the one hand, at first glance Mann's "naturalism" seems to belie the characterization of his cinema as mannerist in the sense that the mannerist revolution in art lay in the fact that, for the first time, art deliberately diverged from nature.[42] On the other hand, Mann's self-conscious display of effect can be seen as part of the stylistic standard associated with mannerism. Again, we find ourselves confronted with the conception of mannerism as the tension or union between apparently irreconcilable opposites.[43] In fact, the very idea of a stylistic standard against which the artist positions him- or herself is a mannerist conception. Hauser explains that whereas artists had previously not been conscious of the stylistic trend of their period, with mannerism style became a program and therefore problematical. It is at this juncture that the phenomenon of historicism made its entrance with Giorgio Vasari and Karel Van Mander, both mannerists. Similarly, intensified continuity was developed during the postwar period, when eminent French historians such as Georges Sadoul wrote canonical versions of film history, and the availability of classic cinema—through film archives and later through television—had never been greater. This availability created a greater degree of self-consciousness among filmmakers and their audiences, who were increasingly trained in picking up on references to a shared pool of media knowledge.[44]

The self-consciousness and allusionism of today's filmmakers and their sense of "belatedness"—that is, the sense that they compete not only with their contemporaries, but also with their predecessors—is perhaps what is most striking about the contemporary Hollywood cinema as Bordwell sees it.[45] Again, the "belated" nature of the contemporary response to classical achievements should not necessarily be cause for negative aesthetic judgment. Bordwell points to several filmmakers who have sought to sustain tradition in refreshing ways, extending and refining its premises while at the same time explicitly alluding to it. Mann is one of these filmmakers, singled out for his innovation of the norms, but what Bordwell finds striking about Mann is the apparent lack of allusionism in his cinema: "It's surprising when *Heat* includes no citations of the classics; Michael Mann acts as if no other crime movie had ever been made."[46] In a later assessment, Bordwell upgrades surprise to praise: "One thing I admire about *Heat* is that it acts as if no other gangster movie has ever been made. Its scenes offer plenty of opportunities for cute citations of old crime movies, especially when Vincent . . . catches his wife's lover watching TV. Instead, Mann treats the material as cut off from cinema, and this saves him from the coyness of so much genre work today."[47] One of the main problems of *Public Enemies* for Bordwell is that it engages in allusionism of the feeblest sort, as when Dillinger watches *Manhattan Melodrama* (1934) and smiles in fascination when Clark Gable says, "Die the way you lived—all of a sudden." Where Bordwell considers the lack of allusionism as a refreshing case of genre purism in the context of an original updating of cinematic classicism, Mann himself sees it as the logical result of his realist aesthetics. In a recent book on Mann's films, the writer F. X. Feeney discusses Mann's reaction to an earlier version of the book's manuscript:

> An earlier version of this book completed by another writer attempted (in a spirit of sincere praise) to treat Mann's films as reactions against film traditions, as subversions of genre. This fetched a rebuke from Mann: "It's irrelevant and neither accurate nor authentic to compare my films to other films because they don't proceed from genre conventions and then deviate from those conventions. They proceed from *life*. For better or worse, what I've seen and heard and learned on my own is the origin of this material. Maybe the film medium by nature spawns conventions, because we all build on what's gone before, but the content and themes of my films are not facile and derivative. They are drawn from life experience."[48]

Bordwell admits to being puzzled by Mann's reasoning: "He insists that his films can't be compared to others along any dimensions, especially thematic ones. Yet in saying that his films are lifelike, he suggests that other films aren't as realistic as his. Moreover, what about comparisons on grounds of technique, surely one of the most striking and admired features of Mann's work? For reasons that are obscure, the director discourages any critical consideration of style; Feeney tells us that Mann hates the very word."[49] Mann's rejection of the very word *style* can be interpreted as a symptomatic reaction of the belated filmmaker bent on authenticity and originality to the perception of his work as lacking in those qualities. The framework in which Mann is working is that of modernism, alternately formalist or realist. In fact, the harshest criticism of Mann's movies would be that they are unexceptional and ordinary, that they do not renew or even intensify, but are just another manifestation of recognizable conventions. "The worst thing I can say about *Public Enemies*," writes Bordwell, "is that it risks becoming academic."[50]

In fact, Bordwell's accusation of Mann's final academicism and Mann's own conception of his cinema as sui generis are anything but irreconcilable, especially within the semantic field of mannerism. Both mannerism and academicism are dialectical in that they incorporate innovation into tradition and tradition into innovation, respectively. The dialectics between tradition and innovation, as Arnold Hauser has made clear, is but one among many such principles in mannerism, including the dialogue between idealism and realism/naturalism as well as the dynamic between disruption of form and harmonic composition: "A completely satisfactory description of the style would . . . emphasise the tension between conflicting stylistic elements[,] which finds its purest and most striking expression in paradox."[51]

How, then, can we think through Mann's cinema as expressive of paradox without considering it the passive embodiment of a period of transition, representational crisis, that resumes the most elementary alignments of mannerism with postmodernism? Indeed, why adopt mannerism as a means to a better understanding of Mann's cinema if all we mean by it is the neobaroque embrace of Hegelianism?[52] In his discussion of Gilles Deleuze's work on the baroque, Dutch philosopher Sjoerd Van Tuinen has given us a clear way to distinguish the neobaroque from mannerism as stylistic tropes expressive of the "break" or "crisis" of our historical moment. The baroque, says Van Tuinen, is defined by its social and religious function, whereas mannerism constitutes the baroque's aesthetic potential.[53] The social and religious function of the baroque is, perhaps paradoxically, conservative: to restore the spiritual and material crisis of the Renaissance, thus becoming, as Deleuze puts it, a "schizophrenic reconstruction of a regime of form and spirituality on another stage."[54] This certainly tracks with John Beverley's reading of the Spanish baroque as the response to a crisis of power, denying classicism in favor of a return to authority and discipline as grounded in spectacle. At the same time, Beverley stresses that besides being a technique of power of a dominant class, the baroque also figured the limits of that power.[55] Both functions, argues Sean Cubitt, appear in the turn toward the transcendental and the sublime and in the sublime's appeal to self-loss: "For the neo-baroque sublime to conquer, it must sublimate the sense of self. . . . The new world needs to be utterly absorbing."[56] This is where Cubitt, resuming a logic borrowed from Fredric Jameson, situates the spatial turn of contemporary cinema in its immersive qualities. Bordwell, in contrast, sees a much more active role for both the viewer and the filmmaker:

> The new style suggests that we can't adequately describe the viewer's activity with spatial metaphors like "absorption" and "detachment."

At any moment, stylistic tactics may come forward, but viewers will remain in the grip of the action. The mannerism of today's cinema would seem to ask its spectators to take a high degree of narrational overtness for granted, to let a few familiar devices amplify each point, to revel in still more flamboyant displays of technique—all the while surrendering to the story's expressive undertow. It would not be the first time that audiences have been asked to enjoy overt play with form without sacrificing depth of emotional appeal. Baroque music and Rococo architecture come to mind, as does the cinematic oeuvre of Yasujirô Ozu and Kenji Mizoguchi. The triumph of intensified continuity reminds us that as styles change, so do viewing skills.[57]

Where Cubitt comes to a diagnosis of the contemporary media space, Bordwell refers to its aesthetic function, preferring the term *mannerism* to *baroque.* Van Tuinen, with Deleuze, goes one better, assigning to cinema the potential to free sensibility from a "televised and informatized economy of representation."[58] For this purpose, he turns to Deleuze's open letter to French film critic Serge Daney, published in *Ciné Journal* in 1986, just after the publication of Deleuze's two volumes on the cinema, *Cinéma 1: L'image-mouvement* (1983) and *Cinéma 2: L'image-temps* (1985).

In the letter, Deleuze congratulates Daney for having developed the concept of mannerism. Daney first developed his concept of mannerism in his review of *One from the Heart* (1982), the "small" movie Coppola made following the baroque spectacle of *Apocalypse Now.*[59] *One from the Heart* is a love story set in Las Vegas, the locus classicus of postmodern visual culture and subject of Robert Venturi and Denise Brown's seminal *Learning from Las Vegas* (1977). Venturi and Brown later turned to a conception of our times and its architecture as mannerist precisely because of its contradictory dimensions and paradoxical allegiances.[60] These dimensions and allegiances are exactly what Serge Daney sets out to stress in his review. Refining Jean-Luc Comolli and Jean Narboni's famous conception of "category e" films, or films that try to present the dominant ideology but do so in contradictory ways that reveal the workings of ideology itself,[61] Daney argues that Coppola's movie *One from the Heart* is at once an homage to the past of the studio film, a laboratory experiment for the future, a warning to his contemporaries, and a love letter to a Las Vegas that is even less real than it is in reality and therefore more true. Daney's logic is this: if Las Vegas is the fakest city in the United States, then there is a good chance a studio

Las Vegas is a little less fake. A negative times a negative equals a positive. Fake times fake equals real. The same logic applies to the film's images, created by a director working for the first time with video-preview technology, which absolved him of the necessity to be actually present when the action is captured (receiving electronic feed from different stages where the action is performed, which he could then immediately edit down). The result, says Daney, is an electronic cinema in which nothing happens to the actors—about whom we no longer care—and everything happens to the image. He calls this approach the American "mannerist" school of filmmaking and identifies it with filmmakers such as Brian De Palma and Steven Spielberg. So far so Baudrillard. But then Daney makes an unexpected move in that he *praises* Coppola for showing us, no matter how superficially, what images are. In other words, he turns Coppola's mannerist cinema of the image into a pedagogy. And it is this pedagogy that interests Deleuze. Deleuze starts his letter to Daney by pointing out that, just like Alois Riegl in art history, Daney has managed to identify three ambitions for the artwork: to beautify nature, to give spirit to nature, and to compete with nature.[62] The ambition to beautify nature is that of the classical cinema, conceived to conjure up the impression of depth, to seduce the viewer to "see through" the image and discover "the secret behind the door."[63] The impression of depth is what was lost with the possibility of illusion and theater after World War II. The modern cinema is one of flatness, a cinema that raises the question of the image itself: What is (still) there in/on the surface plane of the image? This is the cinema of seers, Deleuze reasons, which no longer strives to beautify nature, but to give it spirit. How can we ask what is behind the image when we cannot see what is in it or on it, when we cannot see with our mind's eye?[64] Modern cinema, according to Daney, was then annexed to and "automatized" by a different medium, television. In television, the lack of depth and spectacle are the rule, and the lack of "something" behind the image can no longer be denied: behind the image is simply another image. When there is nothing behind the image, when there is nothing in the image, when there is only an endless succession of images moving into each other, the world disappears and becomes "cinema" itself.[65] Where the ambition of classical cinema, according to Deleuze, is to create an "encyclopedia of the world" (one image following upon another),[66] the aim of modern cinema is to provide a pedagogy of perception. Television, however, is neither pedagogical nor encyclopedic, but simply a means for social control. This differentiation between the social function of television and the aesthetic "supplement" of cinema allows Daney and Deleuze to maintain a pedagogical function for cinema after television. This is what inspired Van Tuinen to differentiate between the baroque—the name Daney gives to the cinema of images—as social incarnation and mannerism as aesthetic potential or supplement. The potential of a mannerist cinema such as Coppola's, then, is to provide a pedagogy of the image capable of teaching us new formalist ambitions in relation to new media technologies. It can do this by bracketing its representational qualities, stressing its cinematic materiality, and gaining what Nietzsche called the "powers of the false."[67]

So if our aim is to present Mann's cinema as mannerist in the sense of its being image conscious and thereby both constructive and instructive of viewing skills, what precisely does its pedagogy consist of? One fact we should certainly take into account is that Mann was a television maker first and, in fact, revolutionized the fictional format of the medium by applying hyperinflated aesthetics and firsthand research to formula cop shows just as Daney was writing his first essays on television. Many of the central films in Mann's oeuvre are reimaginings of his television series. In addition, as we have seen, Mann was a pioneer in the development of electronic cinematography, employing Sony's Hi-Def camera for *Ali* (2001) to capture night scenes in Chicago. While George Lucas and Robert Rodriguez were using the same camera to craft the neobaroque spectacle of *Star Wars Episode II: Attack of the Clones* (2002, Lucas) and *Once upon a Time in Mexico* (Rodriguez, 2003), Mann was combining digital cinematography—both the Sony and the new Viper camera—with traditional film stock to create the look of *Collateral*. The ambition was once again to shoot in extremely low-light situations and to "see" the night. By creating a dialectic between classical and contemporary at the level of technology, a dialectic mirrored in the tension between classical plot construction and modernist aesthetics—including the actor's "phantasmal presence" that Daney finds typical of modern cinema and is incarnated by Mann's "detached professionals"—Mann can be said to have installed a double consciousness in the viewer in a much more critical, dialectical sense than Cubitt's "illusory perception of illusion." Moreover, Mann's interest in sharpness of image, in the extreme depth of field allowed for by the digital camera, was what made him want to do a period piece such as *Public Enemies*. The controversy surrounding that movie's extremely sharp image anticipated the reaction to a ten-minute promo of Peter Jackson's new 3D film *The Hobbit: An Unexpected Journey* (2012), which was shot at forty-eight frames per second rather than the usual twenty-four.

Both films were dismissed for what was perceived as their TV-like or video aesthetic. Jackson is a filmmaker whose artistry, Bordwell argues, like James Cameron's and Lucas's, has become increasingly "mechanical, in that [he] see[s] progress to depend almost wholly on improved hardware (and software)."[68] If Michael Mann is a "gearhead" like these titans of contemporary Hollywood entertainment, each an avatar of the neobaroque, he is one who, like Coppola, looks back while looking forward and "has a warning for his contemporaries."[69] *Public Enemies* is essentially today's *One from the Heart:* a classical genre piece, stylistically inflated, that presents itself as "new" in that it relates cinema to the new media that allow the director greater control. Here's Daney on the Coppola film:

> Video is not just a technique, it's a state of mind, a way of seeing images in the future perfect tense. Video's present tendency is in the direction of control. *"Control,"* says Coppola, *"is power and it is what all organisms tend towards."* The organism named Coppola doesn't please everybody. *One from the Heart* didn't go down well in the States. Too Californian for New York. Too independent for the studios. Too modest for a self-proclaimed visionary film. Too pretentious for such a slender subject. Too expensive for a botched job. Cinephiles, however, those fortune tellers who have not given up trying to guess the future of cinema, cannot remain indifferent to *One from the Heart.* Of course Coppola invents machines in which, when the time comes, he has nothing to put. Of course, the exaggeration, the ugliness, the failure are often intense and their poetic effects often stale. But can we begrudge the builder of the cage if, at the crucial moment, he has only an old cat to exhibit in it? Isn't this lack of proportion, this "much ado about nothing," the most sympathetic aspect of the film? Coppola testifies to the abyss that separates the things we no longer know how to do (as they did before) and those we don't know how to do yet (as they will do after). But he is a bridge-builder all the same.[70]

Notes

1. Sean Cubitt, *The Cinema Effect* (Cambridge, MA: MIT Press, 2004), 224.

2. Erwin Panofsky, "Style and Medium in the Motion Pictures" (1934), reprinted in

Film Theory and Criticism: Introductory Readings, ed. Leo Braudy and Marshall Cohen (New York: Oxford University Press, 2004), 291.

3. Angela Ndalianis, *Neo-baroque Aesthetics and Contemporary Entertainment* (Cambridge, MA: MIT Press, 2004), 11. See also Angela Ndalianis, "Architectures of the Senses: Neo-baroque Entertainment Spectacles," in *Rethinking Media Change: The Aesthetics of Transition,* ed. David Thorburn and Henry Jenkins (Cambridge, MA: MIT Press, 2003), 355–73.

4. Scott Bukatman, "The Ultimate Trip: Special Effects and Kaleidoscopic Perception," in *Matters of Gravity: Special Effects and Supermen in the Twentieth Century* (Durham, NC: Duke University Press, 2003), 111–33.

5. Ndalianis, *Neo-baroque Aesthetics and Contemporary Entertainment,* 31–71.

6. Sean Cubitt, "The Supernatural in Neo-baroque Hollywood," in *Film Theory and Contemporary Hollywood Movies,* ed. Warren Buckland (New York: Routledge, 2009), 51, 49.

7. David Bordwell, *The Way Hollywood Tells It: Story and Style in Modern Movies* (Berkeley: University of California Press, 2006), 120, 121, 141.

8. Cubitt, *The Cinema Effect,* 207–16, 235.

9. Jean Baudrillard, *Simulacra and Simulation,* trans. Sheila Faria Glaser (Ann Arbor: University of Michigan Press, 1994), 59.

10. Cubitt, *The Cinema Effect,* 49.

11. Serge Daney's *"Coup de Coeur"* was originally published in *Libération,* September 29, 1982, and first translated in English as *"One from the Heart," Framework,* nos. 32–33 (1986): 171. We have used the English translation by Ginette Vincendeau, available at Steve Erickson's website, http://home.earthlink.net/~steevee/Daney_one.html, accessed May 15, 2012.

12. "How the Directors and Critics Voted: Michael Mann," *Sight and Sound* (2002), http://www.bfi.org.uk/sightandsound/polls/topten/poll/voter.php?forename=Michael &surname=Mann, accessed May 15, 2012.

13. Bordwell, *The Way Hollywood Tells It,* 180.

14. David Bordwell, "(50) Days of Summer (Movies), Part 2," *Observations on Film Art,* September 12, 2009, http://www.davidbordwell.net/blog/2009/09/12/50-days-of-summer-movies-part-2/, accessed May 15, 2012.

15. Doug Liman directed *The Bourne Identity* (2002), and Paul Greengrass took on *The Bourne Supremacy* (2004) and *The Bourne Ultimatum* (2007).

16. All quoted in Bordwell, *The Way Hollywood Tells It,* 188–89.

17. Ibid., 189.

18. Arnold Hauser, *Mannerism: The Crisis of the Renaissance & the Origin of Modern Art,* ed. Eric Mosbacher (New York: Knopf, 1965), 11 .

19. Ibid., 12.

20. Les Paul Robley, "Hot Set," *American Cinematographer* 77, no. 1 (January 1996): 48 .

21. Nick James, *Heat* (London: British Film Institute, 2002), 15.

22. Quoted in Harlan Kennedy, "Castle Keep," *Film Comment* 19, no. 6 (November–December 1983): 16.

23. Cubitt, "The Supernatural in Neo-baroque Hollywood," 56–59.

24. Kennedy, "Castle Keep," 16.

25. Quoted in ibid., 17.

26. Interview in Gavin Smith, "Michael Mann—Wars and Peace," *Sight and Sound* 2, no. 7 (November 1992): 12.

27. Christopher Sharrett, "Michael Mann," in *Fifty Contemporary Film Directors,* ed. Yvonne Tasker (London: Routledge, 2010), 269.

28. Smith, "Michael Mann—Wars and Peace," 12.

29. Both Goodman and Comb quoted in James, *Heat,* 23.

30. Quoted in ibid., 25.

31. Brooke Comer, "*Last of the Mohicans:* Interpreting Cooper's Classic," *American Cinematographer* 73, no. 12 (December 1992): 31.

32. The tableau vivant as an element of neomannerist cinematic style is usually discussed in the context of period films, as in Belén Vidal, *Figuring the Past: Period Film and the Mannerist Aesthetic* (Amsterdam: Amsterdam University Press, 2012).

33. Quoted in Robley, "Hot Set," 46.

34. Ben McCann, "Colour Strategies in the Films of Michael Mann," in *Questions of Colour in Cinema: From Paintbrush to Pixel,* ed. Wendy Everett (Bern: Lang, 2007), 143.

35. Quoted in Jay Holben, "Ring Leader," *American Cinematographer* 82, no. 11 (November 2001): 37.

36. Quoted in ibid., 38.

37. Bordwell, *The Way Hollywood Tells It,* 184. The television background of many of Mann's projects—e.g., *Heat* was first done as the TV movie *L.A. Takedown* (1989), and *Public Enemies* was scripted by TV writer Ronan Bennett—may also account for the flatness and sloppy construction of the narrative that Bordwell finds typical of Mann's late-mannerist films. The almost allegorical abstraction of Mann's plots also adheres, of course, to the imbalance between content and form and the loss of classical qualities of harmony and rationality in mannerist art.

38. Jay Holben, "Hell on Wheels," *American Cinematographer* 85, no. 8 (August 2004), http://www.theasc.com/magazine/aug04/collateral/page1.html, accessed May 15, 2012.

39. Jay Holben, "Partners in Crime," *American Cinematographer* 87, no. 8 (August 2006): 54.

40. See Tom Gunning, "The Cinema of Attraction(s): Early Film, Its Spectator, and the Avant-Garde," in *The Cinema of Attractions Reloaded,* ed. Wanda Strauven (Amsterdam: Amsterdam University Press, 2006), 381–89.

41. Cubitt, *The Cinema Effect,* 255–56.

42. Hauser, *Mannerism,* 4.

43. Ibid., 12.

44. Bordwell, *The Way Hollywood Tells It,* 24.

45. Ibid., 23–26.

46. Ibid., 24.

47. Bordwell, "(50) Days of Summer (Movies), Part 2."

48. F. X. Feeney, *Michael Mann* (Cologne: Taschen, 2006), 21.

49. David Bordwell, "Do Filmmakers Deserve the Last Word?" *Observations on Film Art,* February 10, 2011, http://www.davidbordwell.net/blog/2007/10/10/do-filmmakers-deserve-the-last-word/, accessed May 15, 2012.

50. Bordwell, "(50) Days of Summer (Movies), Part 2."

51. Hauser, *Mannerism,* 12.

52. Cubitt, *The Cinema Effect,* 242.

53. Sjoerd Van Tuinen, "Cinematic Neo-mannerism or Neo-baroque? Deleuze and Daney," *Image and Narrative* 13, no. 2 (2012): 54.

54. Deleuze quoted in ibid., 59.

55. Cited in Cubitt, *The Cinema Effect,* 237.

56. Ibid., 235.

57. David Bordwell, "Intensified Continuity: Visual Style in Contemporary American Film," *Film Quarterly* 55, no. 3 (2002): 25.

58. Van Tuinen, "Cinematic Neo-mannerism or Neo-baroque?" 61.

59. Daney, *"One from the Heart."*

60. See Robert Venturi and Denise Scott Brown, *Learning from Las Vegas* (Cambridge, MA: MIT Press, 1977) and *Architecture as Signs and Systems: For a Mannerist Time* (Cambridge, MA: Harvard University Press, 2004).

61. Jean-Luc Comolli and Jean Narboni, "Cinema/Ideology/Criticism," in *Film Theory and Criticism: Introductory Readings,* ed. Leo Braudy and Marshall Cohen (New York: Oxford University Press, 2004), 812–19.

62. Gilles Deleuze, "Letter to Serge Daney: Optimism, Pessimism, and Travel," trans. Martin Joughin, in *Negotiations 1972–1990* (New York: Columbia University Press, 1997), 68–81. We have used and translated into English a recent Dutch translation of this letter entitled "Optimisme, pessimisme, reizen," in *Een ruimte om in te bewegen: Serge Daney—tussen cinema en beeldcultuur,* ed. Solange de Boer (Amsterdam: Octavo, 2011), 87.

63. The door, like windows and mirrors, is a key "object" in classical mise-en-scène, luring the spectator's gaze. Deleuze, "Optimisme, pessimisme, reizen," 87.

64. Ibid., 87–92.

65. See Serge Daney, "La rampe (bis)," in *Cahier critique 1970–1982* (Paris: Cahiers du cinéma, Gallimard, 1983), 171–79.

66. Deleuze, "Optimisme, pessimisme, reizen," 87.

67. Van Tuinen, "Cinematic Neo-mannerism or Neo-baroque?" 70, quoting Nietzsche.

68. David Bordwell, "The Gearheads," *Observations on Film Art,* May 14, 2012, http://www.davidbordwell.net/blog/2012/05/13/the-gearheads/, accessed May 15, 2012.

69. Daney, *"One from the Heart."*

70. Ibid., italics in original.

THE ETHICS OF CONTRACTS, CONSCIENCE, AND COURAGE IN *THE INSIDER*

David LaRocca

Jeffrey Wigand (Russell Crowe) takes his wife, Liane (Diane Venora), to dinner with Mike Wallace (Christopher Plummer) and Lowell Bergman (Al Pacino) at an elegant Manhattan restaurant. It is the eve of Jeffrey's taped interview with Mike Wallace for *60 Minutes*, but she doesn't know that; she thinks they're just out for a special dinner. When Jeffrey, at last, confirms the purpose of their visit to New York, Liane storms away from the table, embarrassed and alienated, and Jeffrey follows after her. With irritation and impatience, Wallace asks: "Who *are* these people?" Bergman replies sternly: "Ordinary people! Under extraordinary pressure, Mike. What the hell do you expect? Grace and consistency?" This scene, like so much in Michael Mann's *The Insider* (1999), dramatizes individual attempts to weigh the apparently contradictory demands of an ethical life and to commit to action despite fear, doubt, and confusion. Bergman's question can be turned on ourselves: What the hell do we expect of others and of ourselves? Would we presume to be any more or less graceful and consistent than the Wigands? The dinner scene is one among many in the film that amplifies the way in which *The Insider* is a study of two professionals—principally a scientist and a journalist—trying to do their jobs well, trying to determine what it means to do so while also negotiating the terms and conditions of marriage.

Contracts

The film begins with cloth over our eyes. As viewers, we begin blindfolded, not sure where we are and moving onward to an undisclosed location. We are taken to a place where our view of things is obscured (sometimes wholly, sometimes partially) and, in fact, discover that we are not in one place, but many. There are many contexts or worlds in *The Insider:* the corporate office, the newsroom, the field (where interviews are given and taken), the laboratory, the courtroom, and the bedroom. Each context involves its own rules and implies differing (often competing) responsibilities; each place demands that one has a sense about how to conduct oneself—how to speak and listen, how to identify the terms and conditions for action, how to negotiate or know when to cease negotiation, how to discern the truth or achieve resolution.

The primary ethical dilemma at the core of the film's narrative is whether to be a whistleblower or not, and it is something that Wigand and Bergman struggle with in different ways. The dilemma emerges because Wigand and Bergman have to contend with two kinds of contracts. Wigand's contract is referred to as a confidentiality agreement, and it is written in robust legal language, which for most people means obfuscatory prose. When one needs a lawyer to understand a document, chances are that language is not being used in ordinary ways. The cloudy description contributes to a general sense of confusion and anxiety because one doesn't exactly know how to abide by the contract, even if one wants to. Bergman's contract, in contrast, is not something that is imposed on him, but rather something he adopts. And just as it is not clear that Wigand is bound by a confidentiality agreement until questioned about his work, neither is it clear what kind of journalistic code Bergman ascribes to. Perhaps his code is not definitively codified but rather derives mainly from the accumulated knowledge of specific incidents, including his training and practice as a journalist. In this way, many aspects of his journalistic ethics are tacitly understood—meaning they are unsaid but nevertheless binding. Even so, there are institutions—such as the Society of Professional Journalists—that clearly state the nature, definition, and conditions of journalism's code and invite all journalists to adopt and abide by it.[1] Despite the explicitness of such a "code of ethics," there remains much that is unclear in the code. For example, one of the line items is: "Expose unethical practices of journalists and the news media." Obviously, one has to know what constitutes an unethical practice in order to expose it; the criteria for such judgment are not provided. Strangely, this code of ethics does not mention the principle that gains explicit attention in the film and might be considered the core standard for all journalistic integrity: don't burn your sources. In practice, this means a journalist makes a promise—an implied contract—to protect the names and identities of confidential sources.

Early in *The Insider,* Wigand suspects that he has been burned and angrily calls Bergman to say so. Bergman takes the accusation so seriously that he flies from New York to Louisville to personally defend his credibility and to remind Wigand how stupid it would be for him to burn a source *before* he has received any information: "I did not burn you. I did not give you up to any one." Later, when Wigand's *60 Minutes* interview—confirming his breach of contract and status as a whistleblower—is shelved, Bergman feels this does qualify as a burn and spends the rest of the film struggling with how to move on from what he considers his own lapse of integrity. He clearly believes that another aspect of his contract with his sources (confidential or not) is to get the story to air. Even though the decision to withhold the interview was reached by a corporate entity (albeit with the consent of some high-ranking journalists and producers) without his consent and indeed in the face of his defiant disagreement, Bergman still feels culpable, saying, "What do I tell a source on the next tough story? What got broken here doesn't go back together again. How can I ever ask a source to trust me again?"

These different kinds of contracts—Wigand's confidentiality agreement and Bergman's understanding of how to protect and present a source— provide an occasion to think about the nature of contracts. In his remarkably coherent and incisive book *The Theory of Morality,* Alan Donagan says, "The most elementary institution that gives rise to moral obligations is that of contract."[2] Being "elementary" here does not mean simple, but rather foundational, essential, constitutive; and though moral obligations may arise from a contract, the institution of a contract is not *intrinsically* moral. Nevertheless, moral obligations arise out of it. And when they do, such obligations form a bond between promiser and promisee. The two parties, in effect, create an institutional framework in which to understand their relationship. As Donagan asks, though, "Does the institutional bond between promiser and promisee ever constitute a moral bond?"[3]

When Wigand is fired from Brown & Williamson (B&W), the third-largest US tobacco company, he signs a confidentiality agreement. What motivates a great deal of Wigand's anger (as well as despair) and lays the seed for him to become a whistleblower is B&W CEO Thomas Sandefur's (Michael Gambon) demand that Wigand sign—*after* his firing and signing of an initial agreement—an addendum to the agreement, something, as Sandefur describes it, "to expand our zone of comfort with you." The phrase is a euphemism for widening the scope of confidentiality, or as Sandefur glosses it, "Nobody will be able to say, 'Well, hell's bells, Margaret, I didn't know *that* was a secret.'" One gets the sense that *anything* Wigand might say even remotely related to B&W could fall under terms of the agreement. Thus, by signing the supplement, Wigand willingly muzzles himself. And yet it seems misplaced to say that Wigand's assent to the addendum constitutes acting from his own uncoerced volition.

Wigand, Bergman, and, indeed, Michael Mann's film as a whole are all intently focused on the legal and moral implications of whistleblowing. Much screen time is devoted to the question of creating conditions under which Wigand can at the very least *legally* breach his agreement and tell others what he knows; whether the breach is a moral violation is taken as a somewhat secondary, even private, concern that Wigand appears to deal with in conversation with Bergman or to a much lesser extent with his wife, Liane. Bergman similarly undergoes his own torment in trying to determine how to do his job when his boss (along with a lot of lawyers) block Wigand's story from appearing on television. Bergman asks incredulously: "Is CBS corporate telling CBS News 'do not go to air with this story'?" All the warnings from the legal department about tortious interference in fact mean that, as Jim Cooper from the *New York Times* surmises, "*60 Minutes* is letting CBS corporate decide what is or is not news." Bergman has to decide whether to blow the whistle on his boss, his employer, and his colleagues (including Mike Wallace, a longtime collaborator). If he talks and succeeds in getting Wigand's story aired, he will have "burned his bridges" (as Cooper warns); if he fails, the results at work will be much the same—no one at CBS will trust him.

Considering the conditions under which Wigand signs the supplemental agreement, it would seem the contract is invalidated as a moral institution. As Donagan notes, a contract is not intrinsically moral; in order for it to be moral, certain factors must be met. Supreme among them is the absence of coercion: "A contract is null and void if exacted by violence or by credible threats of death or serious injury."[4] Does Sandefur's threat qualify as violent? His lawyer tells Wigand: "If we arrive at the conclusion you're acting in bad faith? We would terminate, right now, payouts under your severance package. You and your family's medical benefits. And initiate litigation against you, Mr. Wigand." Wigand—here expressed by Russell Crowe's talent for showing on his face a complex internal state of affairs—understandably feels deeply threatened by Sandefur's terms, especially as they connect the decision to sign and abide by the agreement with his family's welfare. Even if B&W

were to pursue recompense only through *legal* means—noting something like six hundred million dollars annually spent on legal counsel—might that not amount to a serious kind of violence? At a crucial moment in Wigand's deliberation about whether to testify or not, the Mississippi attorney Richard Scruggs (Colm Feore) offers him a heartfelt and penetrating soliloquy:

> In the Navy I flew A-6's off carriers. In combat, events have a duration of seconds, sometimes minutes. . . . But what you're going through goes on day in and day out. Whether you're ready for it or not, week in, week out. . . . Month after month after month. Whether you're up or whether you're down. You're assaulted psychologically. You're assaulted financially, which is its own special kind of violence. Because it's directed at your kids . . . What school can you afford? . . . How will that affect their lives? You're asking yourself: Will that limit what they may become? You feel your whole family's future's compromised . . . held hostage. . . . I do know how it is.

By this point, of course, Wigand has already been fired and signed an additional confidentiality agreement. While Scruggs is commiserating about possible future torment, he might as well be describing the stress and trauma Wigand has already experienced. According to Donagan, "In exacting a promise by violence or threats of violence, a promisee forfeits his right as a rational creature to its fulfillment. A forced contract is morally void; and the promiser morally owes it neither to himself nor to anybody else to fulfill it. That his self-esteem, or the mores of some group to which he belongs, should demand that he fulfills it, is of no moral significance."[5] Based on the information we have in the film, it appears that Wigand is under no *moral* obligation to honor the supplement Sandefur compels him to sign. That Wigand remains under legal obligation suggests an important cleaving point between morality and the law.

As a story about human obligations, *The Insider* reflects a division between contracts and codes. Contracts are part of corporate culture (at B&W and at CBS) and are drawn up by lawyers; contracts try to make rights and responsibilities explicit in order to avoid misunderstanding, to limit liabilities, and to articulate rules. Codes are entirely different from contracts, as we see in the culture of science and journalism that Wigand and Bergman respectively represent. Codes of ethics or codes of honor are often implied and cannot be exhaustively articulated. To follow a code requires a constant reassessment of orientation and action. Not surprisingly, it is rather easy to be graceful and consistent when following a contract (because one is merely living in conformity with clearly stated rules), whereas attempts to maintain a code may contribute to rather sweaty, fumbling lurches that may or may not hit the mark. On this point, compare Thomas Sandefur's smug poise with Jeffrey Wigand's uncertainty and disequilibrium. Sandefur's confidence derives largely from the presence and protection of contracts, whereas Wigand feels the pressing demand to reassess his codes of behavior.

The parallel between contract and code appears also in *The Insider*'s depiction of marriage. The marriage contract is meant to cover rather boiler-plate rights and responsibilities: fidelity, conjugal rights, the raising of children, contributions to family economy and welfare, care during illness and infirmities, and the like. A marriage code, though, is rather more compli-cated and much more vague because it entails a ceaseless flow of conversa-tion between parties. A conversation is not a recitation of rules and clauses, but a dynamic, unrehearsed experiment in communication.

Needless to say, or perhaps it is necessary to say, honoring a code is a higher sort of calling than obeying a contract. The challenge of fulfilling a code lies in part in not being able to fulfill it once and for all: a disclosure of truth in one conversation doesn't preclude the need for more conversa-tions. Similarly, although it may be easy to fulfill a contract negatively (e.g., in the case of Wigand's confidentiality agreement, *not talking* is the stan-dard of his success), a code appears in constant need of positive action, such as innovative ways of addressing new situations (e.g., Bergman's adaptive responses to Wigand's reticence, finding ways to "draw him out"). Similarly, in scenes showing the Wigands' marriage, we see how Wigand upholds his marriage contract (e.g., by providing for his family) but violates the codes that make a marriage worthwhile: being unwilling to involve his wife in the most vital aspects of his daily life, especially and including those parts that affect her life. In Doug Liman's recent film *Fair Game* (2010), another portrait of a marriage put under stress by an act of whistleblowing, we see how Joe Wilson (Sean Penn) doesn't consult with his wife, Valerie Plame (Naomi Watts)—or even seem to consider the possible consequences to her hard-won and much-loved career—before blowing the whistle. Wilson acts recklessly. And his wife suffers the loss of her job and her vocation as well as damage to her name and reputation. Not surprisingly, they both suffer a catastrophic stress to their marriage—a marriage that, despite grave obstacles and perhaps even beyond reasonable expectation, appears to survive the ordeal. Wilson's lack of deliberation and discussion with his wife, although motivated by justified moral outrage, culminates in both professional and personal losses and trauma. Even though we should not expect "grace and consistency" from Joe Wilson and Jeffrey Wigand, we might consider how their stories of whistleblowing might have been transformed by exploring the codes that define their marriages—if they had, for example, enlisted their wives instead of acting on their behalves.

On another line of comparison, consider the claustrophobia of Wigand's marriage (where the couple seems more likely to walk past one another than speak candidly to one another) with the easy-going intimacy and strict honesty of Bergman's marriage. Here, in a scene from the beach house where Bergman has repaired with his wife, Sharon (Lindsay Crouse), to think over his next steps, we can hear his wife's diligent, empathetic listening along with her unvarnished attempts to make sure her husband isn't being delusional and selfish.

> Bergman: "I'm Lowell Bergman, I'm from *60 Minutes.*" You know, you take the *60 Minutes* out of that sentence, nobody returns your phone call. Maybe Wigand's right. Maybe I'm hooked. What am I hooked on? The rush? *60 Minutes?* What the hell for? Infotainment. It's so fucking useless, all of it.
> Sharon: So, it's a big country with a free press. You can go work somewhere else.
> Bergman: Free press? Press is free . . . for anyone who owns one. Larry Tisch has a free press.
> Sharon: Get some perspective, Lowell.
> Bergman: I got perspective.
> Sharon: No, you do not.
> Bergman: From my perspective, what's been going on and what I've been doing is ridiculous. It's half-measures.
> Sharon: You're not listening. Really know what you're going to do before you do it.

In Wigand's marriage, Jeffrey and Liane argue about superficial things in ways that carry overwhelming emotional weight. They express their sadness, fear, and aggression passively—and therefore inadequately—which leaves both feeling insufficiently understood. Whether it is the absence of soy sauce or the location of a favorite coffee mug or where to wash gardening soil from one's hands, there is a pervasive sense that the genuine causes of their stress are sublimated and remain unarticulated.

> Liane: Please don't wash your hands in the sink.
> Wigand: Where should I wash them?
> Liane: Use the bathroom.
> Wigand: What's the difference?
> Liane: That's for food.

When Mike Wallace asks Wigand why he was fired from B&W, Wigand states: "Poor communication skills." It is the right answer to the wrong question. Wigand's answer better fits the question why his marriage to Liane dissolved. By contrast, Bergman (part of a second marriage, each spouse with a grown son from a previous marriage) shows the range of his communication with his wife, from the mundane news that "they canceled the six o'clock" flight to moments of invited engagement, as when he asks Sharon about the anonymous box of papers he receives: "You understand any of this?" Bergman assumes that his wife is interested in his day-to-day experiences—profound or otherwise, triumphant or despairing. Wigand, in contrast, steps backward into telling Liane he is fired, and despite moments of attempted positive thinking ("We can make this work for us. Okay? More time together. More time with the kids. More time for us, okay? This is gonna be better. This is gonna be better"), Wigand essentially blocks his wife from his inner experience of the stress he is undergoing and the difficult decisions he faces. After Liane tells Jeffrey that she wants a divorce (even stating this bold claim obliquely: "I don't think I can do this anymore"), Wigand responds, "Can we talk about this when I get back?"—suggesting the kind of conversation they should have had long ago but will never have, certainly not when he gets back from giving his deposition. Wigand's hopeful notion that "more time together" will somehow improve their lives is countered by how little time Bergman spends with his wife and yet still manages to have a fulfilling, deep, intimate relationship with her. Bergman's marriage is an extreme case, perhaps, but it is also an illustration that proximity is not a necessary condition—much less a cause—of marital satisfaction.

Though the institution of marriage is pervasive, and the rituals, conventions, and articulation of contractual terms surrounding marriage are ubiquitous, a film such as *The Insider* reminds us of the cliché that there are as many kinds of marriage as there are marriages. But this is a strange state of affairs. Why would so many people agree—bind themselves contractually—to an arrangement of which they know so little? Or why is it that so many only begin to understand the terms of their marriage *after* they are married, as if the contract were drawn up post facto or as if its terms were revealed only incrementally? In effect, the portrayal of marriage made available to us in *The Insider* reminds us of the difference between fulfilling the terms of a marriage contract and a marriage code. With a contract, one can look at the fine print and figure it out for oneself; with a code, each party, in effect, is perpetually called out by the other to testify to his or her experience. As a result, spouses committed to the exercise of a marriage code share parallel duties with different spheres of responsibilities and rights, which they cannot settle once and for all. Though both Wigand and Bergman are "on" their second marriages when we meet them, it seems that Wigand's approach to dealing with his stress (hitting golf balls, drinking scotch, sulking) is not as effective as Bergman's approach (sharing time in bed, taking a minibreak at the beach, saying what is on his mind). The portrait of these two very different kinds of marriage does not just speak to the differences between these two men, but to a quality that seems constitutive of marriages that work, last, and are fulfilling—namely, an understanding that the marriage contract fundamentally requires a constant, ceaseless flow of communication between parties—and thus implies the existence of a more subtle and thus much more difficult code. Bergman's marriage is not perfect, but at least the imperfections are on the table—shared by husband and wife. The marriage that is "perfect" because imperfections are suppressed or kept secret is the one more likely to implode or dissolve. It turns out that it is Liane who fires Jeffrey for poor communication skills.

Conscience

When a corporation produces a harmful or lethal product, who is liable for the damage it causes? The CEO? The people who manufacture it? The farmers who produce the raw materials used in manufacture? How far back, if at all, should responsibility stretch? Jeffrey Wigand was a corporate vice president at B&W at the time he was fired. And he is a scientist. It seems clear that he knew—but simply ignored—evidence that cigarette smoking causes harm in humans. To justify his well-paid position, he might have reasoned that people smoke from their own volition, so they are responsible for their health. However, there came a time when scientific evidence incontrovertibly showed that the "nicotine delivery business" conveyed something pernicious: an addictive drug that causes serious harm, even fatality, to users. Moreover, B&W adjusted the way that nicotine was absorbed into the body: we might consider this alteration no different than changing a recipe— for instance, augmenting or transforming it over time to satisfy changing consumer tastes. But Wigand didn't get in trouble with Sandefur—and subsequently get fired—because he was upset that the recipe was changed. Rather, Wigand objected to using a compound called coumarin. "I wanted it out immediately," Wigand tells Mike Wallace. "I constructed a memo to Mr. Sandefur indicating I could not in conscience continue with coumarin in a product that we now knew, we had documentation, was similar to coumadin, a lung-specific carcinogen." Changing a recipe is one thing; consciously adding poison to the recipe is another.

After a few years of suppressing his beliefs as a man of science, Wigand discerned that he had a duty to others not to poison them. Fair enough. Intuitive enough. But how does one understand that duty (as well as the duty that obtains for one's profession and the corporate or legal contract that presides over and defines that position) when it may conflict with duties to oneself and one's family? As his lawyer Richard Scruggs puts it, Wigand and his family would be "assaulted," "held hostage" if he disclosed B&W's practice of poisoning its consumers.

At least two important questions arise from Wigand's dilemma whether to testify or not: first, whether he can discern what the moral thing to do is; and second, whether doing the moral thing has anything to do with the consequences of his action (e.g., protecting consumers from carcinogens, on the one hand, and subjecting his family to suffering, on the other).

Wigand is, as screenwriters Michael Mann and Eric Roth write in a scene description, "trying to untangle identity and consequence," which is a way of saying that Wigand seeks to separate a crisis of conscience (something that happens internally, in this case, as a reaction to something external) from the *impact* one's act of conscience might have on oneself, one's family, and a world of unknown others. At Scruggs's house, standing by the dock, trying to sort things for himself, Wigand say to Bergman: "I can't seem to find the criteria [to decide]." The few moments that follow, in effect, show a man thinking on film—going through a tumultuous process of self-determination. Yet Wigand seems to decide expeditiously, even recklessly. He turns to announce his decision: "Fuck it. Let's go to court." Can anything like criteria be understood to inform or direct his decision? Did Wigand even *make* a decision—in the sense of considering countermanding principles, competing duties, weighing evidence, costs, reasons, and so on—or did he just pick an option as one would a door behind which nothing can be seen?

With some time to consider Wigand's decision, and granting what may be a salutary impersonal distance from the case, can we determine what he should want to achieve by making a decision to testify? Are we inclined to believe that the decision has moral worth or should do the least amount of harm (to family and to others, and perhaps, if not in this case, also to one's employer and one's colleagues)? What if one can't determine the proper framework—should moral worth supersede harm; should harm override moral worth? In *Foundations of the Metaphysics of Morals,* Immanuel Kant claims that "the first proposition of morality is that to have genuine moral worth, an action must be done from duty. The second proposition is: An action done from duty does not have its moral worth in the purpose which is to be achieved through it but in the maxim whereby it is determined."[6] This means that we should not be concerned with the consequences of action, but rather (and exclusively) with the "principle of volition" that motivates the action. Kant then derives a third principle from the first two—namely, "Duty is the necessity to do an action from respect for law."[7] In the light of Kant's recommendations, we can assess Wigand's search for criteria to make the decision. First, we can tell him that no amount of meditation on possible consequences will help determine the moral worth of his decision to testify. Creating a list of effects—B&W's financial liability and perhaps its bankruptcy, Wigand's prosecution (including fines and jail time), detrimental effects to his children (poor health coverage, limited means to pursue education), further stress on an already fragile marriage, possible alleviation of suffering among millions of smokers, and even the prevention of the deaths of tens, hundreds, and potentially millions of users—will provide no clarity, according to Kant, for determining the moral worth of the action. Instead, these considerations are part of the felicific or hedonic calculus made popular by utilitarians, such as Jeremy Bentham, who insist that we judge moral worth based on the utility some action provides. If Wigand were to look to Bentham's philosophy for criteria to make his decision, he would be directed to the following measures: intensity, duration, certainty/ uncertainty, propinquity/remoteness, fecundity, purity, and extent. By his own admission, Bentham's outlook was informed by Joseph Priestley, who some half-century earlier had written: "The good and happiness of the members, that is, the majority of the members, of any state, is the great standard by which every thing relating to that state must finally be determined," or the way Bentham remembered and proselytized the sentiment: we ought to seek through our actions "the greatest happiness for the greatest number."[8] John Stuart Mill, for his part in the inheritance and development of utilitarianism, conjured the so-called Greatest Happiness Principle, about which he says: "The ultimate end, with reference to and for the sake of which all other things are desirable (whether we are considering our own good or that of other people), is an existence exempt as far as possible from pain, and as rich as possible in enjoyments, both in point of quantity and quality. . . . This, being, according to utilitarian opinion, the end of human action, is necessarily also the standard of morality."[9]

Kant clearly contravenes all these utilitarian approaches, with their focus on effects, outcomes, and maximization of pleasure for the largest quantity of persons, instead pointing to the intention, motivation, and "volition" that underwrite the action of a single agent. "This subjective element is the maxim that I should follow such a law even if it thwarts all my inclinations."[10] Wigand may be inclined to protect himself and his family, to punish B&W, and to help improve the health and even save the lives of untold numbers of smokers, but his desire to act based on these considerations does not, according to Kant, convey to his action any moral worth. To think and act with care for one's inclinations—and for the effects it will or may have—is to indulge a nonmoral calculus that, Kant argues, exists entirely apart from any moral law.

Throughout the film, Wigand is surrounded by people who encourage him to think like a utilitarian. From Lowell Bergman to Mike Wallace, from Richard Scruggs to Liane Wigand, everyone makes some form of a utilitarian case: they list possible, even probable, effects and then let these awful outcomes do battle in Wigand's heart and mind. No wonder he drinks heavily. No person is in a position to determine the moral thing to do when given a list of competing negative effects. Strange as it may sound, one cannot make a *moral* decision if one is motivated to minimize harm that may arise from the decision. When Wigand stands on the dock and says he can't find the criteria to decide whether to testify, he seems to be trying to make a final utilitarian calculation. But I don't think this is what happens. Instead, I believe, he finally realizes that criteria—up to this point in the film offered up as consequences—have nothing to do with his decision. When he declares, "Fuck it. Let's go to court," he becomes a Kantian. He puts aside the calculus and chooses his conscience, which in effect dictates the moral law to him. He ceases the pursuit of justifications and finds a principle for action.

> Wigand: I can't seem to find . . . the criteria to decide. It's too big a
>   decision to make without being resolved . . . in my own mind.
> Bergman: Maybe things have changed . . .
> Wigand: What's changed?
> Bergman: You mean . . . since this morning?
> Wigand: No. I mean since whenever. . . . Fuck it. Let's go to court.

It might be said that Wigand remains utilitarian insofar as his principle of action is the anticipation of changing the way a tobacco company relates to the public. Such a reading would mean that Wigand acts merely to alter the nature of a tobacco company's responsibility to its customers. But the impetuousness, clarity, and force of Wigand's decision suggests otherwise; his narration of internal deliberation lends a clue that Wigand has stopped calculating altogether. He doesn't act to punish B&W, to avenge their wrong-doing to him or others, or even to help prevent further damage. He doesn't seek justice. Rather, he seeks to act definitively from his conscience, to tell what he knows because it is, well, the right thing to do. He wants to restore himself as a man of science and fulfill the code that such a role implies. When Wigand tells Mike Wallace that "there are times that I feel compelled to do it"—to blow the whistle on B&W—he describes his clarity about the force of the moral law. That's what Wigand means when he says, "I mean since whenever": no amount of deliberation about consequences and justifica-tions for action will ever come close to the compelling force of a rational principle of morality. Because he acts from an anti-utilitarian motivation, his testimony at the deposition has profound moral worth; his remarks to the court unimpeachably follow from a clear sense of what it means to exer-cise his will as a rational creature capable of moral action. Wigand does not testify as part of a plan or for instrumental purposes; instead, he aligns his action with the dictates of duty. To this point, Kant writes: "To be truthful from duty is an entirely different thing from being truthful out of fear of untoward consequences, for in the former case the concept of the action itself contains a law for me, while in the latter I must first look about to see what results for me may be connected with it."[11] As we watch Wigand suf-fer—in the wake of being fired, harassed, threatened and then fearing for his family—we sympathize with his effort to understand what he should do.

Indeed, that effort itself is a kind of suffering. Sadly, though, the suffering derives solely from Wigand's—and others'—focus on the utilitarian notion of moral worth. When one turns to Kant, the dilemma evaporates. It is not any easier to act, but at least one acts with the confidence that the action is possessed of moral worth. As Kant notes, "I do not need any penetrating acuteness to discern what I have to do in order that my volition may be morally good. Inexperienced in the course of the world, incapable of being prepared for all its contingencies, I only ask myself: Can I will that my maxim become a universal law? If not, it must be rejected."[12] To the chorus of wife, friends, lawyers, and the like insisting that Wigand sustain the range of possible outcomes, one might say, as Kant does, "To duty every other motive must give place, because duty is the condition of a will good in itself, whose worth transcends everything."[13]

Although Kant's formulation of these moral principles—often referred to more compactly as the Categorical Imperative—reflects his rigorous philosophical training, Kant himself was convinced that the formulations here presented should be completely intelligible to "ordinary human reason" — in other words, "showing that neither science nor philosophy is needed in order to know what one has to do in order to be honest and good, and even wise and virtuous."[14] Perhaps this is just what we see when Wigand decides to testify: his ordinary human reason, not some convoluted philosophical algorithm or calculus, arrives at the moral action he should commit. In fact, Kant, for all his elaborate and often convincing argumentation, believes that "ordinary human understanding in its practical concern . . . is almost more certain" of "hitting the mark" than are philosophers.[15] Wigand follows his conscience, which is his duty, and whatever may come of it, he will at least have committed a moral act. This achievement in itself, an achievement because it seems so daring and so rare, suggests that Wigand is possessed not just of ordinary human reason, but of a true bravery.

Courage

In the *Nicomachean Ethics,* Aristotle stipulates that virtue is any action in accord with excellence, and part of that excellence emerges from achieving a balance in conduct. Moral action depends on avoiding extremes, in finding a way in which to moderate actions and emotions. Courage, for Aristotle, "is a mean with respect to fear and confidence."[16] Yet, as noted earlier, Wigand is presented with an array of consequences to assess. As a result, he is involuntarily led into a debate about the relative worth of different kinds of acts. On the one hand, at one point, thinking of the health and welfare of his children (one of whom suffers from a lung ailment), he seems cowed—ready to give up and give over to B&W's billion-dollar legal (and perhaps illegal) defenses. On the other hand, at a different juncture, when he focuses on his self-identity as a "man of science," he is clear what such a man must do—and the act seems patently to elide the concerns he had when thinking of his family. As Bergman says, "You're in a state of conflict," but then that conflict—which is really an alternation between the extremes of fear and confidence as related to consequences—is exacerbated by remarks such as the following: "Because, look, here's how it lays out: if you got vital, insider stuff the American people for their welfare really do need to know . . . and you feel impelled to disclose it and violate your agreement in doing so, that's one thing. On the other hand, if you want to honor this agreement, then that's simple. You do so. You say nothing. You do nothing. There's only one guy who can figure that out for you. And that's you. All by yourself." Bergman's conclusion that Wigand is by himself belies the fact that Bergman is setting up the conflict—or at least offering one version of how it might be set up. From Bergman's perspective, Wigand is somehow implicated in the welfare of the American people. Wigand's immediate stresses—losing his job, threats of losing his severance package (including health care for his children), legal fees, fines, and possible incarceration, along with marital discord—suddenly become linked with abstract, generalized concerns for an unknown American public. Bergman's underlying utilitarian argument is echoed and reinforced in the next scene when Mike Wallace says indignantly: "He's got a corporate secrecy agreement? Give me a break. This is a public-health issue, like an unsafe airframe on a passenger jet or . . . some company dumping cyanide into the East River. Issues like that? He can talk, we can air it. They've got no right to hide behind a corporate agreement." The journalists—like the class-action lawyers from Mississippi trying to bring a case against tobacco companies—are confirmed in their belief that Wigand's insider secret eclipses any of his concerns about his private welfare. Again, importantly, the journalists and lawyers are careful not to tell Wigand what to do—he is alone, all by himself in making the decision—yet Wigand repeatedly hears about the wider context and consequences of his decision. A class-action lawsuit is tautologically about the "greatest good for the greatest number," and Bergman's 1960s radical, Herbert Marcuse–inflected social politics also speaks to his abiding commitment to helping people achieve justice. (At one point, Bergman's boss, Don Hewitt [Philip Baker Hall] barks, "You are a fanatic. An anarchist.") Even if Bergman doesn't wish Wigand harm, he remains focused strictly on how Wigand can help others by testifying: "You go public, and thirty million people hear what you got to say, nothing, I mean nothing, will ever be the same again. . . . And that's the power you have." Power? Wigand demurs: "And maybe it won't change a fucking thing. And people like myself and my family are left hung out to dry. Used up! Broke, alone!" What does it matter if Bergman believes Wigand is "the key witness in the biggest public-health reform issue, maybe the biggest, most expensive corporate-malfeasance case in US history," if Wigand can't square his position with other values and duties? Given the set-up offered by Bergman and Scruggs, how can Wigand determine what being courageous means? Is it courageous to protect one's family come what may? Or is it courageous to protect the American people even if that protection comes at the cost of great personal loss?

Aristotle says that "he is courageous who endures and fears the right things, for the right motive, in the right manner, and at the right time, and who displays confidence in a similar way. For a courageous man feels and acts according to the merits of each case and as reason guides him."[17] If Aristotle's notion of courage is not to conflict with Kant's notion of following the moral law, we ought to be careful to understand "the merits of each case" in a deontological sense (as the nature of one's duty to follow a moral command) and not in a utilitarian sense (as what we hope will achieve the most propitious results at any given moment). To maintain coherence with Kant's view, the pursuit of the mean should not be measured in terms of outcomes, but only by the degree to which reason guides us to fulfill our duties. To square Aristotle with Kant, we likely have to find a *logical* sympathy between acting from virtue and acting from duty. (Yet to discover what the mean between extreme alternatives might be, do we not necessarily implicate ourselves in some form of utilitarian assessment of empirical factors?) Wigand's case—as well as Bergman's—gives us an important space in which to consider the potential conflicts that may arise between the exercise of virtue and the fulfillment of duty. When Hilary Putnam responds to work by moral theorist Martha Nussbaum, he recognizes a way of logically consolidating the two views: "And if not everything is to be thought of in terms of trade-offs, then the insights of Aristotelian ethics and the insights of Kantian ethics need not conflict."[18] In this way, courage always involves some form of moral action and never can be understood exclusively as a means to an end.

At the extremes, Aristotle finds unattractive behavior: "He who exceeds in confidence in a fearful situation is called reckless. . . . [M]ost reckless men are reckless cowards: they put on a show of confidence when the situation permits, but do not stand their ground when there is something to fear"; "A man who exceeds in fear is a coward: he fears the wrong things, in the wrong manner, and so forth, all the way down the list."[19] For most of *The Insider,* Mike Wallace seems the clearest example of Aristotle's coward. "What do you think? I'm going to resign in protest? To force it on the air? The answer is 'no.' I don't plan to spend the end of my days wandering in the wilderness of National Public Radio. That decision I've already made." Wallace "exceeds in fear," and it leads him to suppress his commitment to a journalistic code in favor of the dictates of lawyers, contracts, and corporate threats—along with his own comfort and the barbed tidings of vanity. It's not until late in the film that he is shocked back into a proper awareness of his power as a newsman—upon reading the accusation that he and colleagues betrayed the legacy of Edward R. Murrow. At last able to control his fear, Wallace speaks with authority and tells his (and Bergman's) boss: "We caved. It's foolish. It's simply dead wrong." Though Wallace scoffed at the lack of "grace and consistency" in Wigand's behavior, he showed himself capable of no better.

Others exclusively frame Wigand's dilemma in extreme terms: there appears to be no middle ground. Either he breaks the confidentiality agreement, or he doesn't. He is either reckless or a coward. Further complicating matters, these terms can be applied in both directions: Wigand might be deemed reckless to testify and reckless to cower. Where is the space of courage in which Wigand can avoid "excess and deficiency" and keep "to the median and behave as he ought"?[20]

Aristotle explores several types of courageous person, including the *citizen soldier,* a term that may serve as an apt description for the kind of courageous person Jeffrey Wigand is. The citizen soldier is, in Aristotle's parlance, "motivated by virtue, that is by a sense of shame and by the desire for a noble object (to wit, honor) and avoidance of reproach as something base."[21] Some scholars have claimed that the citizen soldier exhibits a "specious form" of courage, yet Aristotle says the courage of the citizen soldier "bears the closest resemblance" to the highest form of courage—that is to say, the type motivated by virtue.[22] This account reads like a gloss on what Wigand means by his conscience: the notion that he cannot abide the shame or inglorious state of being a witness—and, worse, an aid—to criminal activity (e.g., the use of coumarin). Wigand's anecdote about how the president of Johnson & Johnson handled a threat to the credibility of his product offers a glimpse of what Wigand believes to be the standard of "a man of science," and he is ashamed about his role at B&W. Given his values, Wigand should never have gone to work for a tobacco company, as Bergman seems to remind him: "You come from corporate cultures where research, really, creative thinking, these are core values. . . . What are you doing? Why are you working for tobacco in the first place?" Wigand's understanding of his role as a scientist is in tandem with the Hippocratic Oath: "I will prescribe regimens for the good of my patients according to my ability and my judgment and never do harm to anyone. I will not give a lethal drug to anyone if I am asked, nor will I advise such a plan."

The visual and emotional tonality of the scene in which Wigand decides to testify is somewhat overwrought, leaning closer to what one might expect of a war film—in particular, scenes in which men prepare for battle. Wigand is surrounded by gun-wielding law enforcement officers, squads of police and FBI cars are in formation, and there is a clear sense that everyone there—every officer of the law—is waiting for Wigand's decision. Wigand is sorting the responsibilities stipulated in his signed confidentiality agreement (or contract) with the dictates of his conscience (aiming to protect his code). Prior to his making the decision, we sense his radical asymmetry with these men of law, order, war, and justice. But once he decides to testify, he is immediately transformed into an advocate of justice: rapidly placed at the center of an impressive, vaunting police procession and hurried to give his deposition. With Wigand's face in profile, the car drives past a cemetery of fallen soldiers. Wigand remains alone and misunderstood by those who surround him. He is not leading a battle for the good of man. He has triumphed in an inward moral struggle, fighting only to assure his own goodness and render the victory of inner peace.

Even as Wigand aims to fulfill the duties of a man of science, which may require brave acts, he is also a father who wants to protect his children. Clearly, part of his pursuit of a noble object and avoidance of shame is linked with his sense of how his daughters will judge his action. Will they think him foolish and reckless for testifying or a coward for neglecting the call? What action will establish the most honor for him in the eyes of his children? Not surprisingly, we are back in the position of predicting the future, which is to say possible consequences and utility value. Such things can't be predicted because the outcome, in this case, the daughters' opinion of their father, will likely be variable and change through time. As children, they might resent his decision to testify (mostly because they aren't in a position to understand what he faces and how it results in the family splitting up), but as adults with children of their own they might empathize and deeply admire him—at last confirming the honor the father so desperately hoped to establish.

Looking again at the scene of decision, Wigand surrounded by lawmen, we may recognize an unspoken but nevertheless palpable sense that these men know what Wigand should do and what they want him to do. Yet although Bergman, Scruggs, and others never compel Wigand to decide one way or the other, there is an atmosphere in which Wigand's desire to be virtuous—to do the right thing, to follow his conscience—is complicated by their attention and promise of protection. As Aristotle notes, "Courageous action ought to be motivated not by compulsion, but by the fact that it is noble."[23] Though Wigand is never compelled or coerced by others to testify, it does seem crucial to a proper understanding of his bravery that he is surrounded by men who may be brave themselves, may appreciate what he risks, but who fundamentally misunderstand the nature of his duty. Wigand can't be deemed brave because he takes a risk to help others or even his family, but only because he at last confirms his commitment to following his conscience and the moral law.

Wigand cannot express his courage in isolation because it is only from within a community that his bravery can be intelligible to himself and others. "A hermit is incapable of acting virtuously."[24] Yet Wigand has no company for his particular kind of bravery—a courage to follow conscience—because he is surrounded by men of the law (lawyers, police officers, judges, corporate businessmen with their contracts, and apparently corrupt FBI agents). Even Bergman, a seeming ally, remains focused on the effects of revealing Wigand's "vital, insider stuff." Through his testimony, Wigand seeks to redress his lapse from a life in science by honoring the code he believed in and aspired to. When he blows the whistle, the noble object of his professional life is immediately restored.

In the screenplay, after Wigand confirms his decision to testify, the scene description reads: "Dick Scruggs and Lowell [Bergman] look at this normal, somewhat flawed, very courageous man." Scruggs and Bergman's sense of Wigand's mixed status—brave but flawed—does not diminish how his behavior, as Aristotle notes, "is characterized by the fact that he endures what is fearful to man and what seems fearful to him, because to do so is noble and to do otherwise is base." Aristotle suggests that it is "a mark of even greater courage to be fearless and unruffled when suddenly faced with a terrifying situation than when the danger is clear beforehand."[25] Wigand does not demonstrate this "greater courage" because he clearly is not a measure of grace and consistency. And yet he stumbles bravely in the right direction.

Notes

I draw all *The Insider* quotations from the shooting script by Michael Mann and Eric Roth (version dated November 5, 1999), available online at http://www.dailyscript. com/scripts/the-insider_shooting.html. There are also vast and useful resources about the film at http://www.JeffreyWigand.com. For constructive comments on an earlier version of this essay, I thank Sheldon Hershinow and Lorna K. Hershinow. And I appreciate helpful input on later drafts from the editors of this volume. For years of generous, incisive reflections on *The Insider,* I'm especially and aptly indebted to K. L. Evans, who knows and lives the truth of John Milton's remark that "A meet and happy conversation is the chiefest and noblest end of marriage" ("The Doctrine and Discipline of Divorce").

1. See the Society of Professional Journalists Code of Ethics available at http://www.spj.org/ethicscode.asp.

2. Alan Donagan, *The Theory of Morality* (Chicago: University of Chicago Press, 1977), 90.

3. Ibid., 92.

4. Ibid., 93.

5. Ibid., 94.

6. Immanuel Kant, *Foundations of the Metaphysics of Morals* (1785), trans. Lewis White Beck (Upper Saddle River, NJ: Prentice-Hall, 1994), 15–16.

7. Ibid., 16.

8. Jeremy Bentham acknowledges Joseph Priestley's influence on this point, in particular by means of the latter's "The Liberty of the People and Public Discussion." See John Towill Rutt, *Life and Correspondence of Joseph Priestley,* 2 vols. (London: R. Hunter, 1831), 1:52, for quotes and discussion of this influence.

9. John Stuart Mill, *Utilitarianism* (London: Parker, Son, and Bourn, 1863), 17.

10. Kant, *Foundations of the Metaphysics of Morals,* 16–17.

11. Ibid., 19.

12. Ibid.

13. Ibid., 20.

14. Ibid.

15. Ibid.

16. Aristotle, *Nicomachean Ethics,* trans. Martin Ostwald (Englewood Cliffs, NJ: Prentice-Hall, 1962), 1115a.

17. Ibid., 1115b.

18. Hilary Putnam, "Taking Rules Seriously: A Response to Martha Nussbaum," *New Literary History* 15, no. 1 (Autumn 1983): 195.

19. Aristotle, *Nicomachean Ethics,* 1115b, 1116a.

20. Ibid., 1116a.

21. Ibid.

22. Ibid. See Lee Ward, "Nobility and Necessity: The Problem of Courage in Aristotle's *Nicomachean Ethics,*" *American Political Science Review* 95, no. 1 (March 2001): 71–83.

23. Aristotle, *Nicomachean Ethics,* 1116b.

24. Martin Ostwald, introduction to Aristotle, *Nicomachean Ethics,* xxiv.

25. Aristotle, *Nicomachean Ethics,* 1117a.

THE COMMODIFICATION OF JUSTICE

Michael Mann and Postmodern Law

Mark Wildermuth

The significance of the postmodern milieu for Michael Mann has been established by such studies as Steven Sanders's "Sunshine Noir: Postmodernism and *Miami Vice*," Steven Rybin's *The Cinema of Michael Mann*, and my book *Blood in the Moonlight: Michael Mann and Information Age Cinema*.[1] Mann's fascination with the contingent nature of knowledge, the breakdown of ethical norms, and the impact of information technologies on contemporary life are hallmarks of his focus on postmodernity, which lends philosophical depth and sophistication to his works in television and the cinema.

In this essay, I focus on Mann's interest in legalism in the postmodern milieu as a means of describing his films' rhetorical stance and their implicit critique of contemporary culture. His televisual and cinematic works show concern for the collapse of collective social action under the influence, in part, of a modern legal system that commodifies the idea of justice and thereby ensures that the law serves mainly the violently acquisitive members of society at the top of the economic hierarchy. Mann shows strong affinities for the postmodern critique of law exemplified by the critical legal studies movement, Jean Baudrillard's philosophy, and developments in leftist legal critiques after the terrorist attacks of September 11, 2001. For Mann, contemporary law becomes another coercive force in today's information-based culture for controlling human identity and corrupting human society in late-capitalist America. Using representations of collectivist, egalitarian, precapitalist tribal law and their modern cultural analogues, as a contrast with today's legalism, he establishes norms for collective social action that may challenge this global legalistic terrorism on the local level—though only temporarily and with limited results. With analysis of select films such as *The Last of the Mohicans* (1992) and *Collateral* (2004) as well as episodes from the 1980s television shows Mann produced, *Crime Story* (1986–1988) and *Miami Vice* (1984–1989), I hope to show how Mann's oeuvre raises important questions about the negative effects of today's legalism and whether viable means still exist for resisting this coercive cultural force. Mann uses contract law and its association with the social contract as a major motif for exploring the collapse of societal collective norms and their replacement with oppressive legalistic agencies.

Backgrounds to Legal Theory

As critics such as Steven Connor have shown, postmodern legal theory is best understood as a response to issues raised by modernist legal theory with antecedents in the eighteenth, nineteenth, and twentieth centuries.[2] Theories such as positivism, formalism, and realism, as Anthony Sebok has shown, struggled with the issue of determinism and law. Specifically, to what degree is law based on purely deductive, objective legal principles that have no basis in empirical, inductive modes of proceeding and can thereby allow the law to be contaminated by subjective value judgments?[3] In short, to what degree can a judge exercise discretion in making a judgment without subverting legal protocol and procedures? As Sebok argues, early positivism, going all the way back to Jeremy Bentham in the eighteenth century, indicated that law and morality should be separated, that law should be deductive, and that its only base of authority is in the sovereign—even if the sovereign will might be represented by the collective will of the people in a kind of legal and societal contract.[4]

Realists and even later proponents of formalism and positivism came to question the deductive and mechanical nature of this philosophy, while still recognizing that the possible result of not following the original positivist norm might be laws and legal decisions that would be inconsistent and full of contradictions. As James Boyle says, some realists eventually came to accept these contradictions and ambiguities as part of the milieu whereby laws are tested, made, and established. Stanley Fish's pragmatic school would later make the same argument and insist that this ambiguity was part of the natural order of things in law.[5]

But in the 1970s and 1980s, the critical legal studies (CLS) movement took issue with such stances under the influence of Marxist theories of law as well as structuralist and deconstructive postmodern philosophy. All of these philosophies pointed to the sinister implications of these contradictions in the law within the context of a growing cultural studies movement that would insist that such contradictions reflected those promulgated by cultural norms and ideologies shaped by postcapitalist social and economic hierarchies. These implications, in turn, raised the possibility that the contradictions pointed to a legal system that promised equal treatment under the law but did not deliver it for people marginalized by class, gender, ethnicity, or sexual preference.

The great Marxist legal theorist Evgeny Pashukanis had said in the 1920s that law is created for profit to protect the interests of the ruling class's hierarchy and represents a form of "organized class terror." Central to this legalism was the idea of the contract, as a social and a legal phenomenon, that was an "integral part" of capitalist law. Under the influence of such an elitist system, "'society as a whole' does not exist." Hence, all "organic bonds between individuals" erode, with justice being no more than a rude form of "retaliation."[6]

CLS scholars in the 1980s focused on the greater significance of contractual social arrangements in the context of contemporary legalism and its attendant forms of government. As E. Allen Farnsworth shows in his monumental study of contracts, all contracts entail a promise involving an exchange of some kind of goods or services to be provided in the future, where both parties theoretically have something to lose if the contract is not honored by all parties involved. Contracts initially focused on the idea of sharing, but with the rise of more materialist cultures from the Middle Ages to the sixteenth century the emphasis shifted from the idea of gift exchange to business enterprise. By the nineteenth century, the contract became the essential "underpinning of the free enterprise system" because it seemed to focus on the freedom of the individual. In truth, however, this notion eroded over time as contracts in business reflected less an egalitarian emphasis of the rights of all individuals in the context of the contract than a notion of contracts reflecting the influence of economic status with the rise of monopolies.[7]

These realities have caused CLS scholars to question the impact of the contract in capitalist societies where the social contract between ruler and ruled is supposed to reflect the same kind of egalitarianism originally presumed to be reflected in the legally binding business contract. In post-eighteenth-century legal theory (after William Blackstone), laws were assumed to be just only if a contractual arrangement existed between the sovereign (or elected government) and the people who participated in the contract. But such post-Lockean and post-Rousseauian ideas have come under attack in CLS theory, influenced by the deconstructive attack on Enlightenment thought. Anne Barron has pointed to the problem of distilling a single will from a multiplicity of wills.[8] Contracts, according to James Boyle's reading of Peter Gabriel's CLS theory, in truth present "as an accomplished fact an equality that is completely spurious," and this "reification . . . conceals social alienation."[9] This legalism, says Peter Fitzpatrick, ultimately "turns against social relations."[10] This thought is especially disturbing because contract, says Roberto Unger, influences many modes of thought in capitalist society.[11] For Clare Dalton, although the contract attempts to provide a private agreement between distinct individuals with distinctive interests and rights, it actually does the opposite. Its private bond is always violated by the presence of public law. Hence, it deconstructs the subjects who participate in it along with the seemingly egalitarian principles for which it stands.[12]

This concern for the destabilization of human subjects, both individually and socially, anticipates the equally great concern in CLS theory for the possibly coercive and subversive effects of the contract and legalism in mediated, information-based, late-capitalist culture. Anthony Carty, under the influence of the visionary social critic Jean Baudrillard, questions the capacity of the social contract to reflect the will of the people in modern media culture. Like Costas Douzinas, Peter Goodrich, and Yifat Hachamovitch, Carty recognizes that law has become a commodity in this society where the contractual has come to stand for human sociality.[13] As Stephen Connor argues, with Baudrillardian philosophy comes the idea that late capitalism turns not only objects into commodities, but abstract ideas such as love and justice as well. When even the noblest and most sacrosanct ideas become commodities, culture undergoes a fundamental change. Unlike the Marxist who believes the material means of production are the driving forces in the society, the Baudrillardian argues that today it is the image of the product, the abstract idea of it, that has become the commodity and thereby the driving force in society. Images become part of a consciousness industry that shapes what we think, who we are, the choices we make, including everything from what clothes to buy to what presidents to elect. In such a world, Connor says, language points not to reality, but to itself; image is all, and society loses its cohesiveness as a force to shape governments and laws.[14] Opposites such as good and evil, justice and injustice, law and criminality will deconstruct when reality is replaced by a hyperreality of images, and, as

Carty argues, we are left only with the simulation of a social contract under the influence of a mediated world run wild.[15]

Not surprisingly, some CLS theorists directly address the fear that law and its contractual underpinnings can use symbols and language to shape consciousness and to replace, as Peter Gabriel and Paul Harris say, "an active community founded upon love and mutual respect." These authors argue that lawyers and legal theorists must subvert these symbols by empowering clients instead of focusing on the clients' legal rights. These rights are provided by a contract that implies that the real source of the individual's power is the legal system and its attendant economic-based hierarchies, not the individual. These theorists therefore recommend that lawyers establish an egalitarian rapport with their clients and teach them to see beyond the constructs of power.[16] Hence, as Farnsworth says, there develops a strong emphasis in CLS theory on "altruism and solidarity" to fight against the selfish, acquisitive tendencies of today's legalism. And as Unger says, there is the continuing hope that weakening the hierarchy will unleash potentialities that have hitherto been hidden by the current system.[17] This hope has been sustained by recent theory, too, even in the milieu of the post-9/11 security state with its emphasis on legalism as a means of combating external and internal security threats. As Wendy Brown and Janet Halley say in their 2002 volume *Left Legalism/Left Critique,* writers such as Judith Butler and legal theorist Duncan Kennedy have offered critiques of the problem of focusing on individual rights in legalism when this focus empowers the system rather than the individual. There is still time, they feel, for discussing the need for collectivist effort.[18]

Legalism and Michael Mann

I am not the first Mann scholar to emphasize Mann's interest in dishonored contracts, covenants, vows, and promises: as Mark Steensland says, the deal gone wrong, the Faustian arrangement with a malevolent agency, is a major motif in Mann's work that often hurls the plot machinery into motion.[19] This is certainly true of *The Jericho Mile* (1979), where R. C. Stiles's (Richard Lawson) agreement to help drug dealer and gangster Dr. D. (Brian Dennehy) goes horribly wrong, and Larry "Rain" Murphy (Peter Strauss) eventually motivates other prisoners to revolt against D. It is equally true of *Thief* (1981), where Frank's (James Cann) deal with the gangster Leo (Robert Prosky) also goes awry and leads him to destroy his gangster ally. And we see this in later Mann films. The murder and mayhem of *Heat* (1995) are predicated when Roger Van Zant (William Fichter) does not live up to his deal with Neil McCauley (Robert De Niro), and war breaks out between them. And certainly it is true of *The Insider* (1999), where Big Tobacco's attempt to change its confidentiality agreement with Jeffrey Wigand (Russell Crow) results in his alliance with CBS News producer Lowell Bergman (Al Pacino) and his decision to testify against his employers in open court. Why does the motif occur, and what is at the root of this contractual breakdown that causes the fracture and leads the protagonists to rebel against the forces that oppress them?

The answer is made clear in *The Last of the Mohicans* (1992), where Mann exposes the flaw discussed by leftist legal critiques in which these seemingly egalitarian contracts merely provide cover for the oppressive legalistic machinery that informs the way contracts are constituted in the real world. Specifically, *Mohicans* reveals the hypocritical application of the British post-Lockean concept of the social contract and underscores how this application poisoned the ability to make any contract on an equal basis, which, in turn, poisoned modern post-eighteenth-century law. Mann represents the problem clearly in the colonial cultural milieu, where he contrasts the tribal law that influences the thinking of the Native Americans and the American colonists with the corrupt, hypocritical law of the English "Yangees."

The conflict between the two systems is set up in an early scene where Hawkeye (Daniel Day-Lewis) and his Mohican brother, Uncas (Eric Schweig), attend a meeting between colonists, Native Americans, and British soldiers who are trying to recruit people to fight against the French and their Native American allies—"for king, for country" as one of the British representatives says. One of the Mohawk representatives indicates that because the French have violated their earlier contractual agreement with the Mohawks by allowing Abenaki and others on Mohawk land, he will strike up a new contract with the British and fight the "Huron and les Francais." He understands these contracts with the whites in clear and unambiguous terms, like his colonial friend Jack Winthrop (Edward Blatchford), who seeks to make his contract directly with General Dan Webb (Mac Andrews) to ensure the terms of the agreement will allow his men to leave the defense of Fort William Henry if their homes are attacked. Only the more sophisticated Hawkeye seems suspicious of these contacts; when the British ask him if he is not "a loyal subject to the Crown," he mockingly replies, "I do not consider myself *subject* to much at all."

And the ensuing action proves him wise, for the British are using the law to refashion these people's sense of subjecthood in order to use them to realize British geopolitical ambitions. This is painfully obvious in the ensuing scene, where Winthrop and the militia make terms with Webb—but only after Webb's staff has threatened them with being pressed into service if they refuse to join. Webb agrees to let the militia defend "their women and children" on the frontier, but it is clear that the contract is merely a means of securing their service. Webb's contempt for anyone not English becomes clear after the militia agree to his terms and leave, whereupon Webb says to Major Duncan Heyward (Steven Waddington), "One has to reason with these colonials to get them to do anything," with the clear implication being that it was the only way to acquire their service. Webb speaks also of the inferiority of his French enemies and refers even to his colleague Colonel Edmund Munro (Maurice Roëves), whose daughters Duncan is to escort to their father's post at Fort William Henry, as "the Scotsman." Munro's children Cora (Madeleine Stowe) and Alice (Jodhi May) are likewise "the Scotsman's daughters." The world of the British is one where global domination, the desire to "make the world England," as Duncan says, is clearly based on a sense of their perceived superiority to all other "races" and cultures.

So too, it soon becomes clear, is their legal system. After Duncan, with the aid of Hawkeye, Uncas, and their father, Chingachgook (Russell Means), brings the daughters to Munro, the contract's integrity is put to the test—and it fails. Despite testimony from all of these men (and later from his daughters) that the colonials' homes are being attacked, Colonel Munro refuses to let the militia leave the fort. His public claim is that he has insufficient evidence to honor this clause of the contract, but he privately cites his real reason to Duncan: "These considerations are subordinate to the interests of the Crown." In short, the terms of the agreement are not egalitarian—they instead reflect the interests of the imperialist hierarchy, just as CLS theory would confirm. Indeed, as Peter Fitzpatrick argues, the universalist thrust of enlightened law depended on identifying colonized people as "others" who defined the superior character of eighteenth-century European law and made law part of the "imperializing project of Enlightenment."[20]

The colonists soon comprehend the hypocrisy involved here. Jack Winthrop says to Munro, "Does the rule of English law no longer govern? Has it been replaced by absolutism?" And later, when Munro has falsely accused Hawkeye of sedition for saying the French might offer a better alternative, Winthrop confides to Hawkeye: "I believe if they set aside their law as and when they wish, their law no longer has rightful authority over us. All they have over us is tyranny." And his vision is shared by Cora Munro, who confronts her father with the falsity of his charges against Hawkeye and the hypocrisy of Munro's decision when she acts as an advocate not only for Hawkeye, but for all of the Americans: "They do not live their lives 'by your leave!' They hack it out of the wilderness with their own two hands, burying their dead and their children along the way. . . . If it is sedition, then I am guilty of sedition too." Sadly, of course, her father does not see the hypocrisy involved here until General Webb fails to honor his implicit contract as a British officer to come from Fort Edwards to fight for Munro, who can only observe (in the original theatrical release of the film): "I've lived to see something which I have never expected—a British officer afraid to support another." When the chips are down, Webb will not risk anything to save "the Scotsman" and his daughters.

All of this is contrasted with the way Native American justice works, as represented in the scene where the great sachem (Mike Phillips) holds council to hear the plaints of Magua (Wes Studi)—who has killed Munro and captured his daughters—and to consider the reply from Hawkeye and Duncan. Everything in the scene conforms to what scholars of tribal or precapitalist law have reported in the wake of leftist critiques of postcapitalist legalism. The function of tribal law in general was adjudicative rather than executive; it was egalitarian and attempted to express the will of the people while appeasing as many plaintiffs as possible. Vine S. Deloria and Clifford M. Lytle confirm this description: law councils and the chief or chiefs presiding over them sought to be "conciliatory," and retribution was sought only if parties involved in criminal acts or acts of violence refused to reconcile with the offended parties. A. S. Diamond makes the same assertions about tribal law.[21]

Hence, the sachem tries to reconcile all parties involved in the conflict precipitated by Magua's actions. Even though he declares Magua's way not to be "the Huron way," he indicates that Magua should take the younger Munro daughter so "Magua's heart is healed" and, incredibly, "so that Munro's seed does not die." Duncan will go back to the English "so their hatred burns less bright." Cora Munro will die, but only to even the score "for Magua's dead children." The sachem attempts to establish justice for all according to customs and mores shared with his people, even helping those from outside the tribe when he can. And when Hawkeye and Duncan raise objections to the sentence on Cora, he listens and allows Duncan to take her place.

His judgments—however naive they may be in the face of the "sickness of" European greed that Hawkeye speaks of more knowingly than do the Hurons in the council—nevertheless seem to underscore what Deloria and Lytle speak to—namely, that tribal social and cultural unity and egalitarianism negated the necessity of the contradictory Western contract with its elitist hidden agendas.[22] The sachem, of course, cannot soothe the heart of the corrupt and greedy Magua, who has vowed to enslave his Native brothers in his psychotic parody of Western justice and imperialism, and so in the end only the oldest form of justice can prevail when Chingachgook seeks retribution for the death of his son, Uncas, by killing Magua. Significantly, none of this can stop the coming of the whites and their system, as Chingachgook's final speech on the death of Native America makes clear. What is to come is systematic injustice, as the rest of Mann's works demonstrates.

Mann's televisual work is especially effective in illuminating this theme, particularly in those instances where Mann himself was responsible for not only producing the episodes, but also penning either the story or the script. As we move into the mid- to late twentieth century with *Crime Story,* set in the early 1960s, and *Miami Vice,* set in the 1980s, we see that modern law is a continuation of what began in the eighteenth century—a contract-based legalism that alienates individuals, supports the economic-based hierarchy, and weakens human potential for collective action. If law's tyranny can be resisted at all, it is only on the local level; the global reach of the system, made even more powerful by modern information technologies, taints or destroys efforts toward egalitarian collective action and can subvert even localized efforts to liberate justice from the manipulative agency of commodification.

A case in point is the *Crime Story* episode "Abrams for the Defense" (October 14, 1986), story by Mann and teleplay by David J. Burke and Kenneth Michael Edwards. Early in the series, defense attorney David Abrams (Stephen Lang) is working as a public defender because, as he explains in the pilot to Major Crime Unit team leader Lieutenant Michael Torello (Dennis Farina) before he joins the unit's crusade against gangster Ray Luca (Anthony Dennison), he wants to help "people who got the wrong color skin, who talk the wrong language." Abrams is clearly on the side of the disenfranchised, and his name appropriately associates him with historic Old Testament leaders, part of the rise of tribal and ancient Israel, whose law, as Harold V. Bennett, Frank Crusemann, and A. S. Diamond concur, was renowned for its egalitarianism in the ancient world and still influences modern Western law today.[23] Abrams's techniques in this episode also associate him with the egalitarian emphasis in Marxist and CLS theory. But the episode shows how modern corruption can pervert the methods of someone like Abrams and ultimately render him or her impotent in the face of the global power of the legal system.

Abrams is impressive through most of the episode. When racist slum lord Stirkowski refuses to provide services to his African American tenants (whom he refers to as "animals!") and provokes tenant Hector Lincoln (Ving Rhames) into attacking him, Abrams stages a brilliant defense of Lincoln. As he explains to his African American journalist colleague (soon to become his girlfriend) Suzanne Terry (Pam Grier), he argues that "the emotional . . . violence instigated by the landlord is tantamount to a physical attack." Terry, recognizing the leftist slant of his approach, asks if he will also quote "Marx and Engels" in court, and Abrams replies, "No, but I'm gonna win." His plan is to ask Terry to provide "third-person confirmation" of this violence in the form of a news article. "Sounds like you're trying to manipulate the press," says Terry. "Absolutely," says Abrams—but she agrees to help anyway.

In Terry's interview with Stirkowski, Stirkowski reveals himself to be an even worse version of the British in *Mohicans*. He offers a shallow definition of freedom—it means "being able to make money, own buildings . . . have rights." And when Terry asks, "What rights do your tenants have?" Stirkowski blithely replies, "They have right to pay rent or move."

This is the kind of social evil Abrams has told Torello that he is fighting; witnessing his dad's rise to power as a mob lawyer, he has seen enough of "all the justice money can buy." He is rebelling against this system and against men like Stirkowski who use it to oppress people like Hector, his wife, and his child, plus all the other families that reside in the building. Abrams is fighting for community and equality. He seeks to unify the jury as a social unit appalled by the injustice of what has happened. Like a CLS attorney, he gains the trust of his client ("I'm here to fight for you") and puts the entire system on trial. In court, he never denies that Lincoln attacked the landlord. But he insists that a bigger moral value is involved here—unlike the more conservative positivist and realist attorneys of the time, he is not afraid to combine ethics and law. He instead raises the bigger question oriented toward community values: "At what point does a man have a right to stand up for his family against social and economic violence?" The real issue, David Abrams insists, is "that all men are created equal in the eyes of God. And that no one, no one, individually or collectively, has the right to abridge that guarantee. . . . And if that is a value to you, your verdict is just as self-evident: not guilty!" The deeply sympathetic expressions on the jurors' faces say it all, as does their verdict later on—they do work as a social unit and, despite the evidence clearly indicating Hector committed assault—they acquit him. Abrams seems to have beaten the system, replacing inequitable contractualism with collective social effort.

But has he? His rhetoric here seems to embody the best leftist principles that would animate the jury's collective sense of responsibility. Nevertheless, his language is still bound up in the "self-evident" logic of contract and rights granted by the system therein. And his rhetoric alone does not win the day. He also flashes a copy of Terry's article "Slum Lord Endangers Tenants" before the jury during the prosecutor's cross examination of Hector in order to manipulate their response—and again their startled facial expressions show that this tactic is working. In a later episode in this season of the series, Ray Luca does the same thing to a jury, but Abrams objects, calling it jury tampering. In short, Abrams has used the power of the press as an icon to manipulate response, much as the courtroom itself does (as CLS theory after Baudrillard confirms) with its images of the flag, the portrait of Abraham Lincoln, and so on. Has Abrams secured a victory against the manipulative system by mirroring its methods?

The shocking ending clearly proves he has not. Abrams stages a block party at the end, a symbol of communal unity, to celebrate the acquittal and to provide Hector with the rent money he needs after losing his job. But as the streetwise Suzanne Terry points out, "Hector may be out of jail, but the situation hasn't changed. Who's gonna force Stirkowski to make this place livable?" And, as it turns out, the answer is no one. Stirkowski crashes the party by serving an eviction notice on Hector, saying to Abrams, "It's the law, you tell them." An altercation takes place, just as in the episode's beginning—but this time Stirkowski hits Hector's wife, and Hector kills him. Torello is forced to arrest Hector for murder, and as the camera dollies back, we see the community of supporters breaking up and a stunned David Abrams utterly isolated from everyone, even as Suzanne Terry looks on in astonishment and sympathy. Abrams's attack on the system could not beat it, either globally or locally. Abrams could not separate himself from it adequately and used too many of its tactics—even the manipulation of symbols and media—to succeed. His defense simulated justice but changed nothing in reality. Could another kind of assault work?

Flash forward to Miami, 1985: the Reagan era in full swing; commodification off the scale, as Baudrillard's criticism of the time attests, with everything from the cola wars to the coming of Iran Contra; America's president stepping out of the celluloid world of Hollywood into the Cold War culture of simulation and nuclear deterrence. Michael Mann and Maurice Hurley write the pivotal *Miami Vice* episode "Golden Triangle Part II" (January 18, 1985), which explains how vice squad leader Lieutenant Martin Castillo (Edward James Olmos) spent five years in Thailand as a US Drug Enforcement Agency (DEA) agent fighting drug kingpin Lao Li (Keye Luke), who used his CIA contact Dale Menton (John Santucci) to attempt to assassinate Castillo and his wife, May Ying (Joan Chen).[24] Castillo comes to Miami only to discover that Lao Li has taken up residence there and has brought May Ying with her new husband to use as hostages to keep Castillo and detectives Sonny Crockett (Don Johnson) and Ricardo Tubbs (Philip Michael Thomas) at bay.

Twenty years have passed since the world of *Crime Story*, but commodification has made an even greater mockery of justice than before as local law efforts are rendered impotent by the globalization of the power of men like Lao Li. As Lao Li explains in his first scene with Castillo, "You don't seem to understand the realities of commodities. In the global market, opium is no different from tapioca or tin ore from Malaysia. It is simply a product for which there is a demand." Through it, he can empower himself by rendering law and its enforcement agencies into commodities. That is why he can come in "under the protection of one of your federal agencies, and you can't do anything about it." By contrast, he argues, Castillo sees "the world through a narrow, moralistic perspective." "That is why" Castillo is only "a local policeman," but Lao Li is here "to become an honored citizen."

By mastering the globalization of commodification and corruption, Lao Li can invade Castillo's private world, steal his wife and domestic happiness from him, empower Lao Li's own extended family, and render Castillo's justice system impotent. Even in Asia Lao Li had been able to pit the CIA against the DEA because, as Menton explains to Castillo, "his junk was financed by politicians in Bangkok," who were the only US allies left "in that part of the world" after the fall of Saigon. Commodification controls world markets and geopolitics, making a mockery of every legal, social, and governmental contract the world over. As Ray Luca of *Crime Story* might say, it all has become the kingdom of money. Cops and robbers, justice and injustice, are all the same when all can be bought and sold as commodities.

The situation is so bad that Crockett fears Castillo might become a "vigilante." But surprisingly Castillo underscores the same egalitarian principles as other Mann protagonists: "I'm a policeman. I enforce the law, equally, no special cases." He decides instead to build a case to bring Lao Li to justice. Yet the case is not against Lao Li, but against his grandsons, who, unlike Lao Li, are blatantly engaging in drug trafficking right in Miami. Castillo, moralist though he may be, brilliantly devises a strategy to use the desocializing commodification process against the Li family. He realizes that greed has fractured the Li family and uses it as the lever he needs against Lao Li. Invading his private realm, Castillo turns the tables on Lao Li by letting the prosecutor post bail for the wealthy grandsons after their arrest. Lao Li immediately picks them up and accuses them of having threatened the family. When the boys reply, "It's our generation's turn" to get rich, Lao Li orders their death, his own rhetoric signifying the disintegration of his social contract with them: "My paternal benevolence towards you ends right now!" Castillo catches the whole thing on tape and arrests Lao Li and Menton for attempted murder. When Menton says, "One call to Washington, Castillo," Castillo replies, "Wrong! You broke the law. This is Miami . . . not Asia." He has caught them in a trap where his localized perspective and powers can take the day. In a brilliant, deconstructive coup, he explains to Lao Li that he knew Lao Li would do anything to simulate being a law-abiding citizen, "including attempting to commit murder." He strips Lao Li of his crutches and puts him into a police car, an impotent old man.

Castillo shows that the damage done by commodification is a two-way street, leaving criminals as vulnerable as the appliers of the law in this world where contracts of all kinds can be deconstructed. It is, of course a limited kind of reprisal and has no more global impact than David Abrams's initial courtroom victory. Yes, Lao Li and Menton are no longer a threat, but the commodities trade goes on. And Castillo can never regain the domestic bliss of his earlier life. He can only accept thanks from May Ying and her husband as they depart from the airport. Castillo—like Crockett, who has lost his wife and first partner in previous episodes, and like Tubbs, who previously lost his brother in New York—remains an isolated figure. The only social bonds for these men are with their traumatized and alienated colleagues. None will enjoy a lasting marriage or a private life in the future. The global can be subverted but not overturned, despite the fact that Castillo, like so many Mann protagonists, is willing to sacrifice almost anything to battle this global conspiracy.

Another twenty years later, in the early 9/11 milieu, Mann's film *Collateral,* like Brown and Halley's leftist law theories discussed earlier, shows that in this new post-2001 security-regime culture nothing has changed. With even greater intensity than Lao Li, the antagonist hit man Vincent (Tom Cruise) parodies and underscores the corruptness of commodified legalism when he commandeers cab driver Max's (Jamie Foxx) services for a mere six hundred dollars one night in Los Angeles to commit a series of murders. Vincent is an odd but fascinating villain, complaining of the very social evil he embodies: LA does not suit him because it is "too sprawled out, disconnected; that's me," which is to say, that's his point of view, but his language betrays the truth: it is indeed *him*. He complains that "nobody knows each other" and cites the example of a dead man who rode on the LA subway for six hours without anyone noticing. But it is this very urban anonymity that allows him to play his role as judge, jury, and executioner, allows him to administer a kind of justice without conscience or compassion, for the right price, in the desocialized environs of the postmodern city. Vincent's interaction with Max enables an even darker assessment of legalism than in the films previously discussed via a more intimate perusal of the impact of legalism on self and society.

The film seems initially to set up a contrast between this desocialized antagonist and the protagonists Max and his first charge, Annie (Jada Pinkett Smith), a prosecutor with the US attorney's office. Max's dream is to create a limo service that will be such a cool groove that you won't want to leave—but he seems already to be creating such an environment in this cab when Annie arrives. He has ignored earlier fares who bicker in the back seat, but, perhaps because this fare is an attractive woman or perhaps merely through chance, at this moment Max chooses to create a more socialized environment in his cab, one where some degree of intimacy and even generosity with a stranger is possible. It is just the opposite environs Vincent would expect and, interestingly, appears also to be the opposite of what Annie herself is associated with. In the back seat, she barks orders to a colleague on the phone, which becomes a technological symbol of human disconnect through the course of the film: "So what? You'll pull an all-nighter. So will I. So save the tears!" She likewise orders Max to take an alternate route to her destination, still on her phone, still not looking at him—but, amazingly, the quiet Max resists, insisting—for her sake, not his own—that they take the present route, which will save her time and money. The subject of money for her (as for Vincent) proves irresistible—and she accepts his offer of a free cab ride if he is wrong. He is not, of course, and his gesture—an honest contract that does not exploit her on the bases of class or gender but offers her an honest chance to save money on an egalitarian basis—brings her into a more socialized space with him. They share music together, intimate details of their life. She is tied up in herself, in the game of winning, not even speaking of her clients or the possibility of a miscarriage of justice (unlike the highly moralistic, if sometimes misguided David Abrams). But Max persists and tells her to "keep that five bucks. Buy yourself something special," gives her a picture of his fantasy island getaway, and is so focused on her needs that he forgets to ask for her telephone number. But she is so grateful that she returns to provide that gift spontaneously, a remarkable personal reward from this otherwise alienated woman of law.

This is the side of human social life that Vincent has missed, that indeed seems to be vanishing since the days of the Mohicans in Mann's America, and it raises questions about the remaining potential for bonding, for informing contractual arrangements with egalitarian and altruistic gestures. But it is all poisoned by Vincent's presence, which will completely divert these people from this better destination. Vincent's contract with Max is the opposite of what just transpired. Like the British in *Mohicans,* like the system in *Crime Story,* like Lao Li in his contract to "protect" Castillo's wife, there are hidden agendas. On the pretext that all it took to involve Max was a "down payment on a Lincoln Continental," Vincent is making Max an accomplice in a murder scenario where he will hold all of the cards and Max none. Worse than that, before the night ends, he will try to assert absolute control over Max's identity by making him more like Vincent—a ruthlessly effective culling agent that judges and destroys for money and the empowerment it brings.

The *Oxford English Dictionary* says that the term *collateral* refers in its adjectival form to things on parallel paths or things descended "from the same stock" and in its noun form to goods held to secure "the obligation of a contract."[25] In this strangely deconstructive scenario, both definitions apply. These men's lives seem distinct as parallel lines yet converge toward Annie's via a contract (a contraction) that brings all of these characters together to reveal the brutality and ineffectiveness of a desocialized legalism. Vincent keeps Max on course by threatening to destroy innocent bystanders, whom he uses as collateral to ensure Max's compliance. Meanwhile, Vincent also implies he is an agent of justice—continuing to exploit Max's humanitarianism to force him to cooperate in acts of utter inhumanity. After the first murder, Vincent consoles Max by saying, "If it makes you feel any better, he was a criminal," to which Max responds, "You were taking out the garbage?"

Later, ironically after killing attorney Sylvester Clark, whom Detective Ray Fanning (Mark Ruffalo) later identifies as a "criminal attorney turned lawyer criminal," Vincent literally takes on the role of a lawyer. When Max's boss complains of damage done to the cab, Vincent, on the radio (which, like the telephone, seems to symbolize social disconnect in human communication) can falsely identify himself as "Albert Ricardo, an assistant US attorney" who will "report the company to the DMV" and prosecute it for "trying to exploit a working man." Vincent takes on the role of the egalitarian lawyer who fights for the rights of the average man—effectively enough to frighten away the employers on two separate occasions. He shares with them a contractual space that in both cases is neither truly fair nor egalitarian—but instead, as the CLS critics and Baudrillard have said, provides a sufficiently real simulation of a justice system to empower those at the top of the desocialized, disconnected hierarchy.

Vincent uses the law, its symbols, and the means to mediation in information culture to control the cab company and Max in this scene. He tells Max exactly what to say to his employers over the microphone, which creates the illusion that Max is an independent agent. Vincent later plays the role of policeman and protector to Max when a gang of street toughs rob Max and Vincent "avenges" him by killing the robbers. This assault on Max's subjecthood continues as Vincent pretends to be a friend to Max when they are visiting Max's mother in the hospital. And again much later, Vincent forces Max to pretend to be him when he sends him to retrieve his lost zip file from Felix, the man who has hired Vincent to eradicate witnesses to his own crimes. Vincent is hell-bent on making Max into a copy of himself, using legalistic structures and rhetoric to render Max as a human subject into an objectified automaton.

The legally sanctioned appliers of the law also seem to engage in this kind of directionless, desocialized miscarriage of justice. Police who see that Max's cab roof is bloody and damaged (after Vincent's first victim lands on it) leave the pair on their own cognizance when a call on their radio (still a desocializing agency) makes them desert the evidence of their own senses to pursue a criminal at another location. Later, Detective Fanning, over the protests of his own police boss (who seems to think any other legal agency but his own should be investigating the cab murders because his squad won't score any points for it), looks at the physical evidence and investigates on his own. But in checking his cell phone in the hospital when he, Vincent, and Max are riding the same elevator, he fails to see them, even as he speaks to them, which prevents him from recognizing them later in police surveillance videos when Felix meets with Max. Although he does eventually hook up with Max in a discotheque where Vincent is murdering yet another witness, Fanning still cannot identify Vincent, who suddenly appears at the exit and kills the detective.

Annie proves to be an equally ineffective applier of the law. Not only has her entire case been annihilated by Vincent on the streets of LA, but she too becomes the object of the hunt when Vincent, after Max's failed attempt to stop him by crashing the cab, comes to kill her in her own office. She cannot elude him despite Max's frantic attempts to warn her on a stolen cell phone, which—naturally, given communication technology's identification with desocialization in the film—fails due to a dead battery. Vincent steals her subjecthood and agency, too.

Only Max can save her—but under circumstances that are even more suspect than those associated with earlier protagonists such as David Abrams and Martin Castillo. Max's agency takes the form of using the same kind of weapon as Vincent—a 9-mm auto pistol, fired at close range on a darkened subway through a door that does not even allow the two men to see one another. It is the same desocialized environment that Vincent spoke of in his first scene, where he now becomes the dead man doing laps on the subway. "Think anybody'll notice?" the dying Vincent asks a stunned Max. And Max has no answer, no more than the disheveled Annie. They stumble out into the morning darkness, no words between them and no attempts to call for help or to secure a police officer, as a massive train pulls in, as if to symbolize the sheer dehumanizing machinelike nature of this act of violence in the heart of the city. The train points to the nature of legalism and its machinery, which ultimately fail morally or methodologically to distinguish good from evil or justice from terrorism. CLS theorists always aver that perhaps some human potential for a better way will emerge in our attempts to resist the unjust nature of our justice system. Mann shows how limited resistance is possible, but he also shows how, as Baudrillard's critique implies, that which we resist is always present in the means of resistance. And, hence, that resistance fails to change the globally oppressive legalism of a commodified informatics. This is what the letter of the law implies, even as we struggle to preserve whatever smattering remains in it of its preindustrial and egalitarian spirit. And that is where the case stands—and it will be no different even if, someday, we begin again by killing all of the lawyers.

Notes

1. Steven M. Sanders, "Sunshine Noir: Postmodernism and *Miami Vice*," in *The Philosophy of Neo-noir*, ed. Mark T. Conard (Lexington: University Press of Kentucky, 2007), 183–201; Steven Rybin, *The Cinema of Michael Mann* (Boulder, CO: Lexington Books, 2007); and Mark Wildermuth, *Blood in the Moonlight: Michael Mann and Information Age Cinema* (Jefferson, NC: McFarland, 2005).

2. Steven Connor, *Postmodernist Culture: An Introduction to Theories of the Contemporary*, 2nd ed. (Malden, MA: Blackwell, 1997), 61–70.

3. Anthony J. Sebok, *Legal Positivism in American Jurisprudence* (New York: Cambridge University Press, 1998), 17.

4. Ibid., 29–35.

5. James Boyle, "Introduction," in *Critical Legal Studies*, ed. James Boyle (New York: New York University Press, 1992), iii; Stanley Fish, *There's No Such Thing as Free Speech and It's a Good Thing, Too* (New York: Oxford University Press, 1994), 21.

6. Evgeny B. Pashukanis, *Law and Marxism: A General Theory*, trans. Barbara Einhorn (London: Ink Links, 1978), 171–73, 121, 174, 180–86.

7. E. Allen Farnsworth, *Contracts*, 4th ed. (New York: Aspen, 2004), 4–6, 19–20.

8. Anne Barron, "Legal Discourse and the Colonization of the Self in the Modern," in *Post-modern Law: Enlightenment, Revolution, and the Death of Man*, ed. Anthony Carty (Edinburgh: Edinburgh University Press, 1990), 108.

9. Peter Gabriel's theories are summarized in Boyle, "Introduction," xviii.

10. Peter Fitzpatrick, "'The Desperate Vacuum': Imperialism and Law in the Experience of Enlightenment," in Carty, ed., *Post-modern Law*, 93.

11. Roberto Mangabeira Unger, *The Critical Legal Studies Movement* (Cambridge, MA: Harvard University Press, 1986), 58.

12. Clare Dalton, "An Essay in the Deconstruction of Contract Doctrine," *Yale Law Journal* 94, no. 5 (April 1985): 1002–3.

13. Anthony Carty, "Postmodernism in the Theory and the Sociology of Law, or Rousseau and Durkheim as Read by Baudrillard," in Carty, ed., *Post-modern Law*, 71–89. See also Costas Douzinas, Peter Goodrich, and Yifat Hachamovitch, eds., *Politics, Postmodernity, and Critical Legal Studies* (New York: Routledge, 1994), 11.

14. Connor, *Postmodernist Culture*, 52.

15. Carty, "Postmodernism in the Theory and the Sociology of Law."

16. Peter Gabriel and Paul Harris, "Building Power and Breaking Images: Critical Legal Theory and the Practice of Law," in Boyle, ed., *Critical Legal Studies*, 367–69.

17. Farnsworth, *Contracts*, 30; Unger, *The Critical Legal Studies Movement*, 23.

18. Wendy Brown and Janet Halley, "Introduction," in *Left Legalism/Left Critique*, ed. Wendy Brown and Janet Halley (Durham, NC: Duke University Press, 2002), 20.

19. Mark Steensland, *Michael Mann* (Harpenden, UK: Pocket Essentials, 2002), 17.

20. Fitzpatrick, "'The Desperate Vacuum,'" 91.

21. Vine Deloria Jr. and Clifford M. Lytle, *American Indians, American Justice* (Austin: University of Texas Press, 1983), 87–89; and A. S. Diamond, *Primitive Law, Past and Present* (London: Methuen, 1971), 185–86.

22. Deloria and Lytle, *American Indians, American Justice,* 194–95.

23. See Harold V. Bennett, *Injustice Made Legal: Deuteronomic Law and the Plight of Widows, Strangers, and Orphans in Ancient Israel* (Grand Rapids, MI: Eerdmans, 2002), 176–77, which points to exceptions to the Israelites' normally egalitarian approach; Frank Crusemann, *The Torah: Theology and Sociology of the Old Testament Law,* trans. Allan W. Mahuke (Minneapolis: Fortress Press, 1996), 112–15; and Diamond, *Primitive Law,* 23.

24. Torello's Las Vegas–based Department of Justice task force also tangled briefly with some of Lao Li's cohorts in 1964. See the second-season *Crime Story* episodes "Seize the Time" (January 12, 1988), "Femme Fatale" (January 19, 1988), and especially "Byline" (March 29, 1988), in which Lao Li is mentioned by name and his operations in the Shan mountains are described in detail.

25. *The Compact Edition of the OED,* vol. 1 (New York: Oxford University Press, 1971).

Subjectivity and the Ethics of Duty in Michael Mann's Cinema

Aga Skrodzka

> But violence does not consist so much in injuring and annihilating persons as in interrupting their continuity, making them play roles in which they no longer recognize themselves, making them betray not only commitments but their own substance, making them carry out actions that will destroy every possibility for action.
>
> —Emmanuel Levinas, *Totality and Infinity*

> Mann has placed us squarely in a technologized empty space where his protagonists will struggle with the elements of this environment that seek to deny the subject any degree of freedom, any sense of a stabilized identity.
>
> —Mark Wildermuth, *Blood in the Moonlight*

With the release of *Drive* in 2011, Nicolas Winding Refn (the young Danish director whose *Pusher* trilogy, portraying the criminal underworld in Copenhagen, has earned him a worldwide cult following) paid tribute to the cinema of Michael Mann. Well received both in Europe, where *Drive* was praised at the 2010 Cannes Film Festival, and in the United States, where critics unanimously embraced it as stylish and heady, the film generated renewed interest among the younger and international audiences in the legacy of Mann, one of Hollywood's commercial auteurs. Initially conceived as a blockbuster project but ultimately sold as an independent film, *Drive* straddles the line between populist entertainment and film art and in doing so mimics the status of the sources that inspired it. From the beginning of his career, Michael Mann has been directing films that use a commercial platform to proffer aesthetically ambitious and philosophically rich texts, which often engage with other texts, most emphatically music and film, in an intertextual dialogue. It is precisely this intertextual sophistication that contributes to the cult cachet now attached to Refn's film, which, via its citations from Michael Mann and Walter Hill, evokes the New Hollywood tradition with its twin messages of ethical failure and "moral ambiguity."[1] The theme of moral ambiguity is also common to the other dominant Hollywood film tradition that both Mann and Refn like to draw on: film noir. Finally, there is the Western, with its penchant for moral testing of the protagonist, that connects the two filmmakers. In an interview with Christopher Rosen, Refn, acknowledging Mann as one of his key inspirations, comments on this textual link: "What I like about Michael Mann is that Michael Mann reminds me very much of a Western director. He would make Westerns, I feel. He would use the landscape of L.A. like a Western."[2]

This essay sets out to discuss Mann's contribution to bringing ethics into cinema, a contribution that Refn carefully acknowledges in his recent tribute, which centers on a character who must decide on his responsibility to face the Other (i.e., the stranger who comes into one's life asking for acknowledgment, somebody exterior to one's being who must be accepted in her or his exteriority). Like Mann's *Collateral* (2004), *Drive* tells the story of a man driving his car for a living in the streets of Los Angeles as he negotiates his obligations to himself, his profession, his dreams, and, most important, the people he runs into. Both films use the expressionistic noir aesthetic to deepen the sense of the protagonist's alienation in the urban landscape and to signal the existential dimension of his plight. Refn's film showcases the aspect of Mann's work that is a part of his auteurial signature—the preoccupation with man's construction of his subjectivity vis-à-vis his human encounters at work and at home. Indeed, the struggle between the public pursuits (the job that needs to be done) and the domestic responsibility to family (often only vestigial family) becomes the recurrent motif that makes Mann's cinema exceed the patriarchal discourse of the action film and move into the realm of art-house contemplation.[3]

In Mann's filmic microcosm, to be a man, to be the man, one has to be a working male (laboring to make a living, even if that consists of committing a crime), who responds to different levels of obligation, especially obligation to a woman. Duty frequently calls from too many directions, testing the protagonist's ability to prioritize response and his loyalty to disparate causes. Dramatizing the man's process of coming to realize his duty is Mann's way of introducing ethical concerns into his work. On a certain level, each of Mann's films is an exercise in deontology: the study of duty. But it is in *Thief* (1981) and *Collateral* that the director foregrounds the laborious process of fulfilling one's duty as well as the dutiful devotion to one's labor. If we agree with Ramon Lobato that these films are "violent, brooding, macho films,"[4] we have to consider to what degree the violence in question stems from the character's grappling with pressing obligations and, more significantly, with the need to formulate one's code of duty in the increasingly cynical late-capitalist milieu. The violence associated with this kind of ethical struggle, at least in part, undermines the "macho" stigma affixed to Mann's screen politics.

Mann's political stance, although necessarily veiled in his commercial Hollywood product, posits duty as part of the rather unfashionable agenda to confront untethered postmodern existence. Equipped with unprecedented freedom of movement and technological prostheses of all sorts, the Western postmodern subject all too often sheds most of the uncomfortable connections (often familial) that might weigh him down as well as the obligations that these connections might entail. This is not the case for Mann's struggling subject, who stubbornly clings to loyalties that Lobato calls "humanist, even Romantic."[5] Mann's protagonists might be physically mobile (*Collateral*'s main characters are featured moving around Los Angeles in a cab for the duration of the film's action), but they are *not* in possession of the kind of mobility that Zygmunt Bauman identifies as the new mobility of the global capital. In Bauman's words, "The mobility acquired by 'people who invest'— those with capital, with money which the investment requires—means the new, indeed unprecedented in its radical unconditionality, disconnection of power from obligations: duties towards employees, but also towards the younger and weaker, towards yet unborn generations and towards the self-reproduction of the living conditions of all; in short, freedom from the duty to contribute to daily life and the perpetuation of the community."[6] Whether it is Frank (James Caan) in *Thief* or Max (Jamie Foxx) in *Collateral*, Mann's protagonist is well ensconced in social relations, including work relations, that slow him down as he deliberates his duty to contribute to daily life and to "perpetuate his community." Unlike Bauman's mobile investor, Mann's subject, who must labor rather than invest for a living, is still aware of his obligation to humanity and very much tied down by his sense of this obligation.

Although Frank and Max begin as subjects obsessed with their own dreams of "making it," both end up working selflessly to protect others.

In the process, they access the aging ethos of man as the protector of the young, old, and weak, reviving for a moment the model of masculinity that has been almost completely phased out in the postfeminist culture.[7] As a result, in their response to the Other these characters define both their humanity and their masculinity. The obligation to extend oneself in an effort to preserve the Other is usually complicated in Mann's films—the character only gradually comes to realize his duty—by the fact that in the late-capitalist society, with its hypermediated and alienating landscape (which the filmmaker carefully stylizes to bring out the hyperreal element), it has become harder to know what one's societal duty is and what responsibility in a human relationship should feel like. Mann's subjects behave in the way Bauman describes in his critique of the disaffected members of postmodern society, who, "feeling easily disposable" and therefore "yearning for the security of togetherness," are paradoxically "wary of the state of 'being related' and particularly of being related 'for good,' not to mention forever—since they fear that such a state may bring burdens and cause strains they neither feel able nor are willing to bear."[8] As a consequence, Mann's films, in their emphasis on the male subject's struggle to define his debt to society, issue a subtle critique of the contemporary status quo. It is thus appropriate that a young, countercultural director such as Refn is putting Mann's work into a new discursive circulation.

Timothy Shary comments on Mann's "fascination with masculine duality, in its contest of innocence versus evil, obligation versus choice, and determination versus resignation." He also argues that Mann's heroes "throw themselves into their work and their causes."[9] Critics differ in their assessment of Mann's preferred model of masculinity. Whereas Shary sees Mann's masculinity as "obsessed with its own goals of conquest and preservation," Christopher Sharrett argues that Mann's representation of masculinity is marked by the male hero's "self-abrogation" and the general sense of the "eclipse of the male subject."[10] Sharrett further argues that Mann's films deliver a form of extended eulogy to the lost male of the previous era. Although disagreeing on whether Mann's masculinity project can be perceived as hopeful or hopeless, scholars share their understanding of the utmost centrality of the crisis mode in which Mann's man repeatedly finds himself. In this respect, the director remains faithful to his artistic roots in film noir, the Hollywood genre obsessed with construction and deconstruction of masculinity and the melodramatic dimension of that obsession.[11] In his neo-noir iteration of the masculine crisis, Mann significantly reduces the role of the female in confronting the struggling male (no flaming femme fatales populate Mann's cinematic world) and instead brings to the forefront the male's confrontation with his doppelgänger Other (always a male subject who embodies the symbolic alterity—inherent otherness always already residing within one's identity), which leads to an obligatory redefinition of the male subject's self.

Another interesting inflection in Mann's noir paradigm is his emphasis on the role of labor in reconstructing masculinity. Whereas classic noir blamed the woman for usurping the man's place in the wartime workforce, neo-noir blames the system, with its hyperstructured hierarchies of labor relations (as in corporate firm or mafia family), for symbolically castrating the working man. Mann's protagonist loves his work and is always good at what he does, but he is in permanent conflict with those who try to regulate his labor. He dreams of being self-employed yet cannot extricate himself from the all-powerful system. In *Thief,* Frank proudly states, "I am self-employed. I am doin' fine. I don't deal with egos. I am the boss of my own body." Yet soon after issuing this proclamation, he finds himself working for the boss of an organized crime unit—in other words, for the system. By dramatizing this very tension of interests, however, Mann turns his protagonist into a locus of the leftist (and existentialist) critique of American corporate capitalism. In his astute analysis of *Thief,* Mark Wildermuth discusses Frank's conflicts as a worker and an employee trapped in the postmodern exploitive economy of "acquisitive consumerism and coercive informatics." The analysis leads to a pessimistic statement: "Mann once again shows how Frank's identification with the system splinters his being and renders him—and presumably all of us who are part of this system—incapable of realizing basic human needs." Yet later in his study, by recognizing the director's investment in ethical resolution, Wildermuth revises the previous bleak assessment and comments, "Mann's complex epistemology will not allow him to dismiss the potential of the complex dynamics of human beings as social entities as possibly having the power to redeem and save our humanity and our capacity to have a meaningful, beneficial exchange with the natural world."[12]

With a closer look at the two films, *Thief* and *Collateral,* it becomes evident that the ethical potential arises from the protagonist's frustration in the workplace and the conflict that ensues between his loyalty to capital and his loyalty to those he cares about. The call to ethical action is heard in the context of dissatisfaction with one's job. More specifically, when the dream of self-employment collapses and the nightmare of servitude becomes evident to Mann's worker, he decides to engage in a transgressive act that violates the established laws and prescriptive codes in order, paradoxically, to find his way back to humanity (at the very least his own humanity). In other words, he takes action not simply to improve the terms of his work contract, but to stage a violent revolution that entails ideological and existential overhaul. In order to conduct this overhaul, he ceases to perform his job. There comes a point in *Thief* when Frank, a professional burglar, stops acquiring and accumulating wealth and decides to destroy all of his possessions in a fiery Armageddon. Max in *Collateral* similarly decides to stop his monotonous labor as a cabdriver who safely navigates the streets of Los Angeles while carrying his passengers to their chosen destinations in order to go off course and crash his cab. Although both actions endanger the lives of the two men and of those in their proximity and in terms of normative ethics should be considered unethical, the films stage them as acts of courage that are pivotal in the protagonists' search for renewed masculine identity. Tempted to dismiss these actions as macho antics so common in action films, one might easily overlook the preliminaries that lead up to the unleashing of violence as well as the self-destructive aspect, sometimes compared to Christ's "martyrlike and therefore selfless sacrifice."[13] Another reason why a viewer might be conflicted in his or her interpretation of these actions is that the logic behind the worker's violent rebellion does not match the prior interests that motivated him. Frank's and Max's excessive behavior strikes the viewer as somewhat gratuitous, even if considered within the conventions of the action genre. These two men are, after all, keen on getting wealthy and living the good life (with Frank being very close to satisfying his ambition and Max still mostly pipe-dreaming his way out of his menial profession). The nihilistic dimensions of their sudden decisions to cease their methodical efforts to fund their dreams by turning against their sources of income play out as the sort of narrative surplus (accompanied by some image surplus) that characterizes the work of auteurs who, working within the confines of commercial cinema, attempt to advance complex content without compromising their product's entertainment value. As such, the narrative surplus invites a more deconstructive, against-the-grain assessment of the text.

In an attempt to provide such an assessment, I apply the writings of Emmanuel Levinas, which focus on the role of responsibility to others in a subject's ethical life. Levinas's conception of ethics constitutes a fitting philosophical framework for Mann's discourse on ethics because it avoids simplistic moralism and rejects the possibility of ever arriving at a finite articulation of ethical imperatives. Because Mann's characters often inhabit the criminal margins of society and are frequently engaged in the dynamic process of subjectivity reconstruction that involves redefining personal ethics, Levinasian ethics—which, as Diane Perpich puts it, requires one "to know that ethics is in danger"[14]—provides a helpful, conceptually mobile paradigm. In addition, much like Mann's cinematic subject, Levinas's subject contends with much violence in the process of his search for ethical life. This violence is both unwelcome and in some situations necessary. In both Mann and Levinas, coming to accept one's responsibility is fraught with an element of violence. Perhaps surprisingly, the ultimate philosopher of altruism, Levinas, also recognizes that "one cannot say that there is no legitimate violence."[15] On some level, in both Mann and Levinas violence works as a catalyst for one's acceptance of the need to invite the Other as constitutive presence and as the necessary path out of the totalizing egoism of the Self.

In *Thief* and *Collateral*, Mann amplifies the violence that leads up to the encounter with the Other and the moment of finally responding to the Other's call. In Levinas's philosophy, the coming together of the Self and the Other constitutes an ethical relationship, and a truly ethical relationship presupposes a certain degree of annihilation of the Self. This relationship is always unilateral: what the Other asks of the Self, the Self should not be asking of the Other. Levinas explains, "For the ethical relationship which subtends discourse is not a species of consciousness whose ray emanates from the I; it puts the I in question. This putting in question emanates from the other."[16] In *Thief*, two scenes portray this encounter. In the first, Frank decides to approach a waitress, Jessie (Tuesday Weld), at a diner he patronizes on occasion with an offer of a committed relationship. Because the two hardly know each other, one might very easily interpret this meeting as the meeting of strangers who come together baring their alterity. In this exchange, it is Frank as the vulnerable Other who addresses Jessie—a man whose life has been a continuous series of violations, including a less-than-ideal childhood in an orphanage and rape during his stay in prison. In order to present the unsuspecting Jessie with his need for family, Frank sets up a dinner date with her. Not only is he late to his appointment with Jessie, but he also violently forces her to listen to his plea, physically controlling her initial rejection. The viewer might assume that Jessie was hoping for a night of semi-anonymous intimacy with Frank. Instead, he assaults her with his demand for long-term commitment. Jessie informs Frank that she is quite happy with her station in life and does not want to enter in a relationship

with him. She explains that she has already survived one traumatic relationship and is determined to be single. She reasons, "Now I get up in the
morning. I take a shower. I go to work. I have a job. I have a Social Security
card. My life is very ordinary, very boring, which is good because it's solid."
At this moment, Jessie is the Levinasian subject, whose comfortably structured totality (i.e., the privately ordered system) resists Frank's call. Desperate and starved for human intimacy, Frank does not give up. He reminds
Jessie of her responsibility to the Other in the following address: "Marking
time is what you are. You are backing off. You are hiding out. You are waiting for a bus you hope never comes 'cause you don't wanna go anywhere."
After hearing Frank's reasons for wanting a family, Jessie literally, in a gesture
of Levinasian hospitality, extends her hand to Frank and accepts the offer.

   The viewer is soon presented with the image of Frank and Jessie's familial
togetherness. Frank buys a house for his future wife and presents it to her in
a scene that is difficult for a feminist viewer to accept. In it, Frank leads Jessie,
who is wearing a braless Mother Nature outfit, into a space that he intends
to fill with children. Jessie's face beams with happiness as she twirls around
the living room, unable to believe her luck. In this embarrassing gesture of
fusing the feminine with the domestic, Mann in fact follows the philosophy
of Levinas, who also places the feminine in the intimate space of home ("the
dwelling"). At the same time, it needs to be noted that both Mann and Levinas reserve a unique role for the feminine. For both, the woman, through
her "primary hospitable welcome," gains and offers access to radical ethical alterity.[17] Her status is privileged as the figure who somehow leads the
subject to the radical Other. What softens Mann's patriarchal discourse is
the fact that Jessie is indeed presented as the ethical subject herself (not just
the Other), something that the specifically masculine philosophy of Levinas never imagines, with the exception of her role as the mother. For Levinas, the figure of the pregnant woman subjected to the claims of the Other
within her body is the perfect representation of the subject weighed down
by the responsibility to the Other, by implication suggesting that a woman
who would opt for an abortion is acting unethically. Significantly, Mann's
Jessie cannot have biological children; she will therefore never become the
dwelling for the Other. She will, however, facilitate her own and Frank's
welcoming of otherness into their new life together through the adoption
of a child that she much desires.

   The second scene in *Thief* that features the ethical subject wrestling
with the clamoring Other and the responsibility that the subject must

accept comes toward the end of the film, when Frank is confronted by his employer, the mafia boss Leo (Robert Prosky), who decides to pay Frank only a fraction of what he agreed to give him for a spectacular robbery that Frank and his partner, Barry (James Belushi), have carried out. Leo, who at the start of his relationship with Frank offers to be his father, explains that he has invested the rest of Frank's share of the robbery proceeds in the (mafia) family's business venture. When Frank questions Leo's decision, the father figure admonishes the son: "You got responsibilities." Frank is obviously unhappy to hear about these new responsibilities. This heist was supposed to be his final, the proceeds of which would guarantee the possibility of a crime-free future with Jessie. He now must decide which call to responsibility he is ready to answer. This ethical conundrum forces him to choose between the two families, the family of men united in crime or the adopted family he has built with Jessie. In Levinasian terms, this is the situation where multiple others present themselves for the subject to exercise a sense of justice, extending the ethical relationship from the single, personal Other to the more general otherness of the social realm.[18] Frank chooses his loyalty to his wife and child. He demands the money he is owed. Leo has no intention of paying it. He anticipates Frank's filial disobedience and proceeds to threaten him by capturing and eventually killing Barry. Worried about his family's safety, Frank decides to extricate himself completely from his previous life. He sends Jessie away with one of his most trusted associates and proceeds to destroy everything he owns and to hunt down Leo.

Critical opinions once again differ in interpreting the finale of *Thief,* which depicts Frank walking away, alone, into the darkness. Although many critics see this last scene as a transgression that frees the masculine subject from all societal obligations in an act of rebellion against the Law of the Father, I see it as affirmative of Frank's acceptance of his duty toward his family. There is no reason to assume that Frank will not reunite with Jessie and his adopted son, David, considering his determination and methodical work to build this family in the first place. The gesture of destroying all of his possessions, which for a man like Frank (who is proud of being able to wear "eight-hundred-dollar suits and silk shirts") had to play an important role in determining his identity, is symbolic of the high price that the subject must pay in forging his ethical bond with the Other. The fact that in the last shot of the film Frank moves away from the viewer into the unknown space offscreen speaks of Levinas's concept of infinity, which he attributes to an ethical experience. The infinite stands for freedom of action, the future, and limitless possibility.

In *Collateral*, Mann synthesizes his discourse on the encounter with the Other as fundamental to one's formation of subjectivity in a minimalist plot that unfolds as a chance encounter between two strangers. One of this film's most impressive aspects is the dialogue that transpires between a cab driver, Max (who is working nightshifts to save money to operate his own limo company one day), and his passenger, Vincent (Tom Cruise), who hires Max to take him around LA as he performs his work as an assassin for hire. Max only gradually realizes Max's mission, at which point he must face his duty to the Other. In this case, his responsibility is to the Other within himself, but also to the woman to whom he gave a ride immediately before Vincent hails his cab—the high-powered attorney Annie Farrell (Jada Pinkett-Smith), whose death has been commissioned by Vincent's employer. The impassioned discourse between the two men who are stuck together in the claustrophobic space of the moving car is a perfect example of the interpellation theorized by Levinas. In *Totality and Infinity*, he explains, "The claim to know and to reach the other is realized in the relationship with the Other that is cast in the relation of language, where the essential is the interpellation, the vocative."[19] Interpellation is an appeal, a form of hailing from the Other that demands a response. "The interpellated one is called upon to speak; his speech consists in 'coming to the assistance' of his word—in being *present*."[20] Vincent hails Max's cab and proceeds to "hail" him as a subject. He pushes Max out of the routine trajectory of his regimented work time into a present that is full of potential. Through his eloquent diatribe, Vincent performs a speech act that is nothing less than a call to action. Mann once again frames this summoning to action as constitutive in the character's work of consolidating his masculinity. In the end, however, the building of the gendered identity is eclipsed by the rise of an ethical human being.

The verbal exchange that constitutes the interpellation in *Collateral* is a deflected face-to-face encounter, whereupon, out of necessity, Vincent and Max see each other's face through the medium of the rearview mirror. In Mann's text, the Levinasian face, which for the philosopher is always a "living presence,"[21] becomes a reflection in the mirror. When Max faces Vincent in this mirror surface, he is also facing the otherness, materialized in Vincent, that has always resided in himself. Vincent is Max's doppelganger. Vincent's reflection in the mirror is Max's reflection. On the surface, the conversation between the two men concerns work. Max wants out of his deal with

Vincent. He realizes the full extent of Vincent's murderous engagement and does not want to participate in it. "Why don't you just kill me and get another cabdriver?" he asks of Vincent in a self-defeating gesture that indicates his divestment of all responsibility. Vincent explains that he chose Max because he is "good," but also because he recognized Max's inability to take action, to bring himself to become someone other than a cabdriver. "Look in the mirror," says Vincent as he mounts his address to Max. "Paper towels, clean cab, limo company someday. . . . Someday? Someday my dream will come? One night you'll wake up, and you'll discover it never happened. It's all turned around on you. It never will. Suddenly you are old. Didn't happen. And it never will because you were never going to do it anyway. You'll push it into memory, then zone out in your Barcalounger, being hypnotized by daytime TV for the rest of your life. . . . What the fuck are you still doing driving a cab?" In the next shot, the camera zooms in on Max's face as he digests Vincent's critique. The prolonged silence and the expression on his face suggest an epiphany. He responds, "Because I never straightened up and looked at it, you know? Myself. I should have." Acknowledging Vincent's push, he adds, "That's the one thing I got to thank you for, bro. Because until now I never looked at it that way." He then steps hard on the gas pedal, and Vincent (along with the viewer) quickly realizes that his words have moved Max into action. In the following series of shots, Max crashes the cab in a desperate attempt to stop Vincent from carrying out his final murder.

In this scene, as in many similar ones in his other films, Mann locates the protagonist's actual plight in his negotiation with himself, while the doppelganger character, here Vincent, provides the fabric for identification or differentiation. As Christopher Sharrett points out, "Mann's nostalgic sense of the eclipse of the male subject is mitigated to a great extent by his questioning of the demarcation of Self and Other."[22] To paraphrase Sharrett's argument, Michael Mann may nostalgically commemorate the great lost male subject of the patriarchy, but his politics remains sound because he is not afraid to show "the thin line between self and other," therefore deconstructing the accepted notions of subjectivity, including the patriarchal notion.[23] The dramatic impetus in this scene comes from the protagonist's deciding how to answer the call from outside himself, the call coming from the Other, who has been repressed from the meticulously constructed edifice of the Self. Mann foregrounds the scene where his protagonist is called upon and confronted with a choice, to which he must respond as a singular individual. Vincent calls on Max, and Max must respond as a singular individual. He must act to show ultimately whether he accepts or rejects Vincent's proposal to be an accomplice. In his radical response, Max decides to open himself up to the call from the Other by positioning himself against the Other's interests, Vincent's interests, but perhaps on some level he accepts Vincent's abject otherness as the messenger of death. He decides to crash the car, risking an encounter with the ultimate otherness, Death. His readiness to enter into a relationship with the Other by putting his own life on the line is, according to Levinas, the *revelation* of the singular subjectivity, which emerges through the event of being with the Other, the event of responding. The event here is different from practice or act. Levinas thinks that the good inheres only in the event of a relationship, not in practices, forms of life, beings, or things. The Levinasian event stands for a social or moral exchange or both. Max comes to the revelation of his true self through the fact of speaking out. The radical meaning of the scene under discussion lies in the fact that Max opens himself up to goodness in the way that Levinas defines it in *Totality and Infinity*.[24] Goodness, Levinas argues, is something that the subject opens up to when she or he rejects the (subjective) world and instead turns to infinity, to the commands and demands of the Other. Max certainly does that. Michael Mann's emblematic vanishing-point shot at the end of this scene, right before Max crashes his cab, when the camera points to the vanishing point at the end of the avenue, suggests a shared horizon for the viewer, thus allowing the viewer to decide whether to converge with the Other on screen or not.[25] As a viewer, I accept the infinity. I accept Max's choice, his state of consciousness (suggested by the point-of-view camera), which is absolutely open to the unknown that lies down the road.

In a sense, Michael Mann's cinema provides the embodiment to Levinas's abstract ethics and theory of the ethical subject. Mann's narrative and formal emphasis on physical labor (whether it's killing for hire, driving a cab, or burning through a vault) as an important part of subjectivity construction offers a subtle, if a bit nostalgic, critique of strictly postmodern ethics, thus expanding the conception of subjectivity proposed by Levinas into a more materially determined subjectivity, much aligned with the "life-world" phenomenology. Mann's films are supremely cinematic, translating materiality into movement, therefore grounding the ethical concerns in specific material circumstances. The element of work, isolated and represented on screen by Mann in the form of a physical event, brings to mind Luce Irigaray's critique of Levinas, where she identifies the creative work ("oeuvre") as part of the relationship with the Other.[26] Likewise, Mann's films propose that the event of work is also a way to encounter the Other, a form of ethical life.

In conclusion, one might ask, What of Vincent, the lean, mean, killing machine so seductive in his cool professionalism? It seems that in order to promote the ethics of duty over the codified law, the law that only pretends to know evil, Mann separates criminality, defined as institutionally assigned alterity, from evil, defined as the fundamental inability to bear with the Other. Mann's evil is ultimately unknowable but can be glimpsed at in characters such as Vincent, a government-issued assassin whose actions are predicated by logic alone, immune to empathy and deaf to the address from the Other, yet awe inspiring in his animalistic revelation. Once again Levinas's philosophy deftly informs Mann's cinematic ethics: like Levinas, Mann defines evil as that which is knowing but unknowable.

Notes

1. Geoff King, *New Hollywood: An Introduction* (London: Tauris, 2002), 32.

2. Christopher Rosen, "L.A. Story: 'Drive' Director Nicolas Winding Refn on His Quintessential Los Angeles Film," *Moviefone,* September 16, 2011, http://blog.moviefone.com/2011/09/16/nicolas-winding-refn-drive-director-la-movies-interview/.

3. Christopher Sharrett comments on this one-sided vision of social relations: "Mann's eulogizing of the male subject raises more than a few questions about his political focus. He cannot seem to posit a world outside of patriarchy, even in its decayed, postmodern moment. Yet this decay seems fairly absolute, making Mann's vision hark back to an earlier (post-Watergate) cinema that encouraged the critical faculties of the audience, and looked beneath the façade of the existing order of things" ("Michael Mann: Elegies on the Post-industrial Landscape," in *Fifty Contemporary Filmmakers,* ed. Yvonne Tasker [London: Routledge, 2002], 262).

4. Ramon Lobato, "Crimes against Urbanity: The Concrete Soul of Michael Mann," *Continuum: Journal of Media & Cultural Studies* 22, no. 3 (2008): 349.

5. Ibid.

6. Zygmunt Bauman, *Globalization: The Human Consequences* (New York: Columbia University Press, 1998), 9.

7. Timothy Shary defines Mann's preoccupation with chivalric males as his "ongoing examination and celebration of these loners engaged in noble battles to achieve harmony under circumstances that corrupt their independence" ("Into the Night," *Sight & Sound* 16, no. 9 [2006]: 18–19).

8. Zygmunt Bauman, *Liquid Love* (Cambridge: Polity Press, 2003), viii.

9. Timothy Shary, "Man to Mann: Masculine Crisis in the Crime Films of Michael

Mann," paper presented at Clark University, Worcester, MA, February 2006, quoted here with the author's permission.

10. Ibid.; Sharrett, "Michael Mann," 255–57.

11. In her study of film noir as the man's melodrama, Florence Jacobowitz explains that both genres "share the overriding principle of constriction and entrapment as a defining motif, whether it be within the family or within the patriarchal social organisations and demands of gender ideals" ("The Man's Melodrama: *The Woman in the Window* and *Scarlet Street,*" in *The Movie Book of Film Noir,* ed. Ian Cameron [London: Studio Vista, 1992], 50).

12. Mark Wildermuth, *Blood in the Moonlight: Michael Mann and Information Age Cinema* (Jefferson, NC: McFarland and Co., 2005), 71, 67, 76.

13. Ibid., 75; see also Mark Steensland, *Michael Mann* (Harpenden, UK: Pocket Essentials: 2002), 24.

14. Diane Perpich, *The Ethics of Emmanuel Levinas* (Stanford, CA: Stanford University Press, 2008), 77.

15. Emmanuel Levinas, "Philosophy, Justice, and Love," in *Entre Nous: Thinking of the Other,* trans. Michael B. Smith and Barbara Harshav (New York: Columbia University Press, 1998), 106.

16. Emmanuel Levinas, *Totality and Infinity* (Pittsburgh: Duquesne University Press, 1988), 195.

17. Ibid., 155.

18. Fleurdeliz R. Altez explains the distinction between the different degrees of otherness in Levinas as follows: "The *autri* refers to the personal Other, while the *autre* refers to the otherness in general. Aside from the Self and the Other, other faces may be involved, thus making up the third party (that is, of the whole humanity which looks at us). Just like the Other, the Self is also responsible to the third party. After all, every human that man encounters is the Other that we personally treat, and such if collectively taken yields what is called the Other in general, the other Others" ("Banal and Implied Forms of Violence in Levinas' Phenomenological Ethics," *Kritikē* 1, no. 1 [2007]: 65, http://www.kritike.org/journal/issue_1/altez_june2007.pdf).

19. Levinas, *Totality and Infinity,* 69.

20. Ibid.

21. Ibid., 66.

22. Sharrett, *Michael Mann,* 255.

23. Ibid., 259.

24. Levinas, *Totality and Infinity,* 304–7.

25. My interpretation of Mann's vanishing-point shot as an opening of the frame is diametrically different from Wildermuth's interpretation. In his analysis of the vanishing-point shots in *Thief,* Wildermuth argues, "These shots are disturbing because they place the film's principle subjects in a *mise-en-scène* that is closed and implies a kind of determinism—there is no place for them to go except where the electric lights point

them. The implication is that these men have not necessarily achieved a liberating synthesis here" (*Blood in the Moonlight,* 58).

26. Luce Irigaray, "Questions to Emmanuel Levinas on the Divinity of Love," in *Rereading Levinas,* trans. Margaret Whitford, ed. Robert Bernasconi and Simon Critchley (Bloomington: Indiana University Press, 199), 109–18.

NATURAL MAN, NATURAL RIGHTS, AND EROS

Conflicting Visions of Nature, Society, and Love in *The Last of the Mohicans*

Alan Woolfolk

> To understand political power right, and derive it from its original, we must consider what state all men are naturally in, and that is, a *state of perfect freedom* to order their actions, and dispose of their possessions and persons, as they think fit, within the bounds of the law of nature, without asking leave, or depending upon the will of any other man.
>
> —John Locke, *Second Treatise of Government* (1689)

> Happy slaves, you owe them that delicate and refined taste on which you pride yourselves; that sweetness of character and that urbanity in mores which make relationships among you so cordial and easy; in a word, the appearances of all virtues without having any. . . . How sweet it would be to live among us if outer appearances were always the likeness of the heart's dispositions, if decency were virtue, if our maxims served as rules, if true philosophy were inseparable from the title of philosopher! But so many qualities are all too rarely found in combination, and virtue seldom goes forth in such great pomp. Expensive finery can betoken a wealthy man, and elegance a man of taste. . . . Today, when more subtle inquiries and a more refined taste have reduced the art of pleasing to established rules, a vile and deceitful uniformity reigns in our mores.
>
> —Jean-Jacques Rousseau, *Discourse on the Sciences and the Arts* (1750)

Michael Mann's *The Last of the Mohicans* (1992, DVD release 1999) opens with a well-known sequence in the lush forests of upstate New York in which the last members of the Mohican Native American tribe—Chingachgook (Russell Means), his son Uncas (Eric Schweig), and his adopted Caucasian son Hawkeye (Daniel Day-Lewis)—are engaged in a speechless, elaborately choreographed hunt for a deer, which Hawkeye proceeds to bring down with a single shot from his flintlock rifle. Set in 1757, during the third year of the seven-year French and Indian War (symptomatically described in the opening credits as "the war between England and France for the possession of the continent"), the events of the story unfold in the same decade that the French *philosophe* and *moraliste* Jean-Jacques Rousseau wrote *Discourse on the Sciences and Arts* (1750) and *Discourse on the Origin of Inequality* (1755). At first glance, the opening hunt sequence appears to evoke images of Rousseau's natural man, the so-called noble savage. In this scene, the last of the Mohicans present images of physically robust, self-sufficient men of the wilderness, making their own way in the world and fending for themselves, living in harmony with each other and nature. Indeed, the scene ends with Chingachgook offering an invocation of respect in Mohican for the slain deer, which implies that these men are not rapacious but reverent toward nature and observe the limits and ways of their ancestors: "We're sorry to kill you, Brother. [Forgive us.] We do honor to your courage and speed, your strength."[1] Clearly, this is no Hobbesian image of the state of nature in which life is "solitary, poor, nasty, brutish, and short."[2]

The State of American Nature

Nor is this scene precisely a Rousseauian image of the state of nature either, for Rousseau's natural man, although free of the manifold diseases of civilization and living in a world dominated by physical senses, is explicitly described as solitary, unreflective, lacking in language and effectively speechless, and without the ability to make moral distinctions, including those associated with "the moral aspect of love."[3] As the viewer soon learns, the last of the Mohicans know no such deficiencies. They are thoughtful, articulate, and effective moral agents. Chingachgook has adopted and raised Hawkeye as his son. Hawkeye, in turn, respects Chingachgook as his father and, as the story progresses, falls in love with the first daughter of the ill-fated Colonel Edmund Munro (Maurice Roëves), Cora Munro (Madeleine Stowe), just as Uncas develops a love interest in the second daughter, Alice Munro (Jodhi May). Individually and collectively, the three Mohicans are decisive moral agents in scene after scene as they intervene and shape the course of personal and historical events, even if they are not always able to prevent tragic consequences.

This world of cogent moral agents is a long way removed from Rousseau's state of nature except insofar as Rousseau's vision of a distant state of nature has aroused, as Allan Bloom has argued, a vague but powerful nostalgia for an earlier uncorrupted nature among Americans that can be traced through the writings of Henry David Thoreau to the established countercultures of the present.[4] Even so, this powerful nostalgia for nature has been far more culturally influential in exacerbating the tensions between the natural impulses of the self and societal constraints in Europe than in America because, as Bloom points out, Lockean notions of natural rights and private property have prevailed in the United States. In *The Last of the Mohicans,* Mann picks up this popularized European myth of a lost natural innocence and projects it backward in time to the very beginnings of the American nation on the frontiers of the New World. In Mann's hands, this European myth is employed, as we shall see, to expose corruptions in European civilization that are straight out of the pages of Rousseau. Whether this myth has any grounding in American history is perhaps less to the point than the fact that Mann has chosen to inject full-blown moral agents into what Rousseau originally conceived to be an amoral natural state. The state of nature has been moralized and pitted against the corrupting influences of European civilization within the American colonies.

Other artistic depictions of the state of nature inspired by Rousseau have presented a more complex and perhaps more European view of the conflict between nature and society. For example, Albert Camus, perhaps the most prominent twentieth-century French *moraliste* and successor to Rousseau, created in *The Stranger* (1942) a more accurate and coherent artistic representation of Rousseau's amoral natural man confronting European corruptions insofar as the protagonist, Meursault (also a man of a frontier province), is defined by his *lack* of agency until the novel's closing pages. Understanding the preternatural maturity of the last of the Mohicans as moral agents in the American wilderness requires looking beyond Rousseau's theory of nature and its popularizations while retaining his trenchant and widely influential critique of modern societies.

The Radicalism of the American Revolution

The second major scene of the film at the frontier home of John Cameron (Terry Kinney) and his family leads into a series of scenes that deepen the social and political dimensions of the film by depicting an emerging American society that is at odds with European aristocratic society, English as well as French. In the initial scene, the Mohicans break bread with the Cameron family and a colonial militia captain, Jack Winthrop (Edward Blatchford), in a domestic ritual that accents the egalitarian nature of the emergent society. We soon learn that John and Alexandria Cameron (Tracey Ellis) are former indentured servants living in a multiethnic, multiracial community in which English, Scottish, Irish, French Huguenots, and Mohawk Native Americans are living side by side. Indeed, the third major scene depicts an English lieutenant attempting to recruit a colonial militia under the leadership of Captain Winthrop with a game of lacrosse about to commence, which includes a variety of European settlers as well as a significant number of Mohawks. The message of the scene is unmistakable: this is a vibrant democratic society in which people (that is, males, at least in public) work and play together and are not subject to the rigid hierarchical social structures of the past that are represented by the presence of the English lieutenant. This horizontal image of society offers a synoptic glimpse of the democratic revolution to come.

"In the mid–eighteenth century most Americans still conceived of their society in a traditional manner," according to historian Gordon Wood. "They thought of themselves as connected vertically rather than horizontally, and were more apt to be conscious of those immediately above and below them than they were of those alongside them."[5] In Mann's vision, what Wood calls "the radicalism of the American revolution" thus began in the democratic experiences, both public and private, of the American frontier. Intimations of the democratic moral and political revolution to come are evident, first of all, in the repeated questioning and challenging of English authorities by Captain Winthrop and Hawkeye. Hawkeye, in particular, makes it clear that he is no "loyal subject" of the Crown, and Winthrop in his frontier brashness proceeds to negotiate terms for the service of the colonial militia directly with the English general Daniel Webb (Mac Andrews) without regard for his military and social standing. More importantly, a profound transformation of heart and mind becomes evident in the awakening democratic sympathies and passion of the aristocratic Cora Munro after the devastating Huron attack on the military column bound for Fort William Henry and the discovery of the massacred Cameron family by the three Mohicans and the survivors of the earlier attack—Cora, Alice, and Cora's English suitor, Major Duncan Heyward (Steven Waddington).

The awakening of Cora's democratic sympathies is deeply intertwined with the transference of her affections away from the aristocratic personages of her father and Major Heyward and toward the democratic persona of Hawkeye. The first pivotal moment in this transformation of heart, then mind, comes when Cora confesses to Hawkeye that he is right, that "we do not understand what is happening here. And it is not as I imagined it would be, thinking of it in Boston and London." In response to Hawkeye's dismissive "sorry to disappoint you," Cora remarks with complete sincerity, beginning with her eyes downcast and then lifting them to meet Hawkeye's gaze, "On the contrary, it is more deeply stirring to my blood than any imagining could possibly have been." With this remark, we as viewers know that Cora is in the midst of a conversion experience that will end with her commitment to the new democratic community and the love of Hawkeye.

Another decisive moment in Cora's conversion occurs when she rejects her persistent suitor, Duncan, with a final negative answer to his proposal of marriage and the comment that "the decision that I've come to is I'd rather make the gravest of mistakes than surrender my own judgment." Although this remark confirms that Cora has decided to reject Duncan's earlier, blatantly paternalistic advice to let him and her father "decide what is best for her," it also signals her rejection of the entire aristocratic social hierarchy in favor of her own individual reason and judgment. At first glance, this decision may not seem to be an especially radical move on Cora's part. It might be read, for instance, as simply a young woman's spirited rebellion against her family and against what appears to be tantamount to an arranged marriage. But in his preeminent work on American democracy, *Democracy in America*, Alexis de Tocqueville pointed to the great trust that democratic individuals place in their own powers of reason and judgment as the definitive characteristic of the democratic intellect and the democratic revolution's unprecedented break with the past: "To be free of the systematic spirit, the yoke of habit, family maxims, class opinions, and, up to a point, national prejudice; to treat tradition only as a source of information and existing facts as useful to study only in order to do things differently and better; to seek on one's own and in oneself alone the reason for things, to strive for results without becoming wedded to the means of achieving them, and to aim beyond form at substance: these are the principal features of what I shall call the philosophical method of the Americans." For Tocqueville, the primary intellectual trait that epitomized all the rest was the individual's reliance on "the unaided effort of his own individual reason." It is inseparable from the American custom of "deriving the rules of judgment solely from within."[6] Together, self-reliant reason and judgment are the keys to understanding the democratic revolution and what Tocqueville called democratic "individualism."[7]

Cora is in certain respects further advanced toward this cultural and personal condition of individualism than Hawkeye because she is in the midst of *self-consciously* throwing off the bonds of family, class, and nation in a way that Hawkeye has not had to attempt because he is the product of a democratic upbringing and to a great extent lacks her attachments to class and nation. Moreover, Hawkeye clearly retains an uncritical attachment to family and, at least to some degree, to the Mohican heritage of his adopted father, Chingachgook, as is evident in Cora's initial conversion scene when Hawkeye states that his father "warned me about people like you" and then again in his subsequent comments about Mohican legends concerning the origins of the heavens. However, neither Cora nor Hawkeye reveals the deeper implications of democratic individualism and its potentially debilitating effects. Mann simply does not address Tocqueville's ultimate concern that "not only does democracy cause each man to forget his forebears, but it makes it difficult for him to see his offspring and cuts him off from his contemporaries . . . and threatens ultimately to imprison him altogether in the loneliness of his own heart."[8] Rather, *The Last of the Mohicans* explicitly indicts the aristocratic heritage that Tocqueville saw as doomed anyhow and affirms much of the Lockean heritage of American democracy in an effort to imagine the thought and passion of the early democratic age that led to the birth of a radically new kind of nation.

Natural Man, Take Two

Viewed through Tocqueville's eyes, *The Last of the Mohicans* envisions an emergent democratic society in which the public enthusiasms of the day, vital civic associations (e.g., the civilian militia), and an enlightened self-interest prevent the debilitating effects of individualism from surfacing. Of these, an enlightened self-interest framed in Lockean terms receives the most sustained attention in the film. It is evident, first of all, in the repeated references throughout the film to the fact that Americans do not bother "asking leave" or requesting "by your leave" of anyone because they assume that they have a natural freedom to come and go as they please, that they are not subject to the will of another. This assumption becomes evident when

Captain Winthrop abruptly exits the presence of General Webb without waiting to be dismissed and again most tellingly during the final confrontation between Duncan and Cora:

> Duncan: And who empowered these provincials to pass judgment upon England's policies in her own colonies? To come and go without so much as a "by your leave."
> Cora: They do not live their lives "by your leave." They hack it out of the wilderness with their own two hands, burying their dead and their children along the way.

Cora's response makes clear that she now has a personal knowledge or understanding of the Americans that she did not before, that the very moral structure of what is permissible and not permissible in social relations has now shifted for her. Without the deferential practices of courtesy implied in the ritual of "by your leave," aristocracy can no longer link "all citizens together in a long chain from peasant to king."[9] The democratic experience of the frontier has broken Tocqueville's aristocratic chain, and Cora has become a severed link.

As a severed link, Cora immediately proceeds in the same scene to express her view of English military (and by implication all English) justice to her father, who has charged Hawkeye with sedition, and to challenge him that "if that's 'justice' . . . then the sooner French guns blow the English army out of America, the better it will be for these people." With this remark, Cora symbolically joins the Americans, who already view the English as having broken their own rule of law and violated the colonists' Lockean sense of justice from the moment General Munro abrogated General Webb's deceitful agreement to allow the colonial militia the liberty to defend their homes and families. Indeed, when Captain Winthrop states that he believes that if the English "set aside their law as and when they wish, their law no longer has rightful authority over us" and immediately follows with the indictment that "all they have over us is tyranny," he draws the same conclusion as John Locke that any government that violates the individual's natural rights to life, liberty, and property is no government at all, but rather in a state of war with its supposed citizens: *Tyranny is the exercise of power beyond right, which no body can have a right to.*[10] According to Locke, the colonials are not engaged in a rebellion, but in resistance to arbitrary power. There is no legitimate government to rebel against.

"The *state of nature*," according to Locke, "has a law of nature to govern it, which obliges every one: And reason, which is that law, teaches all mankind, who will but consult it, that being all equal and independent, no one ought to harm another in his life, health, liberty, or possessions."[11] Insofar as individuals follow the dictates of reason, the state of nature remains a state of peace. But insofar as individuals renounce reason, the state of nature becomes a state of war, and liberty becomes license. In this state of war, according to Locke, individuals have the right to defend themselves and others and to exercise the executive power to punish transgressors of the law in order to hinder its violation.[12] It is in such a fallen state of nature outside the boundaries of any functioning civil society on the American frontier that the last of the Mohicans become cogent moral agents representing and enforcing the natural law.

As agents of the natural law, the Mohicans possess a charisma that is more than simply personal. In the opening hunt scene, for instance, the Mohicans appropriate from nature only what they need for survival and nourishment in accordance with what Locke understands as the common law of nature applied to property, in contrast to the English and the French, who are engaged in a power struggle for "the possession of the continent" and all of its potential wealth.[13] Likewise, in the initial battle scene the Mohicans come to the defense of the Munro sisters and the English military detachment under attack by the renegade Huron war party because the Hurons are clearly the transgressors. In the course of this defensive action, Hawkeye's intervention prevents the Huron war chief, Magua (Wes Studi), from carrying out his revenge killing of Cora. In subsequent scenes, the portrait of Magua as the chief transgressor against the natural law and natural reason is completed as we learn that he is obsessed beyond all reason with cutting out the heart of Colonel Munro and killing all of "his seed" because he holds him personally responsible for the destruction of his family. In the film's penultimate action scene, Magua brutally kills Uncas as Uncas attempts to rescue Alice. This, in turn, sets up the climactic scene in which Chingachgook's skillfully executed killing of Magua becomes not simply an act of revenge, but a justifiable execution of the natural law against a transgressor who, in Locke's terms, has "renounced reason" and "hath by unjust violence and slaughter . . . declared war against all mankind, and therefore may be destroyed as a *lion* or a *tiger,* one of those wild savage beasts, with whom men can have no society nor security."[14]

Rousseau Reconsidered

Although the Lockean reading of *The Last of the Mohicans* is persuasive, it does not offer an exhaustive interpretation because several significant details are left unexplained. Specifically, the systemic hypocrisy and mendacity of the English and French and the repeated references to the greed of the Europeans are better illuminated by Rousseau than by Locke because they appear to be manifestations of the corruption of civilization per se rather than merely aberrations. Indeed, there is also more than a hint of the invidious German distinction between civilization and culture present in the film, in which the Europeans represent the externalities of outward refinement and the hypocrisies and deceptions of courtesy associated with civilization and the Americans exemplify the genuine virtues of a less pretentious, more robust indigenous culture.[15]

Rousseau's wholesale indictment of highly civilized peoples in the First Discourse, which diagnoses their corruption as growing in proportion to their intellectual sophistication and aesthetic refinement, finds its perfect text analogue in the French general Louis-Joseph de Montcalm (Patrice Chéreau), who is the eventual victor in the siege of Fort William Henry. General Montcalm initially gives every appearance of being an honorable officer when, with a great show of respect and refinement, he grants Colonel Munro generous surrender terms. But shortly thereafter he betrays the conditions of the surrender with his implicit authorization of Magua's attack on the retreating party. This appearance of having "all the virtues without having any" may be contrasted with Captain Winthrop's forthrightness and especially Hawkeye's honesty. In fact, the stark contrast between Montcalm and Hawkeye supports Rousseau's thesis that "the taste for ostentation is hardly ever combined in the same souls with the taste for honesty."[16] In the other obvious case, that of the aristocrat Major Heyward, however, the contrast with Hawkeye is complicated by the fact that Duncan, despite his pretentiousness and dishonesty, redeems himself with his final act of self-sacrifice at the Huron village in order to permit Cora and Hawkeye's escape and to regain his honor.

Nonetheless, the Rousseauian motifs in *The Last of the Mohicans* are unmistakable and remarkably consistent: Hawkeye is the American embodiment of the unpretentious, honest man, *un honnête homme*, juxtaposed to the hypocritical and mendacious Europeans.[17] These motifs are expanded and become even more significant in the film's critique of private property and inequality as we learn that Europeans' ambition and greed threaten the Americans with a much deeper and more permanent corruption. When Hawkeye enters the Huron village to make his case to the reigning sachem (Mike Phillips) for the lives of the captives, he is no longer on Lockean territory in his attribution of a range of American ills to the unchecked European desire for gain and power, but rather deep into the theoretical territory of Rousseau's Second Discourse:

> Would the Huron make his Algonquin brothers foolish with brandy and steal his lands to sell them for gold to the white man? Would the Huron have greed for more land than a man can use? Like Francais Black Robes do? Would Huron kill tribes with disease? Would the Huron fool Seneca into taking all the animals in the forest for beads and brandy, but sell the fur to the white man for gold? These are the ways of the Yangees and les Francais masters. Are they the ways of Huron men who hunt and work the land? Or of dogs? Magua's heart is twisted. He would make himself into what twisted him. Magua's way is false. Magua's way will bring only sadness and shame.

For Hawkeye, Magua's wickedness originates more from his imitation of the Europeans' unbridled desires than from his renunciation of natural reason and the natural law. Magua's heart has been twisted by the European sickness of unrestrained greed and power rather than simply by anger and vengeance; however, in his brutality, he wears no European "mask of benevolence."[18] With his charge against Magua, Hawkeye has in effect placed the entire European socioeconomic and moral system—indeed, as suggested earlier, even civilization itself—on trial.

The corruption of European civilization extends beyond the obvious dishonesty, greed, and power hunger of the French, English, and the likes of Magua to include distortions of social and personal relations, such as romantic relations between men and women. This is evident not only in the case of the strained relationship between Duncan and Cora, but also in the inchoate relationship between Alice and Uncas that ends with the unnecessary romantic suicide of Alice after the killing of Uncas by Magua. In contrast to Cora, Alice is a frail creature of European civilization who lacks Cora's self-possession and canny survival instincts. As such, Alice is incapable of following Hawkeye's anguished command to Cora to "stay alive" because she is incapable of exercising moral agency. Alice is no woman of the frontier; she is a victim of her own civilization.

The suggestion that the Europeans' corruption originates in civilization per se rather than merely in a false civilization, which can be reformed or replaced, is intimated by Chingachgook's closing ode to the frontier in the director's cut of the film: "The frontier moves with the sun and pushes the red man of the wilderness forests in front of it. Until one day there will be nowhere left. The frontier place is for people like my white son and his woman and their children." Although Hawkeye responds that this is "my father's sadness talking," Chingachgook's final words of wisdom to his adopted son suggest that the frontier is the only place where a genuine democratic community can exist in which self-possessed individuals can exercise moral agency and control their own lives. It is the last place of refuge from the corrupt unrestraint of civilization and the debilitating ills of progress.

Notes

1. The words "Forgive us" are taken from the screenplay. They are omitted in the film.
2. Thomas Hobbes, *Leviathan,* ed. and with an introduction and notes by Edwin Curley (Indianapolis: Hackett, 1994), 76.
3. Jean-Jacques Rousseau, "Discourse on the Origin of Inequality," in *The Basic Political Writings,* trans. and ed. Donald A. Cress, introduction by Peter Gay (Indianapolis, IN: Hackett, 1987), 56.
4. Allan Bloom, *The Closing of the American Mind,* with a foreword by Saul Bellow (New York: Simon and Schuster, 1987), 157–72, esp. 170–72. For an insightful commentary on these established countercultures, see David Brooks, *Bobos in Paradise: The New Upper Class and How They Got There* (New York: Simon & Schuster, 2000).
5. Gordon Wood, *The Radicalism of the American Revolution* (New York: Vintage Books, Random House, 1993), 23.
6. Alexis de Tocqueville, *Democracy in America,* trans. Arthur Goldhammer (New York: Library of America, 2004), 483–84.
7. Ibid., 585–87.
8. Ibid., 587.
9. Ibid., 586.
10. John Locke, *Second Treatise on Government,* ed. Richard A. Cox (Wheeling, IL: Harlan Davidson, 1982), 123.
11. Ibid., 4.
12. Ibid., 3–10.
13. Ibid., 17–31.

14. Ibid., 7.

15. See Norbert Elias, *The History of Manners,* trans. Edmund Jephcott (New York: Pantheon Books, 1978), 3–40.

16. Jean-Jacques Rousseau, "Discourse on the Sciences and the Arts," in *The Basic Political Writings,* 4, 13.

17. Jean-Jacques Rousseau, "Discours sur les sciences et les arts," in *Oeuvres complètes,* vol. 3 (Paris: Gallimard, 1964), 5.

18. Rousseau, "Discourse on the Origin of Inequality," 68.

Emotion, Truth, and Space in *Heat*

Jonah Corne

Thermometric Extremes: "Dead-Tech, Postmodernistic, Bullshit House"

Returning home in the late, bright Los Angeles morning from the police detective work with which he has been consumed all night, Vincent Hanna (Al Pacino) discovers his wife, Justine (Diane Venora), engaged in a serene domestic moment with another man, what appears to be a kind of replacement husband. Situated in the kitchen, Justine puts the finishing touches on a plate of food for the man, who reclines barefoot on the sofa in the living room watching television and sipping a cup of coffee, seeming more settled and at ease in the house than Vincent does at any point throughout Michael Mann's 1995 film *Heat*. Catching the couple in this quaint aftermath of the act, Vincent behaves blasé, withholding reaction in a manner that Justine reads as incitement: "Don't you even get angry?" she inquires. A confessed chronic weed smoker and Prozac popper, Justine herself remains weirdly unperturbed, almost benumbed, but her manner, we slowly grasp, derives largely from her having effectively contrived the exposure of the affair by taking no precautions to conceal it, doing so as a way of trying to elicit some sort—any sort—of emotion from her unavailable, workaholic husband. Her premeditation, indeed, invests the scene with an aura of theatricality that accounts for the highly caricaturized picture of traditional domesticity on display. Justine does not so much condone the role of a good wife—ensconced in the kitchen, blithely waiting on a man—as assume and play up such a role for momentary effect. Seeking a reaction from Vincent, she stages a mousetrap performance that dispenses with all subtlety.

If at the beginning of the scene Vincent fails to react with the anger that Justine hopes to bring out in him, however, he abruptly meets such expectations and wildly exceeds them. Indulging that penchant for the tantrum that has become the signature of his acting style throughout the later part of his career, Pacino here delivers one of his most memorable, ranting fulminations. When Ralph (Xander Berkeley), whom Justine ironically refers to as her friend and whose banal name contrasts sharply with the portentous, symbolic latinity of "Justine" and "Vincent," begins uttering profuse, milquetoast apologies for being the unwitting agent of Vincent's cuckolding, Vincent berates him with escalating fury: "You know, you can ball my wife if she wants you to, you can lounge around here on her sofa, in her exhusband's dead-tech, postmodernistic, bullshit house, if you want to, but you do not get to watch my fucking television set!"

Ostensibly the only thing in the house that belongs to him, the television, nevertheless receives no special, sensitive treatment from Vincent, who smashes it with staccato blows and tears the cord from the wall, short-circuiting the picture. (Bland Ralph is watching that blandest of things on television, the news weather forecast, which yet holds a special significance in a film whose title's primary meaning refers to temperature.) If ever Vincent was connected to the house, it was through the television, and now he has pulled the plug, severed even this meager, mechanical root. Bearing the battered box under his arm, Vincent makes a grandstanding exit. As Neil McCauley (Robert De Niro), Vincent's criminal object of pursuit and typical Mann doppelgänger, remarks during the celebrated face-to-face scene in the diner, "A guy told me one time, don't let yourself get attached to anything you're not willing to walk out on in thirty seconds flat if you feel the heat around the corner." Unable to take the heat of his own marriage, Vincent flees, reinforcing all the more his secret kinship with the men on the other side of the law.

In terms of affect, which might be thought of as the expression of the self's own internal weather, Mann's film is concerned as much with coldness as with heat. Indeed, from keeping cool to blowing his top to disengaging in his rage, Vincent possesses an inner climate that seems almost entirely to lack moderate (temperate) phases. Emotions are a perpetual source of trouble for him, somehow always in excess or in short supply. Accordingly, sensing a degree of projection in his charge against the house as being unfeeling or "dead," Justine throws back Vincent's own language at him just before he exits, accusing him of "walking through our life dead," as if he inhabits an affective dead zone no matter where he happens to be located. Bearing out this moveable predicament, the more Vincent attempts to demarcate himself from the house, singling out and repossessing the television, the more his attempt seems futile. For what does it mean to be solely identified with (a) television? Is not such a condition synonymous with a kind of incapacity for genuine emotion, implying a self utterly colonized by the external influences of media? As it turns out, a few scenes later Vincent hurls the television out of his car onto a random city street, the delayed culmination of the earlier thrashing. Even allowing the object to stand in for some scrap of a core self, Vincent gets rid of it, abandons it like so much else in his life.

Alluding to postmodernism by name, Vincent's tirade against the house as a space devoid of emotion and truth-value reveals his own struggle with those crises of affect and authenticity much discussed by postmodern theorists. Specifically, Vincent evokes Fredric Jameson's famous diagnosis of "the silence of affect in postmodernism [that] is doubled with a new gratification in surfaces,"[1] "the emergence of a new kind of flatness or depthlessness, a new kind of superficiality in the most literal sense."[2] Interestingly, Vincent perverts the term *postmodern* with the grammatically superfluous suffix -*istic,* a move that seems less a symptom of naïveté or rhetorical blundering than a deliberate attempt both to mock what he takes to be the pretentiousness of postmodern style and to hint at the idea of simulation with which the style is so closely connected. Indeed, to call the house "postmodern*istic*" is slyly to portray the house as a derivative simulacrum, a fittingly inauthentic instance, of this most authenticity-resistant style: the "postmodern." Admittedly, there is something unusual, momentarily derailing, about a character in a mainstream Hollywood movie dropping the term *postmodernism* or a variant of it. Yet lest one object to Vincent's invocation of technical philosophical language as a stretch, a kind of idiolectical intrusion, it helps to recall that the term had entered popular culture by the mid-1990s—Jameson's own writings on the subject date back to the late 1970s. And besides, Vincent fits the profile of a unique breed of intellectual cop, a high achiever who (as McCauley discovers while performing a reciprocal background check on him) has gone to graduate school.

Densely packed, Vincent's description of Justine's exhusband's "deadtech, postmodernistic, bullshit house" fascinates me. I am drawn by its adjectival audacity (three separate compound words in piled-up combination) and especially by the antic questions interweaving emotion, truth, and space that it raises and that I would like to explore more expansively in the pages that follow. What exactly does it mean for a building to be "dead," coldly corpselike, and thus to fail to transcend what would seem to be its intrinsic condition of inanimateness? Similarly, how does a building embody an epistemological (non)value such as "bullshit" over and above its basic material existence or thereness? What are some of the genealogies of these questions leading up to and extending beyond postmodernism, and how does *Heat* dramatically activate them for cinema, elaborating Mann's complex philosophico-architectural vision?

"Against Architecture"

On a phenomenological level, Vincent's rage against the house speaks to something familiar. How often in the midst of rage does the space one inhabits come to bear the blame—or at least the punishment—for one's very rage? Anger can fester, but rage needs to discharge itself; it tends ineluctably toward externalization, and spaces are submissively ready at hand to absorb the blows. So walls are punched and kicked, windows smashed, doors slammed, shelves voided in a glissando sweep of the hand. Yet rooms can also actively menace and provoke, can all of a sudden seem oppressive no matter their size, declaring limits when all rage wants to do is transgress, standing mockingly while one is in disarray. One's surroundings are in incontrovertible collusion; one's infuriating situation is quite literally where one is situated.

Denis Hollier's pathbreaking study of George Bataille, *Against Architecture* (originally published in 1974 as *La prise de la Concorde*),[3] offers much useful guidance on this theme, as one might gather especially from its title in English. Hollier reads Bataille through the latter's intriguingly indiscriminate, totalizing hostility toward the very idea of architecture. As Hollier explains, Bataille views architecture (a word that comprises the root *archè*, meaning "beginning" or "origin") as in essence an embodiment of authority, seeking to control and dominate its designed users in every instance. Regarding all buildings as latent prisons, Bataille writes in an article entitled "Architecture," published in the surrealist periodical *Documents* in 1929:

> In fact it is only the ideal soul of society, that which has the authority to command and prohibit, that is expressed in architectural compositions properly speaking. Thus great monuments are erected like dikes, opposing the logic and majesty of authority against all

disturbing elements: it is in the form of cathedral or palace that Church or State speaks to the multitudes and imposes silence upon them. It is, in fact, obvious that monuments inspire social prudence and often even real fear. The taking of the Bastille is symbolic of this state of things: it is hard to explain this crowd movement other than by the animosity of the people against the monuments that are their real masters.[4]

"Never concerned with architecture itself but with its expansion,"[5] as Hollier points out, Bataille's article concludes by indirectly conjuring Vitruvius and linking architecture with the biomorphological structure of the human body:

The human order from the beginning is, just as easily, bound up with the architectural order, which is no more than its development. If one attacks architecture, whose monumental productions are at present the real masters of the world, grouping servile multitudes in their shadows, imposing admiration and astonishment, order and constraint, one is, as it were, attacking man.[6]

Such a dual, an-archic attack is graphically represented by André Masson's well-known cover illustration for the first issue of the journal Bataille started in the second half of the 1930s and named *Acéphale,* after the Greek word *akephalos,* meaning "headless." An explicit repurposing of Leonardo's *Vitruvian Man,* Masson's drawing shows a nude male figure standing upright with his arms outstretched, a dagger in one hand, a burning heart (which looks like a molotov cocktail) in the other, a skull over his genitals, and no head. Decapitating Leonardo's figure as well as abandoning the circle and square that contain him, Masson does violence to the fundamental, geometric-rationalistic tenet of classical architecture, which takes the human body ("man") as the ideal measure for building.

Heat displays a keen, related interest in such an-archic iconography, repeatedly presenting figures whose heads (and head regions) are subject to forms of disruption. An occlusion of the face through masks recurs in the two big heists that McCauley and his crew carry out, in the robbery of the armored car in the film's opening sequence and in the later, bloodily ill-fated holdup of the bank. Of course, one might cite any number of heist films where the criminals don masks as a precaution against identification, but Mann draws attention to the convention by creating a wider, (ostensibly) juxtaposing field of interest around the exposed face. One thinks of the maximally vulnerable, close-up face of the deafened armored car guard before he is shot by the erratic Waingro, for instance, or the famous "face-to-face" scene already alluded to. As Marco Abel deftly points out, however, the face-to-face scene, for all the intimacy it establishes between Vincent and McCauley, ends up undermining itself as the characters conclude the scene by mutually affirming that they would kill each other without hesitation *despite* now having engaged face to face.[7] The exchange of pitiless taunts effaces the face as a humanizing bulwark against violence.

Strikingly evoking Masson's drawing, an image of an entirely headless figure appears as a decorative detail on the kitchen wall of Justine's exhusband's house. A small, doll-like sculpture, the figure is mounted among a disordered mélange of artworks, including three unframed portrait drawings done in a vaguely primitivist style. Although the sculpture belongs to the aesthetic regime of the house, taking up a place within the house's extensive collection of contemporary art, it also speaks to Vincent's antipathy toward the house—indeed, as if his resentment against the house, his sense of it as a prisonlike space where his autonomy is curtailed by the obligations of marriage, subtly materializes on the wall in the form of an emblem. Down with the house, the sculpture seems to communicate à la Bataille at the same time that it is manifestly of the house.

Such contradictory valencing is typical of postmodernist architecture. As Hollier explains in a discussion of Bernard Tschumi's Derrida-inspired project for the Parc de la Villette in Paris, postmodern architecture aspires to "realize a paradoxical storming of architecture—by itself," to embody "a Bastille in no way different from its own storming."[8] To return to Vincent's antipostmodernist rant, then, we might understand it as something even more involuted, as partaking of a postmodernist rejection of architecture at the same time that it rejects such a rejection, negates such a negation, moving away from Bataillean acephalism in a most pro-architectural direction, to which I would now like to turn.

"On Bullshit"

Regarded as an expression of longing for a *reinstatement* of authority and tradition, Vincent's rant against the house can indeed be seen as assuming a place among the work of a whole panoply of influential writers on architecture who, highly attuned to the *archè* in architecture, promote the medium as the arch or ur-art. As G. F. W. Hegel remarks in the introduction to *Aesthetics* (1835), "Architecture confronts us as at the beginning of art, a beginning grounded in the essential nature of art itself."[9] Similarly, Victor Hugo writes in the famous "This Will Kill That" chapter of *Notre-Dame de Paris* (1831), where he describes how the printed book usurped architecture as humanity's dominant mass medium: "In fact, from the origin of things up to and including the fifteenth century of the Christian era, architecture was the great book of mankind, man's chief form of expression in the various stages of his development, either as force or as intelligence."[10]

This notion of architecture's privileged status among the arts finds a natural corollary in the similarly prevalent idea of architecture as beholden to an obligation to tell the truth about itself, as if by refusing deception and obfuscation the medium takes inspiration from and reaffirms its position at the authentic source of things. Reflecting on the lamentable state of new architecture in modern-day Paris, Hugo thus writes of the Palace of the Bourse: "If it be the rule that the architecture of a building should be adapted to its function in such a way that this function declares itself merely by looking at the building, then we can hardly wonder enough at a monument which might equally well be a king's palace, a house of commons, a town hall, a college, a riding-school, an academy, a warehouse, a law court, a museum, a barracks, a sepulchre, a temple or a theatre. For the present, it is a stock exchange."[11] According to Hugo, the so-called facade of the Bourse serves as an instance of architectural facelessness, an empty cipher legible as anything and thus of nothing. To borrow the key phrase of *Heat*, the Bourse resists entering into a straightforward, "face-to-face" interaction with those who look upon it. Ironically, only in the sense that the building, like the stock exchange it momentarily houses, represents something radically unstable does it achieve any proper alignment between form and function and, as it were, "openly" tell the "truth" about itself.

The epistemological accountability of architecture holds a profound importance, as well, for Hugo's roughly contemporaneous fellow champion of the gothic, John Ruskin. In the chapter entitled "The Lamp of Truth" in *The Seven Lamps of Architecture* (1849), Ruskin declares: "We may not be able to command good, or beautiful, or inventive, architecture; but we *can* command an honest architecture . . . [for] what is there but scorn for the meanness of deception?" Cataloging three main types of "architectural deceits"—

structural, surface, and operative—Ruskin reserves the most and harshest words for the third type, which he defines as "the use of cast or machine-made ornaments of any kind," revealing his broader anti-industrial stance and attendant lionization of the medieval craftsman—that highly skilled but imperfect worker who inscribes onto buildings a unique "record of [his] thoughts, and intents, and trials, and heartbreakings."[12] Later in the book, elaborating the symbiosis of his radiant, poetic laws, Ruskin connects "the Lamp of Truth" with "the Lamp of Life," writing: "All the steps are marked most clearly in the arts, and in Architecture more than in any other; for it, being especially dependent, as we have just said, on the warmth of the true life [Ruskin is here referring to the warmth of the worker's hand as opposed to the coldness of machine production], is also peculiarly sensible of the hemlock cold of the false; and I do not know anything more oppressive, when the mind is once awakened to its characteristics, than the aspect of a dead architecture."[13]

Like Vincent, Ruskin associates coldness and deadness in architecture with a certain epistemological deficiency and takes umbrage at them all. Instead of considering Vincent as an outright ventriloquist of Ruskin, however, we might draw a somewhat finer distinction based on the fact that Vincent criticizes Justine's exhusband's house not in terms of the *false* (the recurrent word, along with *lie*, in Ruskin), but in terms of *bullshit*—a word appearing nowhere in *The Seven Lamps* nor presumably anywhere in Ruskin's stately written oeuvre. A crucial difference exists between the false and bullshit, however, as Harry Frankfurt argues in his belatedly best-selling essay turned minibook *On Bullshit*.[14] According to Frankfurt, the distinction between falseness (or lies) and bullshit is that whereas the liar "thinks he knows the truth," which he then sets about deliberately warping or subverting, the bullshitter "pays no attention to it [the truth] at all." Or, as Frankfurt claims, making the case for bullshit as a "greater enemy of the truth than lies are," "It is just this lack of connection to a concern with the truth—this indifference to how things really are—that I regard as of the essence of bullshit."[15]

Interestingly, Frankfurt draws one of his central, definitional examples from architecture, making an appeal to him in the context of Vincent's rant against the house especially apropos. In order to illustrate what bullshit is not, the opposite of bullshit, Frankfurt cites a verse from Longfellow's poem "The Builders" (1846), which Ludwig Wittgenstein reportedly claimed "could serve him as a motto":[16]

In the elder days of art
Builders wrought with greatest care
Each minute and unseen part
For the Gods are everywhere

Frankfurt interprets the stanza as follows: "These craftsmen did not relax their thoughtful self-discipline even with respect to the features of their work that would ordinarily not be visible. Although no one would notice if those features were not quite right, the craftsmen would be bothered by their consciences. So nothing was swept under the rug. Or, one might perhaps also say, there was no bullshit."[17] Thus, Frankfurt sets up an opposition between such a mode of building and bullshitting, taking the poem as an appeal to the reader not to grow lazy and ignore higher standards (God, truth) in all that he or she undertakes to build.

Reading *Heat* by the light of Frankfurt's reading of Longfellow, I am struck by the emphasis on the nature of work that runs through both.[18] Indeed, much of the language that Frankfurt uses to describe Longfellow's ideal builders of yore—their refusal to "relax," their adherence to "the demands of a disinterested and austere discipline"[19]—can easily be imagined as receiving affirmation from Vincent, who never takes a moment off and prides himself on his stringent devotion to his job, balking at the way Ralph "lounge[s] around" the house. Parsed à la Frankfurt, Vincent's workaholism takes on a distinctly philosophical cast, which he brings to bear on his judgment on the house as "bullshit," an impetuous label that nevertheless flags the house as a crucible (teeming with the ghosts of Hegel, Hugo, Ruskin, and Longfellow) in which the status of truth is urgently being tested—or, more accurately, in which truth is met with a gigantic indifference. Following Frankfurt's definition, a "bullshit house" would be a house too epistemologically negligent even to be against itself, unable to be stormed because there is nothing substantive there to be stormed. And so Vincent storms *out*.

Absent Fathers

On a more everyday level, Vincent's dereliction of the indifferent house shows up more and more his own capacity for indifference, establishing an affinity between him and a second doppelgänger "in" the film—Justine's exhusband, who repeatedly breaks plans with his psychically frail daughter, Lauren (Natalie Portman), without even bothering to inform her, leaving her stranded, abandoned, and exacerbating her condition. Indeed, not once does Lauren's "real" father materialize in his actual person; he is an absent father marked as such by his literal absence from the film. This being the case, our only access to him is through the house, with which he is strongly identified and which, according to Vincent, never ceases to belong to him and bear his anonymous stamp: "her *exhusband's* dead-tech, postmodernistic, bullshit house," Vincent refers to the place, rather than as merely "her [Justine's] house." Reinforcing this identification, the film hints that Justine's exhusband may have even designed and built the house himself. "My dad's picking me up. He's taking me to the new building and then out to lunch," Lauren says with high hopes before the first of the rattling no-shows. Nothing more is mentioned or explained about this "new building"— Lauren is denied the visit—but her remark suggests that her father's career lies in some architecture-related field; and, indeed, in the comprehensive credits listed at the back of Nick James's monograph on the film,[20] Lauren (but not Justine) is given the last name "Gustafson," assumedly that of her biological father, conjuring Scandinavia, world famous for its ultrasleek, modern designs. What is this wildly busy, deadbeat dad so preoccupied with, we are left wondering, other than covering the topography of Los Angeles with a plenitude of the sorts of high-tech, high-fashion structures that Vincent so loathes?[21]

Spiteful of Lauren's father's shirking of paternal responsibilities, Vincent sets himself up as a surrogate yet superior father—a father more "real" than the "real" one, more "authentic" than the "authentic" one, laying a claim to such titles in arenas that count far more than the biological. Such an assumption of the high ground on Vincent's part, the film makes some effort to caution us, cannot entirely be dismissed as pure self-righteous self-congratulation. Near the end of the film, Lauren attempts suicide in the hotel room that Vincent moves into after he vacates the house, and, as Justine remarks to him afterward at the hospital where he has rushed Lauren to be revived—pitting the two men against each other, her ex and her imminently becoming new ex—"She [Lauren] chose you. She came to your place." With this gesture, it is as if Lauren aligns herself with Vincent's rejection of the house, fleeing the space and not heading to what we can assume is another like it—wherever in the city her father currently lives—but opting instead for an elsewhere, even if that elsewhere is a drab, unexceptional hotel room. Like Vincent, she is deeply sensitive to spaces (in an earlier scene she freaks out because her barrettes go missing in the house, as if the house has mischievously hidden or disappeared them), and, as a result, to "choose" someone effectively becomes for her a choice of one person's "place" over another's.

Nevertheless, one might express some legitimate doubts about Justine's interpretation of Lauren's actions. For one thing, Justine has also just told Vincent that there is no point trying to inform her exhusband about what has happened because he is off "somewhere in the Sierras" (a vast, snow-capped mountain range with glacial origins, perfectly suited to a cold, aloof personality), making it possible that Vincent has merely "won" the presumed fatherhood competition by default. Moreover, what does it mean to be the chosen one when the reward for being thus chosen is the discovery of your (step)daughter's bloodied, near-corpse? Contra Justine, might Lauren's choice of suicide site not be read as an act of aggression pointedly directed against Vincent? Indeed, there is something about her plan that rekindles all of the same questions about Vincent's emotional availability and authentic bona fides that arise in the earlier scene at the house with Ralph. Viewed in tandem, the two scenes describe a transgenerational repetition, a loose replaying out of the distraught mother's behavior by the distraught daughter.

Echoing his previous entry into the house, Vincent enters the hotel room oblivious to the melodramatic spectacle that has been specially arranged for him. A television—not his, the one he has already jettisoned, but the standard hotel model—features prominently in the background. Vincent walks out onto the balcony and gazes out into the vast, twinkling incandescence of Los Angeles by night, which McCauley had earlier compared to the Fiji ocean lit up by "iridescent algae that come out once a year in the water" and which many critics point to as the quintessential Mannian view of the city.[22] Stepping back into the room, Vincent notices on the carpet a giant stain of water that has seeped out from beneath the bathroom door. Cautiously looking inside, he finds Lauren floating unconscious in an overflowing bath-tub of blood, her legs and arms slashed on the arteries. Obviously, Lauren's suicide does not possess the same theatrical aspect that Justine's infidelity does; the slashes are more than skin deep, her blood is pouring out, and her life hangs precariously in the balance. However, one has to imagine that an immense amount of deliberation, "staging," went into situating herself just there in the bathroom for Vincent to find her. (How did she get all the way to the hotel and then into Vincent's room? Did he supply her with a key? Did she somehow break in? Or smooth-talk her way in?) In this respect, Lauren's machinations do indeed recall her mother's. Like the infidelity, Lauren's suicide attempt can be read as a methodically desperate plea to

Vincent to emote, to react, to *care*—as an intervention intended to under-score and potentially rectify his "affective disorder": stormy outpourings of rage followed by (or somehow coupled with) deep-freezes of renunciation.

In this case, the urgency of the situation demands more than before that Vincent respond "appropriately" and not flee the scene. Thus, he lifts Lauren out of the water and cradles her in his arms, and, creating some makeshift tourniquets out of ripped towels, rushes her to the hospital. When Vincent bears Lauren into the emergency room, her body draped in a white sheet, the image recalls the dramatically lit *Pietà* in front of the hospital that we see at the beginning of the film as McCauley infiltrates the institution and poses as a paramedic in order to steal an ambulance. Yet Vincent's model parental solicitude does not last long. Once more, work calls. After Lauren is upgraded to stable condition, he shows little to no resistance to Justine's half-hearted reassurance that she'll be OK and that he should do what he has to do. Going back on his earlier remark, "I'll stay right here. I ain't going anywhere," he races off to pursue McCauley, who is in the midst of trying to make his career-capping great escape to Fiji. The show of fatherly heroics turns out to be a momentary parenthesis rather than a final accomplishment that pieces the family back together.

Vincent's last chance for meaningful connection occurs within the sphere of his job. On the roaring tarmac of the Los Angeles Airport, gar-gantuan planes landing and taking off, he and McCauley meet again, this time with guns in a spectacular shoot-out. Each makes good on his prom-ise not to hesitate to kill the other, and yet it is Vincent whose bullet finds its target first. Dying, McCauley uses his last gesture to extend a hand to Vincent, which the latter accepts, providing us with the final image of the movie: a long shot of the two men linked hand in hand, McCauley splayed out on a generator, his dead face aslant yet visible to us, and Vincent stand-ing upright, facing away from us and gazing (presumably) into the vista of night-lit runways. It is a moment of solidarity between the two men, but one overlaid with all the film's characteristic ambiguities, permitted only on the disconnective condition of death. Moreover, the yin–yang placement of the characters—one facing us, the other facing away—suggests not only a state of oppositional interdependence, but a puzzle about identity. Who are these men? If they are indeed doppelgängers, reduplicative simulacra of one another with no original, where is identity to be located? Perversely, the living face is occluded, a blank, while the face that we do see is emptied of life, the face of a corpse.

Adding to this elusiveness, the pair inhabit a zone of pronounced inter-stitiality, the most volatile area on the airport grounds, where they appear as if fixed forever—a quality owing to the painterly tableau as well as to the shot's extended length, some fifteen seconds as the synthesizers on the soundtrack ethereally crescendo. It is as if Vincent and McCauley have arrived permanently in a state of placelessness. Neither makes it "home," either back to the home that he has abandoned (Vincent) or to the future home that he has wishfully erected in his fantasy (McCauley). Indeed, omit-ting the conventional denouement of the crime picture, where a fleet of police and emergency vehicles rolls in ever so belatedly after the hero has single-handedly dispatched the villain and primary source of danger, Mann does not even allow Vincent to repair back to his temporary home at the hotel. In this, the ending of *Heat* looks ahead to Mann's next Los Angeles film, *Collateral* (2004), which consists of one long night of cabbing around the city—all transitoriness in which the domestic sphere drops out entirely.

In the later film, Tom Cruise plays an expert hit man, also named Vin-cent, who, like Pacino's Vincent, raises the problem of "the silence of affect." However, the two namesake protagonists importantly differ from one another. Whereas Pacino's Vincent is manifestly troubled by his emotional incapacities, as when he projectively, overcompensatingly lashes out against the "dead-tech" house, Cruise's Vincent seems immaculately unbothered by his cold-bloodedness. When Cruise throws tantrums, they seem weirdly objectless, almost random or automatically ticlike. Conversely, when Pacino's Vincent suddenly swings from detached to livid, one senses some sort of genuine dilemma of genuineness within himself. For this reason, Cruise's character represents the more absolute figure of affective nullity in Mann, as if the exhusband from *Heat* finally materializes in him with a vengeance and a literal violence—as if the "dead-tech, postmodernistic, bullshit" house finds in him a more perfect "human" cipher. This difference accounts for why *Heat* is often justly described as a neo-noir tragedy—tragedy requiring agonism, resistance—whereas *Collateral* approaches nowhere near tragedy, coming across like some altogether new experiment in deliberately one-dimensional, already-far-gone characterology.

Coda: "Los Angeles Plays Itself"

The scene at the house that I have been dwelling upon at such length makes a notable appearance in Thom Andersen's critically acclaimed, ceaselessly informative essay–film *Los Angeles Plays Itself* (2003). Examining the history of the cinematic representation of Los Angeles, Anderson compiles, cross-references, and offers glosses upon a vast array of clips from films set in the city, intervening from a position of provocative, unapologetically militant geographic literalism. For Andersen, film—especially mainstream Hollywood film—has on a recurrent basis and with an unchallenged and barely subliminal disdainfulness wronged his city through misrepresentation, failing to produce images that correspond with its actual, lived-in fabric. (A parallel might be drawn here with certain early strands of identity criticism, subbing in Los Angeles for the working class, women, or various minorities.)

In a *Cinema Scope* review of David Lynch's *Mulholland Drive* (2001) and *Collateral* (two Los Angeles films released after Anderson had already finished *Los Angeles Plays Itself*), Anderson reminds the reader of how he had "ridiculed" *Heat* "for situating a character [McCauley's girlfriend, a freelance graphic designer who makes ends meet by working in a bookstore] in the Hollywood Hills when her economic station would place her in the plains below and for rechristening the Vincent Thomas Bridge, named after a venerable state legislator from San Pedro, the 'Saint Vincent Thomas Bridge.'"[23] Andersen's problem with Vincent's rant against the house, however, has less to do with demographic and cartographic inaccuracies per se than with an emasculating negativity that links up all too well with the skewered, one-sided, negative portrayal of the city that he is charting. In the essay–film, showing a clip of the scene following a clip from Mike Figgis's *Internal Affairs* (1990), Andersen (or rather his oral stand-in) remarks in voice-over: "Andy Garcia and Al Pacino played cops with arty wives who make them live in uncoplike designer houses." As if far better suited to living in gritty, cramped apartments in New York, a city that has been endlessly, lovingly fetishized on film, the two cops resent their Los Angeles homes—where they never feel quite at home—and by extension the city as a whole.[24]

Andersen, one might usefully consider, stakes a claim for truth in architectural representation in a manner analogous to those critics and writers before him who stake a claim for truth in architecture as such. Like Hugo, Ruskin, and Longfellow, he wants a spatiality of honesty, free of deception and, as Frankfurt would say, bullshit. Indeed, one gathers the impression from his film that the bulk of directors do not so much willfully lie about the city as display a sheer indifference to its reality. Merely concerned with squeezing the most entertainment value out of their illusory Los Angeleses, they construct remotely self-enclosed images of the city that qualify as bullshit in the precise sense described in *On Bullshit*.

In the *Cinema Scope* article, Andersen acknowledges that quite a few "people who live in Los Angeles accuse me of being unfair to Michael Mann." Although willing to concede that *"Collateral* improves on *Heat"*—citing, among other reasons, the more recent film's focus on the basin, "where most of us live," rather than on the hills—Andersen remains firm in his condemnation of *Heat*.[25] Insofar as Andersen judges the film by his own populist, literalist criteria, he is, it must be admitted, hard to quarrel with. Yet it's worth pointing out that if *Heat* commits a slew of "geographical howler[s],"[26] it also treats the problem of truth and architecture reflexively *as a problem*,[27] which resists being simply or easily played out. Further, there is more than a touch of Andersen's own cranky, often rantlike preoccupation with spatial authenticity coursing through Vincent's screed against the house. For these reasons, the two films are perhaps less far away than Andersen is willing to admit. Indeed, although *Los Angeles Plays Itself* might not convert Vincent into a booster for the city, it is a film that I imagine him watching not with rage or indifference, but with an appreciable dose of sympathetic approval.

Notes

1. Fredric Jameson, *Signatures of the Visible* (New York: Routledge, 1992), 60.

2. Frederic Jameson, *Postmodernism, or, The Cultural Logic of Late Capitalism* (Durham, NC: Duke University Press, 1991), 9.

3. Denis Hollier, *Against Architecture: The Writings of Georges Bataille,* trans. Betsy Wing (Cambridge, MA: MIT Press, 1989).

4. Quoted in ibid., 47.

5. Ibid., 51.

6. Quoted in ibid., 53.

7. See Marco Abel, *Violent Affect: Literature, Cinema, and Critique after Representation* (Lincoln: University of Nebraska Press, 2007), 277.

8. Hollier, *Against Architecture,* xi. Hollier's remarks on Tschumi appear in an introduction newly written for the English edition of *Against Architecture,* where he takes stock of critical and cultural developments since the original publication of the book and elaborates on Bataille's status as a kind of poststructuralist *avant la lettre.*

9. Quoted in ibid., 3. Not incidentally, in the closing lines of the introduction, Hegel figures the prime mover of art, the spirit of beauty, in architectural terms: "Now, therefore, what the particular arts realize in individual works of art is, according to the Concept of art, only the universal forms of the self-unfolding Idea of beauty. It is as the

external actualization of this Idea that the wide Pantheon of art is rising. Its architect and builder is the self-comprehending spirit of beauty, but to complete it will need the history of the world in its development through thousands of years" (*Aesthetics: Lecture on Fine Art,* vol. 1, trans. T. M. Knox [Oxford: Oxford University Press, 1975], 90).

10. Victor Hugo, *Notre-Dame de Paris,* trans. John Sturrock (New York: Penguin, 1978), 189.

11. Ibid., 150.

12. John Ruskin, *The Seven Lamps of Architecture* (New York: Dover, 1989), 35, 54. Despite his anti-industrial antimodernism, Ruskin's concern with truth in architecture (especially regarding structural and surface deceits) reveals strong ties to the modernist core value of "transparency," as promulgated by Le Corbusier among numerous others.

13. Ibid., 150–51.

14. Frankfurt's text first appeared as an essay in *Raritan* in 1986.

15. Harry G. Frankfurt, *On Bullshit* (Princeton, NJ: Princeton University Press, 2005), 55, 61, 33–34.

16. Quoted in ibid., 19.

17. Ibid., 20–21. Longfellow's poem quoted in ibid., 20.

18. For a sociologically attuned analysis of Vincent's workaholism that situates the condition within the context of rising concerns about "overwork" in late 1980s and early 1990s America, see J. A. Lindstrom, "*Heat:* Work and Genre," *Jump Cut,* no. 43 (July 2000): 21–37.

19. Frankfurt, *On Bullshit,* 23.

20. Nick James, *Heat* (London: British Film Institute, 2002).

21. Lively, empirically based discussions of the tech-based explosion of growth in Los Angeles since roughly the 1960s, the last two essays in Edward W. Soja's book *Postmodern Geographies: The Reassertion of Space in Critical Social Theory* (London: Verso, 1989) provide useful context for this point.

22. Mann's interest in Los Angeles at night links up particularly well with Jean Baudrillard's chapter "Astral America" in his travelogue *America,* originally published in 1986. Baudrillard writes: "[Los Angeles] condenses by night the entire future geometry of the networks of human relations, gleaming in their abstraction, luminous in their extension, astral in their reproduction to infinity" (*America,* trans. Chris Turner [London: Verso, 1988], 54).

23. Thom Andersen, "Collateral Damage: Los Angeles Continues Playing Itself," *Cinema Scope,* no. 20 (Fall 2004): 50.

24. My thinking on Los Angeles versus New York representation on film has also been shaped by Mark Shiel's insightful essay "A Nostalgia for Modernity: New York, Los Angeles, and American Cinema in the 1970s," in *Screening the City,* ed. Mark Shiel and Tony Fitzmaurice (London: Verso, 2003), 160–79.

25. Anderson, "Collateral Damage," 50, 51.

26. Ibid., 50.

27. Here it's relevant to mention that one of Mann's purposes in "remaking" *Heat* from its first incarnation as the television movie *L.A. Takedown* (1989) was to better represent—one could say more extensively and accurately—the city. As he explains in an interview available on YouTube (http://www.youtube.com/watch?v=fvkFi72cAbY), the small screen (of the pre-high-definition era, of course) presents deep challenges to capturing landscape. "It's not going to be an experience of a place I'm in," Mann remarks of the restrictions he faced making the television movie.

MANN'S BIOPICS AND THE METHODOLOGY OF PHILOSOPHY

Ali and The Insider

David Rodríguez-Ruiz

> I have to put my family's welfare on the line here, my friend. And what are
> you putting up? You're putting up words!
> —Jeffrey Wigand in *The Insider* (1999)

The Battle of Ideas in *Ali*

What is it to be a people's champion? Are there irresolvable conflicts between
being a people's champion and being an individual committed to critical
thinking? What is the nature of patriotism, freedom, and brotherhood? In
Ali (2001), Michael Mann not only explores these decidedly philosophical
questions but also provides a rich context for a discussion about the meth-
odological difficulties involved in trying to answer them. How does one
decide, for instance, what true patriotism and freedom are? Conceptions of
patriotism and freedom are embedded in our laws and institutions, but that
alone is not enough reason for upholding any of those conceptions. Laws
and institutions can oftentimes be flawed, and they need to be challenged.
The public might also widely share some beliefs about patriotism and freedom at any point in time, but being shared by the majority is not what gives
normative value to these beliefs or what makes them true. Individuals might
rightly challenge widely shared views. Then again, individuals are fallible,
and, from an evaluative standpoint, what should matter are the grounds for
our beliefs, not who happens to hold the beliefs in question.

So what could be the right grounds for our beliefs about the nature of patriotism, brotherhood, and other concepts that shape the social order? Are there objective grounds when it comes to these issues, or are there no matters of fact about them, only opinions that become part of certain traditions or that are convenient to those who seek to maintain power? Although *Ali* doesn't attempt to give direct answers to these questions, the film has the merit of showing (or reminding us) that there is much at stake in answering them. Moreover, the historical examples in *Ali* illustrate that precisely because the stakes are high and there are no easy recipes for finding the right answers, individuals have the responsibility to adopt a philosophical attitude and think critically.

Ali is as much about important battles of ideas during the 1960s and early 1970s as it is about a significant chapter in boxing history. Woven into the main story are direct references to the ideological differences within the civil rights movement, the Muslim church, and different sectors of the American public on issues such as racial integration, the war in Vietnam, and women's liberation. The first complete lines of dialogue that we hear in the film are from a speech by Malcolm X (Mario Van Peebles) criticizing the approach of other African American leaders and arguing against the idea that one should "turn the other cheek to the brutality of the white man and the system of injustice that is established right here." A few additional scenes make reference to how Malcolm X not only disagrees with other civil rights leaders and with the interpretation of some Christian principles but also has differences with the leaders of his own congregation on how to conduct the struggle for equality.[1]

With Muhammad Ali's (Will Smith) involvement in religious and political issues, we get to see an additional series of ideological clashes and contradictions: Ali disagrees with Malcolm X's critique of their religious leader, but later he, too, is suspended from the practice of Islam, supposedly for loving the sports world too much, and is denied contact with other Muslims. He disagrees with his first wife (Jada Pinkett Smith) about what her fashion choices represent. In her view, unwillingly dressing according to Muslim precepts would represent submission to the leaders of Ali's religion, whereas Ali thinks that the way she dresses and straightens her hair represents submission to the prevalent white culture and sends the wrong message that her own ethnicity is less valuable. He argues with his second wife (Nona Gaye) about what it means to have a big boxing event in an African country. He argues with his father (Giancarlo Esposito) about what their family name "Clay" stands for. (In Ali's view, it represents their ancestors' slave past, whereas his father believes that they now own the name "Clay" and that it represents their family unit). And more importantly, Ali disapproves of the war in Vietnam and is willing to speak openly about it.

An aspect of these ideological conflicts worth noting is that part of what is at issue is the meaning or symbolic character of certain practices and acts: the name you use, the way you dress, your hairstyle, where you decide to live, and where a big event takes place. Even individuals (especially Ali) have a symbolic value and are targeted in part because of what they are taken to represent. This value adds another level to the question of how to settle disagreements about meaning. Who decides (or what factors determine) the meanings of a person's acts: the person's intentions, the community where the person lives, influential public figures, advertisers and the people they work for, or a combination of these and other factors? Is the meaning of more abstract concepts, such as patriotism and brotherhood, also determined by a combination of similar factors?

Another aspect worth noting about the way in which the debates in *Ali* are presented is how the dialogue oftentimes goes straight to questioning the meaning of the main concepts used in the discussions or criticisms. After the Illinois Boxing Commission goes along with the US government's stance on the war and asks Ali if he is prepared to apologize for his remarks, he challenges the political establishment's notion of war: "I ain't going ten thousand miles to help murder and kill other poor people." When they threaten to put him in jail for refusing induction into the military, he questions their notions of freedom and imprisonment: "You wanna send me to jail? Fine, you go right ahead. I've been in jail four hundred years." And when they try to imply that he is not acting as a people's champion and accuse him of making unpatriotic remarks, he questions their idea of patriotism: "You want me to go somewhere to fight for you, but you won't even stand up for me right here in America, for my rights and my religious beliefs." At times, the directness of the dialogue can be as effective as the punches we see being thrown in the ring. With one of the saddest and most powerful lines in the film, Ali summarizes his opposition to the war and questions the received view on who the enemy is. "No Vietcong ever called me nigger," he tells a reporter who asks him about the war.

The result of these direct replies is not necessarily that they settle the debates, but that they help us to identify the argument's basic assumptions and elucidate the meanings of the concepts in terms of which they are framed, precisely two of the principal tasks of philosophical analysis. Although they are not the only tasks of philosophy, they are essential for achieving effective communication between the parties to a dispute (or among the participants in collaborative dialogue, to put it in less antagonistic terms). An additional and oftentimes more difficult task is to find the right criteria for choosing among the possibly different meanings attached to the terms used in a debate. The importance of having such criteria can be illustrated with several examples from *The Insider* (1999), another Michael Mann biopic that pays attention to public discourse and to the subtleties of language, especially in legal contexts.

Three Key Concepts in *The Insider*

The Insider was released two years before *Ali,* but the events it portrays take place almost three decades after Ali's famous fights in the boxing rings and the political arena. In one of the most important scenes in the film, Jeffrey Wigand (Russell Crowe) is trying to decide whether to testify in court and disclose information that the public needs to know but that would incriminate the tobacco company that he used to work for (Brown & Williamson). It's a momentous decision that will change his life from then on and affect the lives of many others. As he reflects on what to do, he sees four police officers not too far from the court building. The three Caucasian officers in the group talk among themselves, while the only African American officer stands silent at a distance from them. Wigand seems to conclude that nothing has changed "since whenever" and decides to go ahead and give his testimony.

Many things had changed by the 1990s, of course, but not all of them for the best: the film is set in a time when politicians, lawmakers, and corporations had perfected the art of manipulating language in order to protect their interests, avert criticism, and influence public opinion in their favor. At the heart of each of the main conflicts in *The Insider,* there is some term whose definition or whose application is controlled or manipulated by one of the parties involved in the conflict. The model of definitions that emerges from this dynamic is one in which there seems to be enough room for arbitrarily playing with the meaning of certain terms. This, again, leads to the questions whether there are constraints on the definitions of concepts pertaining to the social order and whether we can justify those constraints in an impartial way. A few examples from *The Insider* will help to discuss these questions in more detail.

The first example is concerned with what counts as confidential information. Almost half of the film revolves around the issue of Wigand's being bound by a confidentiality agreement from sharing any information about his former job, including the fact that tobacco companies lace their cigarettes with a carcinogenic ammonia product that enhances their addictive power. Brown & Williamson's CEO Thomas Sandefur (Michael Gambon) knows that Wigand understands the nature of his confidentiality agreement, but he is concerned that it might not be clear enough, so he proposes to add a supplement to the agreement that "broadly defines and expands in more detail what is 'confidential.'" That way, he tells Wigand, "nobody will be able to say, 'Well, hell's bells, Margaret, I didn't know *that* was a secret.' We're very serious about protecting our interests." The specific contents of the agreement are never explained, but it is made clear that the way it defines what counts as confidential is meant to override Wigand's ethical duties as a citizen.

Wigand's deposition in court, the second example, also involves the definition of a concept that has serious ethical and legal implications. He is invited as an expert witness to answer if nicotine acts as a drug and whether it should be considered addictive. He answers, "Yes. It produces a physiological response, which meets the definition of a drug. Nicotine is associated with impact, with satisfaction. It has a pharmacological effect that crosses the blood–brain barrier intact." Wigand's statement contradicts the definition of "addictive" that the seven CEOs of Big Tobacco use when they appear before Congress. Their definition, conveniently, doesn't apply to cigarettes:

Congressman: Yes or no: Do you believe that nicotine is not addictive?

CEO: Congressman, cigarettes and nicotine clearly do not meet the classic definitions of addiction; there is no intoxication.

Congressman: We'll take that as a no. I think each of you believes nicotine is not addictive and would like to just have this for the record.

The reason why it is important for the CEOs to deny any knowledge of the addictive nature of nicotine, as one of the staff lawyers for *60 Minutes* explains later, is that then they can deflect their accountability by arguing that it is the consumers' responsibility to find out about the possible health risks related to using their product. The aspect of this case that is most relevant to the present discussion is the disagreement between two definitions of "addiction," one that fits the tobacco companies' purposes and one that has implications regarding their accountability.

The final example involves the legal concept of "tortious interference," which the CBS general counsel (Gina Gershon) explains as follows: "If two people have an agreement, like a confidentiality agreement, and one of them breaks it because they are induced to do so by a third party, the third party can be sued for damages for interfering. Hence, 'tortious interference.'" It is in part because of the limitations set by this concept that CBS decides to air an edited version of Wigand's interview that doesn't include his statement to the effect that the CEOs of Big Tobacco have perjured themselves before Congress. Interestingly, when reporter Lowell Bergman (Al Pacino) confronts *60 Minutes* executive producer Don Hewitt (Phillip Baker Hall) about the decision not to air the complete interview, Bergman makes his point in terms of how they use language at their convenience. He argues that they are hiding behind legal terminology and are not disclosing their actual reasons for avoiding a possible lawsuit:

> Hewitt: You're questioning our journalistic integrity?!
> Bergman: No, I'm questioning your hearing! You hear "reasonable" and "tortious interference." I hear "potential Brown & Williamson lawsuit jeopardizing the sale of CBS to Westinghouse." I hear "Shut the segment down. Cut Wigand loose. Obey orders. And fuck off!" That's what I hear.

Skepticism about the Grounds for Defining Concepts That Belong to the Social World

Both *The Insider* and *Ali* provide insightful perspectives on the roles that language plays in the quest for justice as well as in the obstruction of justice. Although some of the boundaries established by certain concepts seem to be more arbitrary than others, their practical implications are not less real. Actual people lose their livelihood, might go to prison, and get only second-rate freedoms depending (in part) on how one defines what counts as "equal," "unpatriotic," "conscientious objection," "confidential information," "addictive," "legal drug," "tortious interference," and so forth. Given that the concepts that shape the social world can serve such a powerful role, it is important to have the right tools to challenge, defend, or modify certain definitions when necessary.

According to a skeptical approach to the tasks of assessing and possibly revising our concepts, there are no objective grounds for choosing among the definitions of concepts that apply to social states of affairs, in the sense that such concepts are human made and that there is always an element of arbitrariness to how we choose to divide what we take to be our social reality. With regard to things such as water, it is perhaps easier to talk about an independent nature that can be explained in terms of simpler elements. However, the skeptical view maintains, with regard to concepts such as love and democracy, that talk of an objective and unchanging nature is unfounded. One version of this approach, known as cultural relativism, argues that ethical and political concepts, such as justice and freedom, have different definitions in different cultures and that there are no independent standards for deciding whether the concepts of one culture are preferable to those of other cultures.

As James Rachels points out in *The Elements of Moral Philosophy,* cultural relativism makes some valid points, but its main thesis seems to be mistaken. In other words, there seem to be facts about ethics, and some cultures (including, of course, whatever culture we decide to call our own) might get some of those facts wrong. Depending on one's background assumptions, this view might be considered to be either implausible or obvious enough as to require no defense.[2] To take an example from *The Insider,* if it is found out that a company intentionally sold a carcinogenic product without letting consumers know what they were buying, most people would agree that it is a fact (not just an opinion) that such a practice is unethical regardless of where and when it took place.

Part of Rachels's argument consists of appealing to our ethical intuitions about cases such as the one presented in *The Insider* and spelling out the unintuitive implications of cultural relativism. As Rachels points out, if we seriously maintain that there are no independent standards of justice, we would have to commit to the following statements. First, "we could no longer say that the customs of other societies are morally inferior to our own." Of course, "to condemn a particular practice is not to say that the culture is on the whole contemptible or that it is generally inferior to any other culture, including one's own."[3] But from the standpoint of cultural relativism, we would have to say, for instance, that a society that allows racial discrimination and religious persecution is just different from ours in these respects, not morally right or wrong about their views on equality. Second, "we could decide whether actions are right or wrong just by consulting the standards of our society."[4] For example, if our society accepts that a confidentially agreement with your employer overrides your responsibilities as a citizen, then such a practice is morally right just in virtue of being the customary way of doing things. Or if we want to decide whether it is unethical to discriminate against patients that have preexisting medical conditions, we would just have to take a look at our health-care system, and however things are presently done would have to be considered the right way of doing them. Third, with cultural relativism "the idea of moral progress is called into doubt" because, in this view, there are no culture-independent standards by which past practices, such as racial segregation and denying women their right to vote, may be judged as better or worse than currently favored practices and values.[5]

In addition to pointing out these unintuitive consequences of cultural relativism, Rachels argues that despite the differences among cultures, which oftentimes are overemphasized, "there are some moral rules that all societies will have in common, because those rules are necessary for society to exist." For instance, "any cultural group that continues to exist must care for its young," must encourage its members to tell the truth, and must prohibit murder.[6] Thus, the conditions required for our survival put some constraints on the norms that we can have and, by extension, on the concepts in terms of which those norms are formulated. Considerations about survival, however, should not be expected to provide the answer to all questions about our ethical concepts. We need additional criteria in order to do justice to the fact that there is something ethically wrong about societies where, even though the minimal conditions for survival are met for disadvantaged individuals or groups, they are exploited and disrespected by other members of their society. And because ethical concepts are only a portion of the concepts that apply to human affairs, we also need methods for adjudicating disputes about concepts that are not directly concerned with ethical issues.[7]

Philosophy's Ambivalent Relation with the Public

The traditional method of conceptual analysis begins with the task of identifying clear instances of the concept that one wishes to define. If we are trying to analyze what justice is, we need examples of acts that would be normally classified as just. After gathering those initial examples, the next step is to try to provide a definition that captures the features in common among them. In order to test the proposed definition, we must apply it to actual or hypothetical situations. If there is a situation that intuitively seems to be unjust even though it meets the conditions specified in the proposed definition of justice, then the definition would be considered deficient, and it would have to be either rejected or modified. This method is based on the assumption that our grasp of the contents of our concepts is almost always incomplete and indirect. For even if we are competent language users, it is one thing to judge correctly that racial discrimination is unjust or that knowingly selling a carcinogenic product is unjust and another thing to be able to explain what justice is.[8]

Despite the widespread use of the method of conceptual analysis in philosophy, there are still some disagreements about its main features, including whether experts' conceptual intuitions should be given the same weight as the general public's conceptual intuitions. In many cases, it is clear that experts have a better understanding of a concept. If one asks people on the street what "tortious interference" is, most of them will probably reply as Bergman did in *The Insider*: "That sounds like a disease caught by a radio." In other cases, we can make a distinction between ordinary and technical definitions. For example, competent speakers of ordinary language may use terms such as *addiction* and *depression,* but their use should not be confused with clinical uses of the same terms, even though the two may be related. Finally, in yet other cases, it is not clear whether anyone can claim to have a special kind of expertise in using certain concepts, in the sense that both the general public and specialists in different fields have the same level of competence. Perhaps that is the case with concepts such as "justice," "patriotism," "love," "knowledge," and so on.

Things get complicated when there are different definitions of technical concepts, when there are differences among competent speakers about which cases should be classified as instances of a given concept, and when we need to choose only one definition and apply it in a broader context than the one for which it was originally intended. In these cases, conceptual analysts tend to give emphasis to consensus, either among experts or among competent speakers of ordinary language. Most conceptual analysts agree that we can make some adjustments to our concepts and still call them by the same names they currently have. But, at the same time, they argue that if we have made too many (or substantive) adjustments to a concept, we would not be providing a proper analysis or theory of it. As Brian Weatherson puts it, "While a theory can be reformist, it cannot be revolutionary. A theory that disagreed with virtually all intuitions about possible cases is, for that reason, false."[9]

Although this view might sound utterly conservative, to be fair, if a definition of the concept "addictive," for example, implied that water is addictive because we have to consume it every day, we would reject the definition for going against the way most people understand the concept in question. So we do give some emphasis to consensus when defining our concepts. The crucial questions are: How much emphasis should we give to consensus and how much tinkering with an ordinary concept counts as too much of an adjustment? In some cases, there are aspects of a definition that must be rejected even if there is widespread agreement to the contrary. In the early 1960s, when Muhammad Ali won a gold medal for the United States at the Olympics and his first heavyweight championship, interracial marriage was still illegal in twenty-one states. In those states, being of the same ethnicity was a necessary condition for getting married; the consensus (or at least the view that prevailed in the law until the 1967 Supreme Court decision) was that the concept of marriage couldn't apply to interracial couples. Needless to say, consensus about that aspect of the definition of marriage had to be challenged.

According to a recent alternative to conceptual analysis, we should investigate the goals that our concepts are supposed to help us achieve and then try to find the best conceptual tools for achieving those goals. As Edward Schiappa describes this proposal, "Instead of posing the questions in the time-honored manner of 'What is X?'" we should "reformulate the matter as 'How *ought* we use the word X?' given our particular reasons for defining X."[10] This shifts the focus of the discussion to questions about the purpose of words that shape the social world, which is undoubtedly a valuable discussion, but one where we still have to negotiate conflicting ideas and sometimes challenge the consensus on what our goals should be.

So, in the end, we are left with a dilemma similar to the one that the heroes in Mann's biopics had to face—not nearly as momentous, of course, but at least similar. On the one hand, both Ali and Wigand seek some recognition from the public, and their political battles are won when the court of public opinion rules in their favor. On the other hand, they know that the public is oftentimes manipulated and misinformed. And they are committed to being independent thinkers first: Wigand as a man of science and Ali as a people's champion who is not afraid to speak his mind and who is willing to challenge the public when necessary. Here is how he responds to a reporter when, a few days after wining his first heavyweight championship, he is asked whether he plans on being a people's champ like Joe

Louis: "Now I'm definitely going to be the people's champion. But I just ain't going to be the champ the way you want me to be the champ. I'm gonna be the champ the way I wanna be." Years later he reiterates this commitment when his friends warn him about the possible consequences of voicing his unpopular (at the moment) views on the war: "So what? I ain't got to be what nobody else wants me to be; and I ain't afraid to be what I wanna be, think how I want to think."[11]

Notes

1. *Ali* is somewhat ambiguous about the reasons why Malcolm X was suspended from the Nation of Islam. The film doesn't mention Malcolm's critique of Elijah Muhammad's womanizing or their disagreements about Malcolm's proposal to assassinate members of the Los Angeles Police Department in retaliation for the police shooting of seven Nation of Islam members at a mosque. See Manning Marable, *Malcolm X: A Life of Reinvention* (New York: Viking Press, 2011). For present purposes, however, it is not necessary to discuss the historical accuracy of the events portrayed in Mann's biopics.

2. James Rachels, *The Elements of Moral Philosophy,* 3rd ed. (New York: McGraw-Hill, 1999).

3. Ibid., 25, 33.

4. Ibid., 26.

5. As to the theses of cultural relativism that are on the right track, Rachels points out that the theory "warns us, quite rightly, about the danger of assuming that all our preferences are based on some absolute rational standard. They are not. Many (but not all) of our practices are merely peculiar to our society, and it is easy to lose sight of that fact. In reminding us of it, the theory does a service" (ibid., 34). Moreover, "by stressing that our moral views can reflect the prejudices of our society," cultural relativism helps us to keep an open mind and provides an antidote for dogmatism (35).

6. Ibid., 30, 29.

7. In addition to considerations about survival, Rachels suggests that we should also take people's welfare into account: "We may ask *whether [a] practice promotes or hinders the welfare of the people whose lives are affected by it.* And, as a corollary, we may ask if there is an alternative set of social arrangements that would do a better job of promoting their welfare. If so, we may conclude that the existing practice is deficient" (ibid., 32, emphasis in original).

8. For recent interpretations and defenses of the method of conceptual analysis, see Frank Jackson, *From Metaphysics to Ethics: A Defence of Conceptual Analysis* (Oxford: Clarendon Press, 1998), and Alvin Goldman, "Philosophical Intuitions: Their Target, Their Source, and Their Epistemic Status," *Grazer Philosophische Studien* 74 (2007): 1–26. For critiques of the method of conceptual analysis, see Hilary Kornblith, *Knowl-*

edge and Its Place in Nature (Oxford: Clarendon Press, 2002), and Kristoffer Ahlström, *Constructive Analysis: A Study in Epistemological Methodology* (Göteborg, Sweden: Göteborg University, 2007). For a discussion of different approaches to the use of intuitions in conceptual analysis, see Michael DePaul and William Ramsey, eds., *Rethinking Intuition: The Psychology of Intuition and Its Role in Philosophical Inquiry* (Lanham, MD: Rowman & Littlefield, 1998).

9. Brian Weatherson, "What Good Are Counterexamples?" *Philosophical Studies* 115 (2003): 8.

10. Edward Schiappa, *Defining Reality: Definitions and the Politics of Meaning* (Carbondale: Southern Illinois University Press, 2003), xi.

11. In Mann's most recent biopic, *Public Enemies* (2009), there is also an ambivalent relation between the main characters and the public. The fight between cops and robbers is in part a fight to win the public's respect and admiration. However, the public is also portrayed as naive and subject to manipulation by the media.

ACKNOWLEDGMENTS

We are grateful to Michael Mann for creating a body of work so deserving of the appreciation, analysis, evaluation, and exploration found in this book. We also want to thank our contributors for both the hard work that went into their chapters and their patience as the volume slowly took form. Mark T. Conard, editor of the Philosophy of Popular Culture series, has our appreciation for his dedication to the cause of bringing philosophical discussion to bear on areas such as film and television. We are grateful to University Press of Kentucky senior acquisitions editor Anne Dean Dotson, acquisitions assistant Bailey T. Johnson for providing such a congenial atmosphere for the books in the Philosophy of Popular Culture series, and assistant editor Iris A. Law for her work during the editing stage. We are also grateful to the readers of the manuscript for their helpful comments and suggestions. We thank Blair A. Thomas, marketing and electronic publishing assistant, for timely and informative communication as well as for the fine work the Marketing Department staff has done to publicize Michael Mann as the major American filmmaker he is. Our manuscript was copyedited by Annie Barva, who brought to her task insight, understanding, and an admirable feel for the material as well as indispensable technical skills. We deeply appreciate the work of the staff of the Production Department for their creation of the dust jacket cover. We could not have asked for a more apt congruence of theme and design than that conveyed by the photograph of Michael Mann behind the camera, an image that reflects his well-known reputation as a hands-on director who has often operated the camera himself.

Steven Sanders would like to thank his coeditors and each of the participants for their contributions to his understanding of the issues outlined in his introduction to this volume. He is also grateful to Christeen Clemens for helpful comments on the introduction and for her extensive assistance in the preparation of the manuscript.

Aeon J. Skoble would like to thank Steven Sanders, R. Barton Palmer, and Lisa Bahnemann for their support and assistance.

R. Barton Palmer is grateful to the Calhoun Lemon family for their continued support of his research and to the College of Art, Architecture, and Humanities at Clemson University, especially its dean, Richard Goodstein, for release time from teaching and myriad favors and conveniences that make his commitment to scholarly research possible.

Contributors

Vito Adriaensens is a PhD student and teaching assistant in the Department of Theatre and Film Studies at the University of Antwerp and researcher and lecturer at the School of Arts, University College Ghent. He is working on a dissertation that investigates the influence of nineteenth-century theatrical and pictorial strategies on the visual rhetoric of feature-length productions by Gaumont and Nordisk between 1908 and 1914 and, by extension, on the pan-European style of the 1910s. At the School of Arts, he is working on a project that focuses on the cinematic representation of fine arts, from living statues in early cinema to murderous wax museum artists. His research focuses on the interaction between visual arts, theater, and film, with an emphasis on silent cinema. In 2013, he has been a visiting scholar at the University of Copenhagen.

Robert Arnett is associate professor at Old Dominion University in Norfolk, Virginia. He teaches film history, criticism courses, and screenwriting. He has published in *Creative Screenwriting, Journal of Popular Film and Television, Film Criticism,* and *Quarterly Review of Film and Video.* His screenplays have won national awards and representation by RPM International in Hollywood. Also, his screenwriting students have won national awards and have gone on to MFA programs and graduate screenwriting programs.

Jonah Corne is assistant professor in the Department of English, Film, and Theatre at the University of Manitoba. He received his PhD in 2008 from Cornell, where he wrote his dissertation on architecture in modernist literature. His essays and reviews have appeared in *Film International, Literature/ Film Quarterly, Screening the Past, Modernist Cultures,* and the anthology *Georg Simmel in Translation* (2006).

David LaRocca is writer-in-residence at the New York Public Library and fellow at the Moving Picture Institute. He is the author of *On Emerson* (2003) and *Emerson's English Traits and the Natural History of Metaphor* (2013) as well as the editor of Stanley Cavell's *Emerson's Transcendental Etudes* (2003),

The Philosophy of Charlie Kaufman (2011), and *Estimating Emerson: An Anthology of Criticism from Carlyle to Cavell* (2013). He is the director of the documentary film *Brunello Cucinelli: A New Philosophy of Clothes* (2013) and is currently editing a new volume—*The Philosophy of War Films*—for the University Press of Kentucky Philosophy of Popular Culture series. He has also contributed essays to the press's volumes on Spike Lee (2011), the Coen brothers (updated edition, 2012), and Tim Burton (2014) in this same series. His articles on aesthetic theory, American philosophy, autobiography, and film have appeared in such journals as *Epoché, Afterimage, Transactions, Liminalities, Film and Philosophy, Midwest Quarterly, Journal of Aesthetics and Art Criticism,* and *Journal of Aesthetic Education.*

R. Barton Palmer is Calhoun Lemon Professor of Literature at Clemson University, where he also directs the Film Studies Program. He is the author, editor, or general editor of more than fifty books on various cinematic and literary subjects. Most recently, he has written To Kill a Mockingbird: *The Relationship Between the Text and the Film* (2009), *Hollywood's Tennessee: The Williams Films and Postwar America* (2009, with Robert Bray), and *Shot on Location: Real Space in Postwar American Film* (forthcoming). He has edited or coedited several works, including *Larger Than Life: Movie Stars of the 1950s* (2010), *The Philosophy of Steven Soderbergh* (2012, with Steven Sanders), *"A Little Solitaire": John Frankenheimer and Postwar America* (2012), *Modern American Drama on Screen* (2013), and *Modern British Drama on Screen* (2013).

Tom Paulus teaches film studies in the Department of Theatre and Film Studies at the University of Antwerp. He is the former curator of film and digital media at the Museum for Contemporary Art and former editor of the media journal *AS/Andere Sinema.* He has published on issues of genre and film style in such journals as *Film International* and *Foundations of Science.* His essays on pictorial style in the films of John Ford have been published in three edited collections: *John Ford in Focus* (2007); *Westerns: Movies from Hollywood and Paperback Westerns* (2007); and *New Perspectives on* The Quiet Man (2009). He is also the editor, with Rob King, of *Slapstick Symposium: Essays on Silent Comedy* (2010).

Murray Pomerance is professor in the Department of Sociology at Ryerson University. He is the author of *An Eye for Hitchcock* (2004), *Savage*

Time (2005), *Johnny Depp Starts Here* (2005), *The Horse Who Drank the Sky: Film Experience beyond Narrative and Theory* (2008), *Michelangelo Red Antonioni Blue: Eight Reflections on Cinema* (2010), *Edith Valmaine* (2011), *Tomorrow* (2012), *Alfred Hitchcock's America* (2013), and *The Eyes Have It: Cinema and the Reality Effect* (2013), as well as editor or coeditor of more than a dozen volumes, including *The Last Laugh: Strange Humors of Cinema* (2013) and *Cinema and Modernity* (2006). He edits the Horizons of Cinema series at the State University of New York Press and the Techniques of the Moving Image series at Rutgers University Press and coedits the Star Decades and Screen Decades series at Rutgers with Adrienne L. McLean and Lester D. Friedman, respectively.

Ivo Ritzer is assistant professor in the Media and Film Department at Johannes Gutenberg University of Mainz. He has widely published on film, media, and cultural theory. His work includes monographs and edited or coedited books on the dialectics of genre theory and auteurism (*Walter Hill: Welt in Flammen,* 2009), the gangster film (*Mythos der Pate,* 2011), representations of the body in the media (*Global Bodies,* 2012), transgression in TV series (*Fernsehen wider die Tabus,* 2012), French crime cinema (*Polar,* 2012), intercultural perspectives on the Western (*Crossing Frontiers,* 2012), and genre hybridization and cultural globalization (*Global Cinematic Flows,* 2013). Current research projects focus on performativity of film and TV, inter- and cross-mediality, and new approaches to mise-en-scène criticism.

David Rodríguez-Ruiz is a PhD candidate at the State University of New York at Buffalo. He received the Patrick Romanell Dissertation Award for his research on cognitive ontology and the methodology of epistemology. He has a BS in mathematics and an MA (ABD) in philosophy from the University of Puerto Rico. He has taught courses in mathematics and philosophy and worked as graduate assistant to the editor of the *Transactions of the Charles Sanders Pierce Society* and as research assistant to the director of the National Center for Ontological Research in Buffalo.

Steven Rybin is assistant professor of film at Georgia Gwinnett College. He is the author of *Terrence Malick and the Thought of Film* (2011) and *Michael Mann: Crime Auteur* (2013) as well as the coeditor of *Lonely Places, Dangerous Ground: Nicholas Ray in American Cinema* (2014). He is currently writing a book about the performance of courtship in classical Hollywood cinema.

Steven Sanders is professor emeritus of philosophy at Bridgewater State University. He works primarily in the areas of philosophy, film, and television, ethics, and analytic existentialism. He is the author of the critical monograph *Miami Vice* (2010), editor of *The Philosophy of Science Fiction Film* (University Press of Kentucky, 2008), coeditor with Aeon J. Skoble of *The Philosophy of TV Noir* (University Press of Kentucky, 2008), and coeditor with R. Barton Palmer of *The Philosophy of Steven Soderbergh* (University Press of Kentucky, 2011). His essay on Orson Welles has appeared in *Film Noir: The Directors* (2012), and he has contributed essays, articles, and entries to *The Philosophy of Film Noir* (University Press of Kentucky, 2006), *Hitchcock and Philosophy* (2007), *101 Sci-Fi Movies You Must See Before You Die* (2009), *The Philosophy of Martin Scorsese* (University Press of Kentucky, 2009), *Film Noir: the Encyclopedia* (2010), *A Companion to Film Noir* (2013), *Lonely Places, Dangerous Ground: Nicholas Ray in American Cinema* (2014).

Aeon J. Skoble is professor of philosophy and chairman of the Philosophy Department at Bridgewater State University and senior fellow at the Fraser Institute. He is the author of *Deleting the State: An Argument about Government* (2008), the editor of *Reading Rasmussen and Den Uyl: Critical Essays on Norms of Liberty* (2008), and the coeditor of *Political Philosophy: Essential Selections* (1999) and *Reality, Reason, and Rights* (2011). Besides his academic writing, he has frequently lectured and written for the Institute for Humane Studies and the Foundation for Economic Education. His main research includes theories of rights, the nature and justification of authority, and virtue ethics. In addition, he has written widely on the intersection of philosophy and popular culture, including such subjects as *Seinfeld, Forrest Gump, The Lord of the Rings,* superheroes, film noir, Westerns, Hitchcock, Scorsese, science fiction, and baseball, and in these areas of interest he is also coeditor of *Woody Allen and Philosophy* (2004), *The Simpsons and Philosophy* (2000), and, with Steven Sanders, *The Philosophy of TV Noir* (University Press of Kentucky, 2008).

Aga Skrodzka is assistant professor of film studies in the English Department at Clemson University. She is the author of *Magic Realist Cinema in East Central Europe* (2012). Her research focuses on the notion of European periphery and the alternative aesthetics used in cinema to communicate the sense of peripherality. Her next book-length project, focusing on kinetic bodies and paralyzed subjects, addresses the figure of the eastern European sex slave in recent films about human trafficking, with an emphasis on mobility and labor. Both in research and teaching, she engages with transnational theory, film theory, feminist theory, and critical race theory. She has published articles and book chapters on films by the masters of Polish cinema (Jan Jakub Kolski, Krzysztof Kieslowski, Walerian Borowczyk), but also by Hollywood auteurs, including John Woo and Martin Scorsese.

David Sterritt, chair of the National Society of Film Critics and chief book critic of *Film Quarterly,* is a film professor at the Maryland Institute College of Art and Columbia University, where he also cochairs the University Seminar on Cinema and Interdisciplinary Interpretation. He is contributing editor at *Tikkun,* contributing writer at *Cineaste* and *MovieMaker,* and an editorial board member of *Cinema Journal, Quarterly Review of Film and Video, Journal of Beat Studies,* and *Hitchcock Annual.* His writing has appeared in *Cahiers du cinéma,* the *New York Times, Journal of the American Psychoanalytic Association, Journal of American History, Journal of French and Francophone Philosophy, New Review of Film and Television Studies, Journal of Aesthetics and Art Criticism,* and many other publications. His twelve books include *The Films of Alfred Hitchcock* (1993), *Spike Lee's America* (2013), and *The Beats: A Very Short Introduction* (2013).

Mark Wildermuth received his PhD in eighteenth-century literature from the University of Wisconsin at Madison. He is professor of English and Dunagan Research Fellow at the University of Texas of the Permian Basin. His work has appeared in *Philosophy and Rhetoric, Rhetoric Society Quarterly, Journal of Popular Film and Television, The Age of Johnson,* and *The Eighteenth Century: Theory and Interpretation.* He has recently published two books: *Blood in the Moonlight: Michael Mann and Information Age Cinema* (2005) and *Print, Chaos, and Complexity: Samuel Johnson and Eighteenth-Century Media Culture* (2008).

Alan Woolfolk is vice president of academic affairs at Flagler College in Saint Augustine, Florida. He holds a PhD in sociology from the University of Pennsylvania and previously taught at Oglethorpe University and Southern Methodist University. He has published extensively on contemporary culture, public intellectuals, and film. Woolfolk has twice been a National Endowment for the Humanities Fellow and is a member of the editorial board of *Society.*

INDEX

White of the Eye (1987, Donald
    Cammell), 95
Whitinsville, Massachusetts, 133
Wigand, Jeffrey (character), 41, 52, 83,
    148, 160–79, 186, 244, 247–49, 253
Wild Bunch, The (1969, Sam
    Peckinpah), 142–143
Wildermuth, Mark, 7, 17, 200, 204
Wilson, Colin, 37–41, 43, 46, 49n6,
    49n11
Wilson, F. Paul, 98
Wilson, Michael Henry, 13n20
Wiseguy (Pileggi), 33
Wittgenstein, Ludwig, 234

Wolf, Dick, 3
Wölfflin, Heinrich, 144
Wood, Gordon, 218, 225n5
Woolfolk, Alan, 8
World Trade Center, 72

X-Files, The (TV show), 3

Year of the Dragon (1985, Michael
    Cimino), 73n1, 76
Yerkovich, Anthony, 13n6, 17, 56

Zanuck, Darryl F., 3
Žižek, Slavoj, 78, 80, 94

The Philosophy of Popular Culture

The books published in the Philosophy of Popular Culture series will illuminate and explore philosophical themes and ideas that occur in popular culture. The goal of this series is to demonstrate how philosophical inquiry has been reinvigorated by increased scholarly interest in the intersection of popular culture and philosophy, as well as to explore through philosophical analysis beloved modes of entertainment, such as movies, TV shows, and music. Philosophical concepts will be made accessible to the general reader through examples in popular culture. This series seeks to publish both established and emerging scholars who will engage a major area of popular culture for philosophical interpretation and examine the philosophical underpinnings of its themes. Eschewing ephemeral trends of philosophical and cultural theory, authors will establish and elaborate on connections between traditional philosophical ideas from important thinkers and the ever-expanding world of popular culture.

SERIES EDITOR

Mark T. Conard, Marymount Manhattan College, NY

BOOKS IN THE SERIES

The Philosophy of Stanley Kubrick, edited by Jerold J. Abrams
The Philosophy of Ang Lee, edited by Robert Arp, Adam Barkman, and
　　James McRae
Football and Philosophy, edited by Michael W. Austin
Tennis and Philosophy, edited by David Baggett
The Philosophy of J. J. Abrams, edited by Patricia Brace and Robert Arp
The Philosophy of Film Noir, edited by Mark T. Conard
The Philosophy of Martin Scorsese, edited by Mark T. Conard
The Philosophy of Neo-Noir, edited by Mark T. Conard
The Philosophy of Spike Lee, edited by Mark T. Conard
The Philosophy of the Coen Brothers, edited by Mark T. Conard
The Philosophy of David Lynch, edited by William J. Devlin and Shai Biderman
The Philosophy of the Beats, edited by Sharin N. Elkholy
The Philosophy of Horror, edited by Thomas Fahy
The Philosophy of The X-Files, edited by Dean A. Kowalski
Steven Spielberg and Philosophy, edited by Dean A. Kowalski

www.ingramcontent.com/pod-product-compliance
Lightning Source LLC
Chambersburg PA
CBHW030259100426
42812CB00002B/506